Do You Really Know What Goes on in Nursing Homes?

D1520844

Do You Really Know What Goes on in Nursing Homes?

An Insider Tells All

Shirley Ann Kraemer, Ph.D.

VANTAGE PRESS
New York

FIRST EDITION

Published by Vantage Press, Inc.
419 Park Ave. South, New York, NY 10016

Manufactured in the United States of America
ISBN: 978-0-533-16220-8

Library of Congress Catalog Card No: 2009902443

0 9 8 7 6 5 4 3 2 1

To Our Respected Elders

Contents

Foreword

I've had the pleasure of knowing Shirley Kraemer for many years and consider her to be a dear friend, so I was deeply honored when she asked me to review the manuscript of this important new book. Knowing Shirley as I do, I wondered if I would be up to the task! I knew I would find it interesting, challenging, unique, insightful, honest, and helpful. It is bold, it is daring, and it is challenging.

From the very first few words, Shirley's compassion for older persons and those who care for and about them becomes clear, as does the breadth and depth of her understanding of so much about who and what the elderly really are—and are not!

As forthright and even critical as her book is at times, it is always hopeful. Shirley admonishes, accuses, and advocates, always with a hopeful eye to making things better—not repeating the mistakes of the past. She does not shy away from controversy, always with the goal of making things better. She discusses where we have been and where we are going (or where she would like to see us go), but perhaps most importantly, the why of both so that even though we can't change the shortcomings of the past, we can certainly learn from them. She shares heartwarming stories and sad stories, because both are part of life as it is and part of what she has experienced in her many years of serving others—"patients" (as older persons are too often called) staffs, families, and the broader community.

And whether you agree or disagree with her critique of elements of "traditional" care for elders, past and present, I think you will find it impossible to miss her passion for trying to make things better. Some may look askance at one or more of the newer, "nontraditional" forms of treatment, therapy, and lifestyle, but don't miss the courage of her convictions. She is not afraid to insist on accountability, just as she is not afraid to take risks. How will we know unless we try? Shirley proposes unique and varied approaches to elder care, including a strong, integral, and unabashed faith—one of the core elements of the very lives of many of those about whom she writes. Shirley is, as always, honest—painfully so at times—and candid in her assessment of what is right and wrong with our society's system and approach to care for older persons. Those of us who are aging (and we all are!) should welcome a champion for our interests in having a better, healthier future. I truly believe the reader will be fascinated and enlightened by her knowledge of and approach to the utilization of holistic, homeopathic, art, pet, remotivation, aroma, and other therapies, some as old as civilization itself and some viewed as more cutting edge.

I may not agree with everything Shirley says (most, but not all), and perhaps it is because I came from a more traditional medical (nursing) model and am not as familiar with all of them in actual practice. But as a measure of the respect I have for her, it would not be fair to her if I did not at least raise my questions. I have certainly learned—and had my mind and eyes opened—by reviewing this manuscript. Maybe it is the old dog learning new tricks adage!

I emphasize again, that in the end, after all is said and done, Shirley's book is hopeful—hopeful that we as a society can and must do better. As the poet Browning said, ". . . come grow old with me, the best is yet to come." There should be more truth and comfort in that sentiment for all of us because of the efforts in this book by Shirley Kraemer.

Jim L. Brown, R.N., B.S. Ed., J.D.

Preface

Do you know why elders continue to fear nursing-homes? Are there politics in the care of the elderly? Why a nursing shortage? Why the high cost of care? Do you want to know how nursing-homes can change? YOU DESERVE TO KNOW!

With a thirty-year career in nursing-homes, Kraemer not only tells all, but provides answers in a higher level of spiritual consciousness. Kraemer, as a friend, teacher, and counselor, compassionately walks over the bridge of change, embracing new, innovative teachings.

We are like caterpillars on a cabbage leaf prepared to become beautiful free butterflies.

—Dalai Lama

What really goes on in a nursing-home? With an insider telling all, the reader will find myths and truths about those who reside and work in nursing-homes, never told stories about the families, religious institutions, and consultants; the day-to-day incidents, joys, sorrows, and challenges. All is true. Nothing has been changed to protect the innocent as there are few, if any, innocent persons involved. All have chosen to become part of a nursing-home setting for either money, a karmic debt, out of deep compassion for the elder person, and/or to learn lessons about being an aged, dependent, person.

It has been said that those of us who have chosen to care for the elderly in a nursing-home setting have the desire to know what our future holds . . . just as caregivers in a child day-care setting wish to remember what it is like to be a child again.

Society needs to ask if it has created the nursing-home crisis by relinquishing its responsibility in the care of our elders. Have we, the nursing-home staff, been no more than followers? Have not nursing-homes bowed to every governmental edict regardless of cost and paperwork?

The nursing-home industry must wake up and be leaders once again. All of society must move the care of our elders to a higher level of consciousness. It is a beginning that we in the nursing-home industry, must mend our *own* ways before we demand that others change. The past . . . is done; it's over. Let us begin again to walk and listen to one another and awake to the new future. Let us respond with deep compassion.

Can we accept new and innovative therapies that do no harm? The answer is in the heart of staff, residents, nursing-home owners, families and community.

This is the Age of Aquarius, the age of information and exciting paradigms, when many truths will be revealed if we but remember that we are gods in training.

May this book bring about personal catharsis, new thoughts, spiritual enlightenment, change, and many blessings.

Introduction

The question needs to be asked. If nursing-homes were not available for the elderly and disabled, who would be caring for them? What events took place that brought the Federal government into the care of the elderly? Nursing-homes started to be built in the 1950s with the greatest growth in the 1960s. Why did society place their elders and disabled family members in nursing-homes when children, private homes, or county homes, had been the primary caregivers?

Today, the outcome is that many nursing-homes are often maligned, rarely credited for being good Samaritans, and frequently thought of as a "horrible place to work and live." Betty Friedan in *Foundation of Age* stated that in ten years of research no data has emerged to counteract her impression of nursing-homes as nothing more than death sentences . . . the final interment from which there is no exit but death. Why do families and society unfairly vilify nursing-homes? Are families transferring their guilt unto nursing-homes because they are not taking responsibility for the care of their elders? Or is society angry over the cost of nursing-home care for those they perceive as "useless?"

Arnold Kling, holding a Ph.D. in economics from the Massachusetts Institute of Technology, writes that payroll taxes for Medicare are less than the benefits being paid out for hospitalization under Medicare. It is estimated that in fiscal year 2003 about one-third of Medicaid's budget for a total of $45 billion went for long-term care. Dr. Kling is proposing that Medicare and Medicaid that pays for long-term care be scaled back. He has also proposed that Medicaid's eligibility rules for long-term care reimbursement be restructured. In regards to the Medicare system, when billionaires, judges, and politicians with bloated pensions, turn sixty-five-plus years of age, they are just as qualified for free hospital care and physical therapy in a nursing-home as the working class is. In fact, when President Johnson signed the Medicare system into law, the first to sign up was former President Truman.

Cannon and Tanner (Cato Institute of Health Policies) sum it all up with the statement, "It is unlikely that Congress would allow Medicare's growth to crowd out other areas of government spending, such as national defense. It is equally unlikely that Congress, even over many years, would be able to increase taxes as dramatically as will become necessary to maintain existing benefit levels. Thus, it is almost certain Congress will have to cut Medicare benefits." Today, the Federal government seeks to reduce Medicare spending by $183 billion over a five year period. Plans are in motion to freeze payments to skilled nursing facilities and reduce payments by $17 billion over five years. These cuts will not only impact the reimbursement rates but will change services to beneficiaries, limiting the number of elders and providers receiving Medicare payments and benefits.

Nursing-homes are a beleaguered industry. Over the past eight years, forty eight nursing-homes have closed in the state of Minnesota. The decline is due to the cost of maintaining older buildings, the method of reimbursement and the general shift in the attitude of consumers who are looking for alternatives to the traditional nursing-home. Today, nursing-homes are inundated with paper work, regulations, lawsuits, inflationary costs and staff who have lowered educational abilities due to the "dumbing down" of educational systems, loss of morals, work ethics and spiritual insights as to who they are and what their purpose is in life.

The nation as a whole is suffering from millions of lost jobs, industries transferring overseas, the health and welfare system besieged with not only illegal immigrants who demand services but jobless, hard-working middle-class Americans in need of basic services. Foods and medications shipped in from other countries are often tainted with unknown chemicals and unhealthy fillers. Most important is the loss of a sense of who we are as a people and the destruction of Godly teachings in our homes, religious institutions and educational systems. Our Nation is in trouble, which directly affects the nursing-home industry.

Philosophically, when a way of life dies, it makes room for the new. The nursing-home way of life is now in the throes of the dying stage making way for a new rebirth to provide a more compassionate and spiritual environment for elders, the disabled and staff. Nursing-homes must make that quantum leap forward. The dark side (powers that be) is terrorized in the teachings of love, compassion, the truth and the way. The dark side will stand against any changes.

Steve Shields, nursing-home administrator writes, "The time has arrived to let the nursing-home (concept) go. Some would say it's broken. I say it never was fixed. It was never a healthy nourishing thing." (*Old Age in a New Age*, p. 7).

In my book *An Insider Tells All,* I will attempt to give the reader an inside look at what really goes on in a nursing-home and provide reasons for why elders are in nursing-homes; why staff work there; how staff, families, community, church, and society can assist in supporting an institution that plays an integral part in our society; provide ways to alleviate the shortage of nurses; decrease cost of elder care in nursing-homes, and reveal the truth about the politics played that not only cost the taxpayer but are rarely in the interest of elders who reside in a nursing-home setting.

Do You Really Know What Goes on in Nursing Homes?

A Letter to My Readers

Let all who read this book know, without any doubt in their minds, that I hold no animosity toward any individual or profession.

My ministry is now, and always has been, in the compassionate care of our respected Elders; to bring spiritual peace to those who reside and work in a nursing-home setting.

My "soul" intent is to present a golden opportunity for change.

I am writing this book as a service to others. However, I am also doing this for myself to create a way to share my thoughts and feelings throughout the many years of walking beside the elderly and nursing-home staff.

This book is an expression of my spiritual self from the depths of my soul. If this book were never to be published or read by many, it would still be a satisfaction to me to have created, in words, my service to all those whom I was called to serve.

The astrological influences for the next few years suggest humanity is crossing a threshold and is in need of a new and expanded spiritual awareness. The old life is disappearing . . . The influences are not only affecting the world stage but also every individual in the world. Each of us will have the opportunity to be part of the problem or part of the solution.
Raye Mathis, astrological counselor

To create a very readable and enjoyable text, I occasionally give credit within a paragraph or at the beginning or ending of a paragraph; however, all resources can be found in the bibliography. I add professional research and comments to back up my experiences.

I am not alone in the desire to see what needs to be done and work toward change.

1

The Shofar Is Sounded

To love, respect, and care for the elderly is like a shofar sounding, calling one into battle or prayer for their namesake. The shofar, usually a ram's horn, blown by the ancient Hebrews in battle and during religious ceremonies, was sounded. My battle to bring even the simplest change in the care of the elderly and to see my prayer life intensify was beginning. No one ever promised me a rose garden.

I owe much to my parents, who agreed to bring me into this Earth life, at this time, and in a rural setting, where there was opportunity to live in a small northeast Nebraska village neighborhood surrounded by elderly persons; where neighbors cared for one another; where windows were opened in the evening to hear Don play the latest tune on his piano and where one would sit in the swing on the front porch to watch villagers walk by or stop for a moment to pass on the latest gossip.

Our neighborhood was filled with "grandmas." Everyone was "grandma" to me. I loved Grandma Smith, so petite and wrinkled and so bent over. She was kindness unparalleled. Grandma Smith owned a pump organ. My memories are of me sitting under the old organ, pumping the pedals as Grandma Smith played "Jesus Loves Me." And the smell of old woolen carpet in the middle of the floor surrounded by old, heavy furniture, pretty oil lamps and red flowered oilcloth on the kitchen table, where pots of feathery ferns basked in window sunlight.

I hold the vision of Grandma McCoy toddling over to our house bringing mysterious and delicious home-canned jellies and jams that always tasted awesome.

And then there was Grandma Mittlestadt, whose house I cleaned. She had this habit of following me around with her magnifying glass to make sure I was getting the dirt out of each corner. I was paid twenty-five cents for a day's work.

Then there was Grandma and Grandpa French. Grandma French always turned her aprons backwards in the middle of the week so the apron was good for the rest of the week. After all, everyone washed only on Mondays, and heaven knows washing of clothes was hard work in those days. Grandpa French had a goat to keep the weeds down in back of the house. But secretly I think the goat was to keep erring neighborhood kids from sneaking across his place. Personally, I was afraid of that old goat! (The animal, not Grandpa French.)

I occasionally stayed overnight with Grandma Maun when she was sick, as she had no family close by. I remember sleeping next to the old oil burner with an eisenglass door. The flames danced to and fro all night long, surrounding me in warm company.

Of course, my favorite was Grandpa Mallatt, an Irishman to the hilt with his red hair, beard, and mustache. He was a farmer who raised race horses and traveled the countryside not only as a horse trader but also racing his horses.

I spent the summers walking through cornfields, jumping into the cool sandy-bottomed Bow Creek on hot days, drinking from the well pump, gathering eggs, and running from mean ducks. Grandpa Mallatt taught me to not be afraid of long-legged spiders, to gently catch them and ask, "Where are the cows?" And then the spider would point with one of his long spindly legs.

That was my neighborhood and my childhood . . . walking barefoot in summer rain puddles, roller skating up and down sidewalks, helping with Mom's Victory garden during WWII, sleeping outside under the stars, searching the lawn for four leaf clovers, playing "ante I over" ball until the sun set, hearing the 7:00 a.m., twelve noon, and 6:00 p.m. village whistles blow, being the envy of the neighborhood kids with a metal hoop and wooden driver made by my dad out of an old barrel, hitchhiking five miles to the Belden swimming pool or swimming in the Logan Creek (with cows upstream), delivering newspapers on my bike to many elderly households, and when night fell, trying to get home before the nine o'clock curfew house lights went on.

Elders were part of my life. I loved them, even those who were a bit crotchety.

As an adult, I delivered meals to housebound elders. It was here I saw the impact of the need for touch. As I entered the house of Grandma Marie, I saw her sitting on her sofa with tears in her eyes. I sat beside her to ask if I could help her in some small way. This was her story, "I have the finest of children. I am so proud of them. They treat me so good and visit almost every day. But since my husband passed away, no one has touched me or given me a hug. I miss being touched."

So, with Grandma Marie and all the grandmas and grand-pas memories instilled in my soul, my ministry of caring for the elderly in nursing-homes was beginning. Hugs and touch are my pattern EACH DAY plus hugs for many of the staff who need to know they are valued, too. The shofar had sounded.

Who Am I, Really?

I was born in Wynot, Nebraska in a newly built chicken coop. It was 1935. Times were hard. The chicken coop never had chickens in it, so my parents rented it for my three brothers, and a new baby born on June 21. As years passed, if my brothers wanted to make me really mad, they would tell me I was "hatched." My mother often said she did not know how any of us could have any "smarts" as we grew up on homemade pancakes made with skim milk and sugar-boiled syrup. Dad was a very good mechanic, but times were such that he often would bring home twenty-five cents a day. However, I do not remember those years as "hard times."

A move to Laurel, Nebraska set my love of neighborhood el-ders into motion. I attended the public schools until the tenth grade and left because I was terribly bored (while in college, a college professor told me the school system did not meet my needs so I was never to blame myself for being a "drop-out.") In those times, this was not unusual as many farm kids were needed on the farm and simply did not go beyond the eighth or the tenth grade.

I married at the old age of fifteen. Seven children were born in fourteen years. I knew hard work with a regular washer and no dryer, several acres of garden, and as a dedicated community volunteer.

I received the Woman of the Year award on the local level and; the Lewis and Clark award for work with Scouts and Camp Fire Girls; worked as an area newspaper correspondent, and substituted as a community radio broadcaster. As my mother was the school Dietary Manager where 550 students and teachers were fed every day, I was asked to be the substitute kitchen worker. I shared the community work, as this was to be the background for my being hired as a social worker. No one should ever feel they are not qualified for a job in a nursing-home with community service in their background.

In 1974, I entered Wayne State College at the encouragement of Mrs. Ruth Wills, whose husband was a professor at the college. Mrs. Wills, the GED teacher, said I was college material. What she saw, I will never know. I was thirty-seven. At that time, "old" people just were not students on a college campus. I was often mistaken for a teacher.

I registered for the winter semester before I took the GED test plus I took the CLEP test, which granted me nine credit hours. Taking classes throughout the summer months, I advanced quickly. Graduating in the winter of 1976 with a bachelor's degree in Community Service Counseling, magna cum laude, I successfully completed both a nurse aide course and the Nebraska nursing-home administrator license test in 1977.

I applied for a newly created social work position and was hired not only because of the college degree but due to my past community work and awards. I knew very little about the nursing-home industry. What an awakening I was to have!

I was to be interviewed by four nursing-home administrators and a Regional Manager for the position as a new Consultant Social Worker.

As I pulled at the large, heavy metal doors, I entered the nursing-home foyer. The first image was a floor-to-ceiling caduceus emblazoned on a brick wall. In this era, a caduceus was symbolic of the medical profession. So, what was this caduceus doing in a nursing-home? Only years later would I connect the relationship between nursing-homes built on hospital models.

And then my eyes fell upon three residents sitting near the door. One had a bag of yellow liquid dragging under her wheelchair, the other a soiled blouse, and the last had one hollowed out eye without a patch. I knelt down so I could be eye level with the one-eyed man. I took his hand in mine and said, "Hi, my name is Shirley."

A broad smile came over his face. At that moment, I seemed to be enveloped into a thin, blue mist, hearing a voice say, "Love him as you love me." The moment disappeared as quickly as it appeared. It was to be a confirmation of my ministry in caring for elders in nursing-homes, for better or for worse.

In 1981, I completed the master's program in Educational Counseling. At that time I accepted my first position as a nursing-home administrator at a city-owned facility.

In the years that followed, I worked toward and received a nursing-home administrator preceptors certificate (which permitted me to train those who wished to become an administrator); and a medication aide certificate, was licensed as a massage therapist, obtained a bachelor's in divinity and was ordained, became a Registered Guardian/conservator, and in 2007 received a Ph.D. in Philosophy. I attended the School of Law, University of South Dakota, Vermillion, South Dakota for Elder Law and Health Care and the Law classes. I am a student of Edgar Cayce, whose philosophies, spiritually and psychologically, changed my life. I believe deeply in the philosophy of karma and reincarnation taught throughout the ages by early religions and hold to the Truth that we are all spiritual/energy beings encased in flesh bodies.

Today, I hold three nursing-home administrator licenses—in the states of Iowa, Kansas, and Nebraska.

I have presented workshops throughout the states of South Dakota, Nebraska, and Iowa. I was invited to tour a new, innovative facility in Ohio and was a guest speaker in Duluth, Minnesota, introducing massage therapy into nursing-homes.

I was selected as a Cambridge "Who's Who" for the

7

2008/2009 Executive and Professional registry. I am a member of the Nemenhah Lodge, Medicine Woman.

I write this book sharing my most intimate experiences. All is true to the best of my memory. Bless those who walked beside me and helped me along the Way.

Residents may not remember my name, nor are they interested in titles or degrees. They will remember my love and all those hugs.

Many Mentors Along the Way

Who were my mentors? Ruth Ebmeier encouraged me during my college years; B.T. Christensen, a nursing-home regional manager, who hired me for my first position as a consultant social worker, had faith in me, and taught me what I needed to know about nursing-home politics; Jim Brown, attorney and a former Director at the Nebraska Health Care Association, who later became my CEO; Mary Newman, a forever friend and all those across the Midwest who traveled beside me in my spiritual quest and the wonderful nursing-home staff who taught me everything I know today. What the reader must remember is that in my entire career, for the better and the worst of times, I always had beside me the essence of my Ascended Master Jesus of Nazareth, Mother/Father God within, my guardian angel Kazela, my spirit guide Matilda (a Greek Amazon in full warrior apparel), and my traveling angels Michael and Grace. One powerful group of mentors, would you not agree?

Now, let us get on with the story of my years as a consultant social worker, administrator, preceptor, workshop speaker, and regional manager. May you laugh when you recognize yourself or others, may you cry as you read truths, may you become upset as you feel I have been too hard on a particular department, but most of all, may you come to the conclusion that nursing-homes are a godsend to many lonely elders and the disabled who have no family. However, you may come to the conclusion that nursing-homes of yesterday can be an instrument for change in today's world and that change will come only with YOU!

Fundamental change begins in the human heart. If we really don't believe that people are still people because they have a dementia, we will not care for them as a person, but as objects of medical maintenance. If we really don't believe that elderhood can be a great age of enlightenment and societal participation, then we will continue to relate to elders as retirees on the golf course. Each of us must work deeply on our own journey of aging, transforming our traditional fears and uncertainties into a hopeful, joyful embrace of who we are and our new capacities for growth and giving.

Bill Keane, longtime culture change leader, in *Old Age in a New Age*, p. 183).

May each chapter be an inspiration!

2

Aging Well

The social and economical visibility of elders has increased dramatically. Ample food, clean water, high work ethic, good housing, technological innovations, and programs have increased life expectancy from age fifty in 1910 to the eighties and nineties in 2008. "Father time is not always a hard parent, and though he tarries for none of his children, He often lays his hand lightly on those who have used him well." (Charles Dickens in *Barnaby Rudge*.)

Health care professionals agree that:

1. Attractive, good tasting, and nutritional food is essential to good health.
2. The aging body becomes increasingly sensitive and less tolerant of certain foods ingested successfully as a younger person.
3. The aging process is usually accompanied by a change in activity; therefore, food habits of the past are usually inappropriate. As the body processes slow, so does that ability to digest and metabolize food. As the body demands proper, nutritious food, it is essential that the elderly maintain a "gestalt" diet, one that is a combination of all foods plus vitamins and minerals, within every twenty-four-hour period. The goal of any nutrition program for the nursing-home resident should not be to just keep him/her alive but with an outcome of contentment . . . socially, psychologically and physically. (*Remedies for Life Extension* by Gerontologist and Pharmacist Stephen Fulder, Ph.D. Destiny Books, 1983.)

Hippocrates said the beginning of old age was forty-two years. In the 1970s we said over the hill was somewhere between the ages of forty and fifty. Then we entered that era of the 1990s. An elder was considered to be in the seventies and an elder-elder in the late eighties and nineties.

The great physician Avicenna (1000 A.D.) said, "Every person has his own term of life . . . the art of maintaining health consists in guiding the body to its *natural* span." (Emphasis mine.) So what is this thing called "natural?"

Let us take a look at those who have lived a long and healthy life. Long-lived humans are mostly isolated and rural dwellers, poorer but seemingly healthier, engaged in agriculture and living frugally. There seems to be no consistent use of special herbs, foods, or health-care practices with the exception that the meat and foods were farm-grown, farm fed with no chemicals.

From 1950 to 1970 life expectancy only increased 3.4 years despite the trillions of dollars spent on medical research, drugs, and medical equipment.

Nursing-home resident Mary P. ate garlic every day of her long life. She was a German immigrant, rural dweller, with family support close by, worked in her garden and kept her own home until she was ninety-nine. She rarely saw a doctor. Gradually her family felt she needed nursing-home care. When I met her, she still spoke fluent German, her mind clear with a contented personality. At this time, she was wheelchair bound. My opinion was that her inability to walk was due to obesity. She lived to be 103.

Call her an "elder-boomer." Centenarians are the fastest-growing segment in the United States, right on their heels are the eighty-five-plus-years. In 1985 there were about 25,000 centenarians and today there are 72,000 centenarians. By the year 2050 the projection is more than four million.

Researchers have found that centenarians are a select group of people who have a history of aging slowly and escaping many of the diseases normally associated with getting older. Lynn Adler, a lawyer and founder of the National Centenarians Awareness Project, identifies traits that contribute to longevity:

- A love of life and a good sense of humor
- A positive yet realistic attitude
- A strong religious or spiritual belief
- Personal courage
- A remarkable ability to renegotiate life at every turn
- Incredible self-determination
- Staying interested in life
- Exercising the brain and the body
- Acceptance of losses
- The ability to change and move forward

Many elders had a quiet faith, never boasting, never proud. Just faith. The most beautiful tape I found and use on a frequent basis is "The Lord's Prayer" with background music.

Nursing-home residents, regardless of religion, need to be encouraged to say "The Lord's Prayer," remembering that Master Jesus directed that we say this prayer, not in rote, but to meet our needs. We have the freedom to change the words on a daily basis.

As the day may bring pain or thoughts of our ills, we may pray like this:

*Our father, mother God who art in heaven
Holy is Thy name
Thy kingdom come
Your will be done
As in heaven, so in earth.
Give us for tomorrow the needs of the body.
Forget those trespasses as we forgive
Those that have trespassed and do trespass against us.
Be Thou the guide in the time of trouble,
Turmoil and temptation.
Lead us in paths of righteousness
For Thy name's sake.

*Edgar Cayce reading 378–44 from the Source.

Our elders must be provided "aging well" therapies and prayer in a nursing-home setting just as they did in their home life. And who are our elders in nursing-homes? What are their needs? Two examples:

Precious Souls Who Have Walked Through the Portals of a Nursing-Home

Anna: The door quietly opened. I was working near the receptionist desk. I hardly heard anyone standing near me. It was more like a feeling. I turned and saw a neat, petite, gray-haired lady. She was carrying a suitcase. I smiled and asked if I could help her. "Yes," she said. "I would like a room for the night." I chuckled a bit. "Was this a joke?" I thought. No one *wants* a room in a nursing-home.

I took her hand and asked her if she would like a cup of coffee, and perhaps a cookie. As we walked into the dining room, I noticed tears forming and her hands shook. She was such a little mite that I just wrapped my arm around her shoulders, pulling her close to me. "Whatever it is, we will work things out."

"Well," she began ever so softly, "It's time to come. Things are just getting so bad. When I make my meals at home, I forget and the food burns. I caught the stove on fire more than once. Then last week, I had a car accident and I am so afraid when I leave home, because I can't remember the way back. So here I am. Do you have a room for me?" I wiped away her tears with my ever-ready handkerchief (which always please elders more than using tissue). The daughter was called, who confirmed what her mother had told me. This little sweet soul became a resident of our facility that very night. Later, she related to me that now she felt safe at night, and did not worry anymore. A happy resident, indeed!

Robert: A hug proved to reveal Robert's psychological pain. His entire body was covered with keratosis (warts). He was surprised when I touched him for, according to Robert, most people

13

shunned him. He became a recluse in his own home. His only family was a niece and nephew.

Then came the day when family decided he could no longer care for himself. He walked into the nursing-home, appearing much younger and more agile than most nursing-home residents. The activity directors were overjoyed to have a resident able to take part in most of their activities. But our joy was not long-lasting. Robert retired to his room and his bed. Nothing we offered or said would change Robert's mind. He had come to the nursing-home to die. He refused all water and food. The family came daily but made no impact.

Coming to my office, they requested that somehow I get Robert to eat. I ordered two trays from the kitchen, one for Robert and the other for me. I set up a small table in Robert's room. In my chatter, Robert remained passive. The trays were delivered. Without words or warning Robert picked up his tray and threw it at me, dishes and utensils clattering, food spilling to the floor. No words needed to be said. Robert was not going to eat. This day was followed by seven more. I was witnessing a suicide by starvation. There seemed to be no pain, just the knowledge that Robert was in control of his life. Death came quietly. A socially acceptable death . . . more acceptable than society had accepted Robert in this life.

Understand? How can we? We are not them. We have never walked in their shoes. We never tasted their desires, hopes, loves, disappointments. Who are these beautiful people who have been entrusted to our care? Have we met in other lives? And what is the purpose of our meeting in a nursing-home? What is the staff's purpose in the caring of the souls like Anna and Robert?

14

3

How We Got to Where We Are

Gerontologist Robert Butler wrote, "Old age in America is often a tragedy. We pay lip service to the idealized images of beloved and tranquil grandparents, wise elders, white-haired patriarchs, and matriarchs. But the opposite image disparages the elderly, seeing age as decay, decrepitude, a disgusting and undignified dependency."

We are born to age. We are born to die. Should we not age with dignity? Should we not live in dignity? Should we not die with dignity?

From time immemorial, elders and disabled persons were cared for by family. Herbs, home-grown foods, and home cures for any ailments were utilized. Most importantly, elders often headed the family in decision making, thus their need to be needed was honored. Their work, however limited, was valued.

During Eastern Shore settlements in the New America, disabled elders without family were brought to a community meeting, where their care was bid on by families in financial need. The lowest bidder took the elder into their home. The family received payment by a collection from the wealthier inhabitants of the community.

Eighteenth-century Americans devoted very little energy to devising and enacting programs to isolate the dependent person. Dependency did not equate to disease or old. Communities handled their needs. Moreover, churches, mutual aid societies, families, and neighbors supported those in need. One of the most influential organizations in dictating American attitudes toward the poor and elderly was the Protestant church. They made the treatment of the elderly as much a religious as a secular matter.

15

They asserted that the presence of the poor, elderly, and disabled was a God-given opportunity for men to do good.

Later, so-called Poor Houses and County Homes were developed on the single-family concept with a family being the sole caretaker. Expenses were paid by the county taxpayers. The poor, the sick, the old, and women without spousal support and her children were taken into Poor Houses and County Homes.

All were expected to pull their share of the work to pay their way. The work included gardening, cleaning, cooking, doing chores, caring for livestock and doing field work according to their abilities. All were made to feel as if they were "working" for their keep.

Regardless of the caretakers, elders were taken care of by their own family or placed in a Poor House or on a county farm. Most were compassionate. And then there was Annie Cook.

Evil Obsession: The Annie Cook Story

Evil and greed was the impetus for the closing of single-family-operated homes for the indigent and elderly. The Annie Cook story is true. The year is 1923.

Prior to being called a Poor Farm, institutions were known as County Hospitals and Poor Houses. Patients (hospital term) were called inmates (prison term).

For twenty-five years paupers throughout the county were cared for by compassionate women. The county paid for all linens, towels, and patient's clothes. Guardianships were unknown. The county paid the local doctor to do inspections. County Commissioners frequently transported the elderly, the indigent, and the disabled to County Poor Houses or private homes, or the county would hire the local funeral director with his hearse. A contract for the care of the poor was awarded annually to the lowest bidder. Typical bids were:

$.75 a day for a pauper who could work (men, women, and children).
$1.00 a day for a person sick or injured.

$1.25 a day for the insane.

$.25 per meal and $.25 per night for the transient.

Annie Cook's farm was located in western Nebraska—Lincoln County. The farm had a large farmhouse with a myriad of outbuildings surrounded by old cottonwoods, orchards and gardens. Annie Cook, known for her stinging tongue and her horsewhip, ran this forty-acre Poor Farm supported by county funds.

Kind, lonely desolate old men and women who could no longer care for themselves and with no family or family who disassociated themselves from their elders ended up at the Cook Poor Farm.

Some, with tears in their faded, sad eyes, would tell of children who persuaded them to deed over the farm to them in return for perpetual care and then were turned over to the Cook Poor Farm to again work and labor from sun up to sun down, to be cold at night and always hungry.

When elders first came to the Cook farm, they often brought with them nice and ample clothing, which Annie would then take from them, rip up and also throw away their dentures.

Annie attended church every Sunday to establish her standing as a Christian, even though she ran a whorehouse and gambling casino in North Platte, Nebraska. When attending church services, the "patients" were noted to be in faded clothes, cracked and ill fitting leather shoes, looking poorly and shabby. Interestingly, many knew of the cruel treatment and abuse, but no one seemed to have the courage to take action against Annie Cook or remove the persons being abused.

Back on the farm, the male patients shared a double bed. A mother, with as many children as she had with her, was also placed in one double bed. The more fortunate had a cot to themselves. One "room" was actually a storeroom. The pointless iron beds and old dressers were the only contents of the small, usually overcrowded bedrooms. No chairs, tables, or lamps were furnished. Linens were ragged and dirty. No bedroom had heat. The floors were encrusted with urine and vomit. Clothes were often donated. Annie frequently called the women "damn lazy sluts and lazy bastards."

17

Punishments were dealt with by denying the person a meal. Breakfast consisted of thin oatmeal gruel and watery soups and one slice of bread for the noon and evening meals. No one received second helpings. Patients were emaciated, emanating foul body odors mixed with the smell of ammonia and all had that frightened look.

The old and frail were frequently found dead, in irrigation ditches, drowned, pushed there by Annie, because they could no longer work. The county mortician, who received numerous favors from Annie, would sign death certificates stating cause of death was "old age" regardless of the fact the bodies were filthy, emaciated, and full of sores.

Regardless of a truancy law, Annie would keep children out of school to work the farm.

No patient was allowed in the parlor where Annie "entertained" her guests—such as the physician who came to inspect and was well paid by Annie to give her a good report. Prayer meetings were held for church members in this parlor where no patients were allowed. Did the minister visit? Yes and always came back with a glowing report plus boxes of fruit, vegetables, poultry, and a twenty-dollar bill.

There were lines of family rigs that came to the farm to purchase fresh cider and garden produce, poultry, and fresh eggs. However, reports of abuse and starvation went unheeded as Annie and the local sheriff were good friends, due to the fact she favored him with kickbacks. Annie's house of prostitution was frequented by the local judge. Lavish parties were thrown for Annie's county friends, who included the county treasurer, clerk, commissioners, and the sheriff, not only providing rich and plentiful food but a supply of girls from her whorehouse. When a commissioner won an election, it was Annie who hosted the victory party with her daughter as the "prize" for the night.

Reelection brought out Annie's ill-begotten money as "whore" monies were used to pay for newspaper ads and posters for elected officials, who then looked the other way at her greedy discretions. The editor of the local papers also capitulated to Annie in fear of losing ads and printing jobs.

Those who contested the continual contract with Annie for

the caring of the poor and elderly were ignored. The outcries would die away sooner or later and life went on as usual.

The Door Opens for Government Control

With the Annie Cooks of the world, the need for change was imperative! The federal government became involved in the care of the elderly. Social Security checks could now pay for nursing-home care. The Social Security Act, established as a federal-state public assistance program for the elderly, was called the Old Age Assistance (OAA). Because the drafters of the legislation opposed the use of public poor houses and poor farms (the Annie Cook-type farms) to care for the poor elderly, the act prohibited the payment of OAA funds to these places.

Passage of the Social Security Act of 1935 was patterned after a similar act in Germany. The United States government saw the program as one that would rarely issue checks to a person meeting the sixty-five years of age requirement, as after WWI longevity statistics revealed the old to be an average of fifty years. The taking of Social Security taxes out of the working class paycheck would, then, be a windfall for government coffers. However, one future factor changed. Elders began to live far past fifty years of age.

Social Security checks stimulated the growth of voluntary (private and religious based) and proprietary (corporate) nursing-homes. By the time of the first national survey of nursing-homes in 1954, there were 9,000 homes classified as skilled-nursing or personal-care homes with skilled-nursing facilities—86 percent were proprietary, 10 percent were voluntary, and 4 percent were public.

In 1950, amendments to the Social Security Act authorized payments to beneficiaries in public institutions and enabled direct payments to all health-care providers.

The majority of nursing-homes at this time were called intermediate care facilities (ICFs), receiving Medicaid payments only, and were not documented as "skilled." Less than honorable insurance companies would often sell Long-Term-Care policies to elders that would pay for skilled care only. As elders needed nursing-home care they would discover their policy would not pay for ICF care.

In this same era, society saw a mass movement of the younger working class, lured into jobs across the states often leaving elders behind to fend for themselves.

With few elder and disabled persons in-home support services in place, the United States government stepped in, providing low-interest loans to religious organizations, private parties, cities, counties, and corporations to build what were to be coined "nursing-homes" as (and often nonlicensed) nurses were the only staff needed to care for the elders. One of the caretakers was the manager or administrator. The administrator was the activity director, social worker, often the maintenance person, and assisted as cook and bottle washer.

In 1950, legislation required that participating states establish programs for licensing nursing-homes, but set no standards. The nursing-home resident gave up his/her Social Security check to the facility, with the balance being paid with government Medicaid checks.

By the 1970s, simple standards were put into place. 80 percent of nursing-home residents were private pay or with postal or veteran benefits; 20 percent were Medicaid. The 80 percent carried the deficit created by low reimbursement for those on Medicaid.

There were three levels of care: low, moderate, and heavy. The average cost per diem was $17.50. There were two completely different sets of surveyors, one for Medicaid recipients only and one who represented the state who inspected the entire physical plant as well as the care of the residents. Nursing-homes of the '70s had two annual inspections plus the Fire Marshal inspection. If corporately owned, each nursing-home was paid a monthly visit by the Regional Manager. There were no consultants nor management firms. Policies and Procedures were in one three-ring binder. Competent nursing-home administrators, and Directors of Nursing were held accountable for resident care.

Nursing-homes, built on the hospital model, usually had

double-occupancy rooms, one or two wards with four beds, small closets, shared bathrooms, long hallways, nurse stations, medical charts, communal dining rooms, shower rooms, and nurses dressed in white.

Hospitals were for the acutely ill and dying. With this hospital concept in the collective conscious minds of the elderly, nursing-homes were also seen for the sick and dying. Today, we continue to say "nursing-homes," and we wonder why elders are so fearful of going to a nursing-home.

Sad to say, if the truth is known on a soul level, society and families heartily endorsed the nursing-home industry. Elders, no longer valued or needed, were placed out of sight and out of mind just as family, the church, and the community deserted elders in the Annie Cook story. Starting in the '50s, the family turned their elders over to the government, the medical and pharmaceutical industry although over the past fifty years medicine has proven to be of little help for the so-called newly diagnosed disease called "old."

With a nursing-home in nearly every community an entire industry was born, i.e. state surveyors, inspectors, licensed nurses, administrators, dietitians, social services, activity directors, physical therapy, podiatrists, gerontologists, elder law attorneys, managing firms, accountants, medical directors, pharmacists, consultants for every department, mandatory college classes and workshops, policy makers, and architects and builders of hospital-designed nursing-homes.

And at what cost to the taxpayer? And at what cost physically, emotionally, and spiritually to our elders? What is the spiritual cost to society's collective consciousness?

Today nearly 60 percent of long-term care facilities are in the hands of corporations. Their primary purpose is to make money. Research reveals corporate facilities have less staff and a higher rate of staff turnover. Is this not a harbinger for continued sufferings for our elders who reside in a corporate facility?

Today, the average cost for a private pay nursing-home resident is approximately $60,000 per year. Public funding (your tax dollar through Medicaid and Medicare) pays 80 percent of the $100 billion bill sent directly to the taxpayer every year.

Filing for Medicaid, the elder must sell all possessions, forfeit the majority of their Social Security check and become a ward of the state in which they live. All services and medications are then funded by Medicaid (the taxpayer). The elder can have no more than $3,000 in the bank and that is be used solely for clothes, personal items, radio, TV or a comfortable chair and a pre-paid funeral.

The cost of caring for one Medicaid nursing-home resident annually can easily exceed three years take home pay earned by the average worker.

Private pay residents not only pay for nursing-home care, but physician contacts, medications, dentist, optometrist, transportation, and incidentals in the nursing-homes such as disposables and all personal care items.

In 2007, about nine million men and women over the age of sixty-five needed long-term care for short-term rehabilitation or for permanent residency. By 2020, twelve million older Americans will enter a nursing-home. A study by the U. S. Department of Health and Human Services says that those who reach age sixty-five will likely have a 40 percent chance of entering a nursing-home. Ten percent of those who enter a nursing-home will stay there five years or more. By the year 2020, it is projected that the elder population will reach 72,000,000. At the same time there will be approximately 66,000,000 persons under the age of eighteen years. Thus we have the "sandwich" generation subsidizing two sectors of society . . . the young and the old.

Dr. Deepak Copra says we can live to age 120. It is obvious that for the purpose of sustaining life, your allopathic physician is an important figure. He/she is a friend in need when you break a bone or incur an acute and life-threatening disease.

The allopathic physician's general response to a problem is the prescription pad for medication that tends to suppress the underlying cause of the problem. We are asked why our elders are living so long, if not for modern medicine. Careful research has shown that much of the increase in life span has occurred in the past 100 years because of *public-health* measures such as clean water, sanitation measures, control of rodents and mosquitoes, etc., and not the use of allopathic medicines.

Elders of the late 1890s enjoyed excellent sanitation measures, better water, tending their own gardens, nutritional food minus the chemicals, homemade meals, hard work, and close family ties. Drugs came into full bloom in the 1950s along with processed foods, chemicals, loss of family connections, and government interference in the ability to care for himself.

According to Dr. Fulder, gerontologist, there is reliable data showing those now in their elder-elder years (eighty-plus) have had very little prior contact with the misuse of drugs.

Modern medicine cannot guarantee a ripe old age but combined with good public health measures, nutrition, natural health therapies, and medicines, most elderly will live to a ripe old age . . . with the dignity they deserve. But the responsibility lies with each of them, or their family, not with a dependence on drugs alone. Taking responsibility for good health leads to a higher level of life satisfaction, more years for prayer for family and country, time to grow spiritually, to volunteer time to those in need, and less taxation on the Medicaid and Medicare programs.

Today, the allopathic physician, often a specialist in his/her designated field, has made great strides in the medical field, albeit the excessive use of synthetic pharmaceuticals, surgeries, and medical equipment, which have proven too often to do more harm than good. The medical profession is taught to suppress symptoms with synthetic drugs without understanding the true source of healing—the God-given life force that is often neglected and forgotten (McGarey, p. xix). No one knows all the possible problems synthetic drugs are causing for the elderly who reside in a nursing-home (R. Strand, p. 197).

Currently, $150 billion is spent annually on nursing-home care in the United States. Geriatric care is a specialty. The Alliance for Aging research has documented a need for 20,000 geriatric-trained physicians to adequately care for thirty-five million elderly, of whom 1.7 million are in 18,000 nursing-homes across the nation. Of the 650,000 allopathic physicians, only 9,000 are gerontologists. By the year 2030, if the system does not change, the United States will need 36,000 gerontologists (N. Gingrich, p. 29).

Ninety percent of today's long-term facilities are acknowledging there is a severe shortage of nurses, which, in turn, jeopardizes the care of its elderly residents. By the year 2020 there will be a 400,000 nurse shortage nationally. (N. Gingrich, p. 28).

Medical school applications have fallen for the fifth year in a row (N. Gingrich, p. 29). There will be 200,000 deficits within the medical profession by the year 2020 (N. Gingrich, p. 29). This deficit has opened the door for foreign doctors to be welcomed into the United States due to the fact that foreign doctors will work for less money and will adhere to the dominance of the pharmaceutical industry, which, again, will directly influence the health of nursing-home elders. (Lecture by M. Myers).

With the growth of government controlled nursing-homes, the care of the elderly elicited six new social behaviors:

1. Ease in placement of elders in nursing-homes
2. Displacement of guilt feelings by families and society upon the nursing-home industry
3. The practice of polypharmacy
4. The relinquishment of personal care assistance by the family, the church and society
5. The rapidly escalating cost for the taxpayer
6. Loss of spiritual care for both the elders and the staff

Stephen A. Moses in his Policy Analysis No 549 says it all very well: "LTC is an 800-pound gorilla of social problems that lurks just around the bend. If we wait to deal with Medicaid and LTC until after we handle Social Security and Medicare, it will be too late."

What does Moses mean when he says Long Term Care is an 800-pound gorilla of social problems? Let us examine this comment.

4
Nursing-Homes of Today

In the past thirty years, I have found most nursing-homes to be safe havens for the elderly and disabled—warm in the winters and cool in the summers; a hospice for the critically ill; a home for the homeless; a home that provides food for the body and a bit of food for the soul; clothing for the indigent; a home for contemplation, for memories; for working through anger, despair and hopelessness; meeting new faces; finding new friends; creating a neighborhood; finding companionship; developing a new love; petting a puppy, a kitten, a bird; watching the seasons come and go; anticipating a new grandchild, a wedding, Christmas, a Fourth of July picnic; an occasional visit from family or a friend; an occasional van ride; a visit from the doctor; medications delivered to the door; no more worries; no work; no laundry; no cooking; no dishes; no field work; clothes clean; baths taken; a roommate that is very precious; a little money in the bank and in the purse; controlled pain, dying and release from this earth. What more can an elder want?

The following note was written by Anna Mae Halgrim Seaver, who lived in Wauwatosa, Wisconsin. Her son found these notes in her room after her death.

This Is My World

This is my world now. It's all I have left. You see, I'm old. And, I'm not as healthy as I used to be. I'm not necessarily happy with it, but I accept it. Occasionally, a member of my family will stop in to see me. He or she will bring me some flowers or a little present, maybe a set of slippers—I've got eight pair. We'll visit for awhile

25

and then they will return to the outside world and I'll be alone again.

Oh, there are other people here in the nursing-home. Residents, we're called. The majority are about my age. I'm eighty-four. Many are in wheelchairs. The lucky ones are passing through—a broken hip, a diseased heart . . . something has brought them here for rehabilitation. When they're well they'll be going home.

Most of us are aware of our plight—some are not. Varying stages of Alzheimer's have robbed several of their mental capacities. We listen to endlessly repeated stories and questions. We meet them anew daily, hourly or more often. We smile and nod gracefully, each time we hear a retelling. They seldom listen to my stories, so I've stopped trying.

The help here is basically pretty good, although there's a large turnover. Just when I get comfortable with someone he or she moves on to another job. I understand that. This is not the best job to have.

I don't much like some of the physical things that happen to us. I don't care much for a diaper. I seem to have lost the control acquired so diligently as a child. The difference is that I'm aware and embarrassed but I can't do anything about it. I've had three children and I know it isn't pleasant to clean another's diaper. My husband used to wear a gas mask when he changed the kids. I wish I had one now.

Why do you think the staff insists on talking baby talk when speaking to me? I understand English. I have a degree in music and am a certified teacher. Now I hear a lot of words that end in "y." Is this how my kids felt? My hearing aid works fine. There is little need for anyone to position their face directly in front of mine and raise their voice with those "y" words. Sometimes it takes longer for a meaning to sink in, sometimes my mind wanders when I am bored. But there's no need to shout.

I tried once or twice to make my feelings known. I even shouted once. That gained me a reputation of being "crotchety." Imagine me, crotchety. My children never heard me raise my voice. I surprised myself. After I've asked for help more than a dozen times and received nothing more than a dozen condescending smiles and a "yes, deary, I'm working on it," something begins to break. That time I wanted to be taken to a bathroom.

I'd love to go out for a meal, to travel again. I'd love to go to my own church, sing with my own choir. I'd love to visit my friends.

Most of them are gone now, or else they are in different "homes" of their children's choosing. I'd love to play a good game of bridge, but no one here seems to concentrate very well.

My children put me here for my own good. They said they would be able to visit me frequently. But they have their own lives to lead. That sounds normal. I don't want to be a burden. They know that. But I would like to see them more. One of them is here in town. He visits as much as he can.

Something else I've learned to accept is loss of privacy. Quite often I close my door when my roommate—imagine having a roommate at my age—is in the TV room. I do appreciate some time to myself and believe that I have earned at least that courtesy. As I sit thinking or writing, one of the aides invariably opens the door unannounced and walks in as if I'm not there. Sometimes she even opens my drawers and begins rummaging around. Am I invisible? Have I lost my right to respect and dignity. What would happen if the roles were reversed? I am still a human being. I would like to be treated as one.

The meals are not what I would choose for myself. We get variety but we don't get a choice. I am one of the fortunate ones who can still handle utensils. I remember eating off such cheap utensils in the Great Depression. I worked hard so I would not have to ever use them again. But here I am.

Did you ever sit in a wheelchair over an extended period of time? It's not comfortable. The seat squeezes you into the middle and applies constant pressure on your hips. The armrests are too narrow and my arms slip off. I am luckier than some. Others are strapped into their chairs and abandoned in front of the TV. Captive prisoners of daytime television; soap operas, talk shows, and commercials.

One of the residents died today. He was a loner who at one time started a business and developed a multimillion-dollar company. His children moved him here when he could no longer control his bowels. He didn't talk to most of us. He often snapped at the aides as though they were his employees. But he just gave up; willed his own demise. The staff has made up his room and another man has moved in.

A typical day. Awakened by the woman in the next bed wheezing—a former chain smoker with asthma. Called an aide to wash me and place me in my wheelchair to wait for breakfast. Only sixty-seven minutes until breakfast. I'll wait. Breakfast in the dining area.

27

Most residents are in wheelchairs. Others use canes or walkers. Some sit and wonder what they are waiting for. First meal of the day. Only three hours and twenty-six minutes until lunch. Maybe I'll sit around and wait for it. What is today? One day blends into the next until day and date mean nothing.

Let's watch a little TV. Oprah and Phil and Geraldo and who cares if some transvestite is having trouble picking a color-coordinated wardrobe from his husband's girlfriend's mother's collection.

Lunch. Can't wait. Dried something with pureed peas and coconut pudding. No wonder I'm losing weight.

Back in my semiprivate room for a little semiprivacy or a nap. I do need my beauty rest, company may come today. What is today, again? The afternoon drags into early evening. This used to be my favorite time of the day. Things would wind down. I would kick off my shoes. Put my feet up on the coffee table. Pop open a bottle of Chablis and enjoy the fruits of my day's labor with my husband. He's gone. So is my health.

This is my world.

The question to be asked is, "Could this be your nursing-home?" Have nursing-homes changed in the past fifteen years? Could your elder family member who resides in a nursing-home write this exact same letter? What part did religious organizations play in Anna's life in a nursing-home? Could not their ministry pick up elders in nursing-homes for weekly services? Did she even mention prayer, meditation, natural therapies which would have decreased her time of idleness and feelings of despair? What organization could have provided a once a week game of bridge? Where was pet therapy? Could not family have purchased her a new and perfect-fitting wheelchair?

Where was the Social Service Director to listen to her needs? Where was the striking clock and battery movement calendar to keep her oriented to time and date? Could not she have a glass of Chablis every evening, kick off her shoes and relax after a busy day?

Where was the Dietary Manager concerning her weight loss? The waiting time for meals was inexcusable. Where was the Activity Director to provide an activity and prayers before meals? Where was the family? An editorial appeared in the *To-*

ledo Blade on May 9th, 2006 that says it all in essence: "Americans are just too busy. Here is twenty bucks to visit Grandma." And the facility would say that no one knew of her needs. And I ask why did they not know?

The Ascended Master Jesus of Nazareth gave us the Book of Love carried forth by the teachings of the first messengers, the Mandans and the Cathars, who taught universal truths about spiritual mankind. With the destruction of these teachings, most residents, staff, families, and society are spiritually lost and all suffer.

The Barry Corbet Story

Permit me to introduce you to a writer, author and filmmaker, who, with a disability, wrote so insightfully about his experiences in a nursing-home. His name is Barry Corbet and here is his story, entitled *Searching for a New Beginning Amongst Those Who Are Searching for an Ending:*

It happened so fast, it stunned me. At the age of sixty-seven, after one week in a hospital, I found myself in a nursing-home. Maybe I should not have been surprised. We think nursing-homes are just for old people, but that's not always true. Nursing-homes also exist for people like me. Most people in nursing-homes are old, but it isn't age that gets them there . . . it's disabilities, the kind that make us unable to get in and out of bed or get dressed or go to the bathroom on our own.

In 1968, I was in a helicopter that crashed while I was filming a movie near Aspen, Colorado. My lower body was paralyzed, and I started using my arms and shoulders as others use their legs and hips. Now, my bones are eroded by abuse and arthritis and muscles and tendons are long gone.

For thirty-five years it's been slow-motion demolition. Performing everyday tasks has become so painful, my functioning so balky, that I'm ready to try a partial shoulder replacement, the only remedy medicine offers. Recovery will certainly take many months. That certainly causes real fear. So equally does the uncertainty. No one can predict how long I'll lose my physical independence. But I've done my homework and made my decision.

29

One September morning I wake up very early and hoist myself out of bed on a ceiling-mounted lift. I ride the lift to the bathroom and deal with my bags of waste, liquid and solid. Then I shower, put on jeans and a T-shirt.

This is my morning routine . . . for years the same. What's different is how hard it is to do (anything) with ruined shoulders. In my power wheelchair, I roll out of the now empty house and into my lift-equipped van. I turn to the front, snap my chair into the driver's space, take up the hand controls, and I'm off to the hospital. It's 4:30 a.m.

An hour out of recovery, I wake up in a tiny hospital room. An opaque curtain separates me from my roommate, Joel, also a paraplegic. When not in the hospital, he lives in a nursing-home. Fourteen years after his injury, he's forgotten how to live in the world. We never see each other face-to-face but become buddies in a way . . . troubled souls living four feet apart for an entire week.

I pulled every string to avoid going to a nursing-home after surgery. I wanted to go to a rehabilitation facility. But eventually, we all get to a point where our strings aren't enough. Most people with longtime disabilities are terrified of nursing-homes. Many of the young disabled arrive on one-way tickets and spend years or decades attempting to make beginnings amid people occupied with endings. (It is my belief, in talking with young disabled persons that they have special needs and need a place of residence that provides innovative therapies and activities.)

Nursing-homes are environments of isolation and disempowerment. They dictate when to get up, when to go to bed, when and what to eat, when to take showers and who will help, and when and if to leave. The disability-rights movement resists. "Our homes," we chant, "not nursing-homes." But living with a disability at home takes nerve, know-how, and resources . . . resources the movement is trying to build but that are not yet adequate for most. But too many of us languish in nursing-homes until the desire to live in the outside world evaporates. We become lifers, sometimes unable even to get out of bed. It's not going to happen to me, I tell myself. I'm too well informed. Too proactive.

I am discharged from the hospital. My daughter drives me in my van to a small town only a few miles from my home in Golden, Colorado. I am delivered to a low brick building tucked away from the highway. No sign announces its name or purpose.

30

Impressionable Entrances to a Nursing-Home

On entering, I am met by a wall of fetid air. So many colostomies have passed this way, and here I am, bearing another. I wheel down the hall, and there's a new assault, an olfactory Doppler effect, as I pass each door. So it's true what they say, I think. Nursing-homes stink.

The Emotions. The Feelings. The Needs.

The next morning I smell nothing. Have I so quickly surrendered my senses, or is the smell really gone? On my own, in my power chair, I roll outdoors. Immediately I'm overcome by the extravagance of color and warmth. I haven't realized how thoroughly my senses and my freedom have been deprived. I had forgotten what fresh air and sunshine can do to a vulnerable mind. I'm embarrassed. For two days, I weep.

My Space

My room in the nursing-home is small, but it does have a window and it's private. This is extraordinarily lucky. Most of the rooms, just as tiny as mine, are double occupancy because that's what Medicare covers. But before I signed on with this facility, the management agreed to provide a dedicated phone line for my computer. Now it seems giving me a room with two phone connections and no roommate is the easiest way to get me online. After some experimentation, I conclude the new speech-recognition software doesn't work as well for me as one-handed keyboarding. It's clumsy, torture at first, but it links me to the world beyond this place. I can do some writing. I'm an accidentally embedded journalist with a different kind of war to report.

The rehabilitation wing, where I am, is nominally separate from the long-term nursing wings, where the permanent residents are, and the secured unit, where many of the Alzheimer's residents reside. But the borders leak. Almost every day some confused stranger wanders into my room. Negotiation seldom works, so I use my wheelchair to bar the door against intruders. Some of our crowd, too, are temporarily unhinged because of head

31

injuries, drugs, who knows what. We are not tolerant of the people we think are crazier than we are.

Here, doctors are the ultimate authority of irreversible destiny. They are also rarely seen. My medical care is usually supervised by physician assistants. Medicare calls them physician extenders—an odd term—sounds like Hamburger Helper.

My Nurses

To my pleasant surprise, the day to day authorities—the nurses—are good, helpful people who generally respect my thirty-five years of experience with spinal cord injury. Every night an aide gives me a bed bath. Aides are at the bottom of the pay scale—the grunt labor, the lifters, the bathers, the meal servers, the toileters, the people who spend the most time with residents. They are the glue that holds this place together. Most are men in their late teens or twenties, people who can take the hard work and want the long shifts. Some work four sixteen-hour shifts a week and hold down a McJob besides. Racially and culturally, they are an accurate sampling of modern America. A couple have degrees . . . some are headed for nursing school or taking business courses; one has EMT credentials. Some look like angels and some like hard cases, but none look as if they relish bathing a sixty-seven-year-old paralyzed man with holocaust legs, bilateral toe amputations, and multiple rearrangements of his personal plumbing. Some of them look as sensitive as rocks. I fear exposing myself to these men. I think how I would have hung back from such work at their age, but they show no resentment. They take the time required and attend to the task with something approaching good cheer, even tenderness. They tell me about their lives as they bathe my body. And I am touched.

My Identity

For thirty-five years riding a wheelchair has been a distinguishing mark of my identity. In the group photos, the wheelchair is what makes me easy to spot. Not here. Here my persona is preempted by all these stupendously old women . . . there are very few men in the long-term care sections . . . who create gridlock in the dining room and accidentally lock wheels passing one another in the halls. Practically everyone's in a wheelchair, but I'm the only one not new to wheels. Wheelchairs are engines of liberation to me. They enable me to go where I want, when I want. This place reminds me why nondisabled people think they are tragic.

Their Identity

In the custodial sections, residents are propped up and seat-belted in their chairs, left with nothing to do but the impossible task of getting comfortable on old, unupholstered bones. Their heads hang down and they wait, their chairs no more than movable restraints. Some residents still move themselves. Heading back to their rooms after meals in the big dining room, they run out of stamina and stop in their lanes (like) toy race cars whose batteries have run down. For others, the bid for locomotion is Sisyphean (futile) labor . . . as heads are bent forward, they strain to gain a few yards. Then tragedy . . . somebody whisks them away to wherever they came from. There is usually a bright announcement of the staffer's intention, "Hi, Maria, let's go back to your room." But no request for permission.

The Names We Use!

The diminutives! The endearments! The idiotic "we's!" Hello, dear, how are we today? What's your name, dear? Eve? Shall we go to the dining room, Eve? Hi, hon, sorry to take so long. Don't we look nice today! You've got to eat, sweetie. Sweetie, would you take a pill for me? A little prune juice, sweetie? Chirpy singsong voices. Who thinks we want to be talked to (in) this way?

The Invasion

The ceaseless din of television sets and alarms. So many people with so little to do. The constant pill pushing. The nighttime visits by aides. The preemptory bang on the door, the room suddenly flooded by light, like a drug raid. The unending need to educate. My safety depends on the staff's knowing the arcane of how to handle my body and its odd attachments, but each shift brings new helpers to teach.

The World of Worries

The errors. I normally do my own monthly catheter change. I'm more immune to my bugs than to other people's and the years have given me more experience than most nurses ever get. I can't do it one-handed, so I consent to a nurse changing it. Trouble. They don't have the right size catheter. The nurse wants to install a different one, then replace it in a couple of days. Not a chance . . . major infection risk. Two days later, the correct catheter arrives. Nurse Anita changes it efficiently and expertly. She once worked in a urologist's office. Sometimes, I worry too much.

Medication Errors

Or maybe not. There are repeated staff errors with my medication, even though I myself administer all my medications but one. It's easy for me to spot the errors, but what about all the residents who have no idea what they are taking?

Appointments not Important . . . to Them

The nursing-home schedules any necessary doctor appointments, and I am supposed to get my sutures removed two weeks postsurgery. The day before the date specified by the surgeon, I ask a nurse if everything's arranged. "I made an appointment," she says. But she delegated the job, so she has to check. She comes back: "The appointment isn't until October 2." That's a week late. She doesn't know why it shook out that way. It's scheduled. Can't change what's scheduled. I consider accepting what is given, but instead I make my own phone call and reschedule the appointment for the next day. A small rebellion, which I am able to pull off because, with access to my own adapted van, I am not dependent on the home to get me there.

What Our Ears Hear, the Eyes See and the Heart Feels

That night, Squawk Lady calls for help. I've never seen her, but she's a constant aural presence with her amplified communication device. It's loud, and she can and does crank it louder. Squawk Lady is not happy with her circumstances. Now, she wants to get out of her room. Often it's something else she needs. "Help! Help! Help! Help!" she cries. It's piercing, unvarying, insistent, like a baby bird crying for food. It's hard to ignore and hard to listen to, and it's not her fault. I feel terrible calling her Squawk Lady. One day Squawk Lady falls silent. I miss her protests.

Overheard . . . a man: "Oh, for Christ's sake. I'm going home right now!" Another man: "Goddamn it! Get out of my room!" Yet another calling forlornly for his absent daughter, "Allie! Allie!" Then scolding . . . "Allie!"

Overheard . . . a male aide addressing Emma, a tall, elegant woman who came into my room a day or two ago: "Oh, hi, sweetheart, let's get you back to your room." "No! I'm going to get something to eat!" "Come on sweetheart, you can't be walking around like that. Let's go back to the room." "I said no! No!" The next morning, Emma wants to walk, and she doesn't want to discuss it with the devil's instruments, the aides. Emma is wired for altitude. If she starts to stand, an ear-piercing alarm sounds and aides immediately appear. When she really wants to stand, her alarm is a constant din. "Emma, honey, you've got to sit down." "I said no! Goddamn it! Get your hands off me!" "Then stop hitting us." Patiently, "the doctor says you can't stand up. He doesn't want you to break your hip." "Bullshit!" says Emma. "Bullshit!" Emma is not cowed by medical authority.

Emma sits, but a moment later her alarm is sounding. Soon it becomes evident from her creative cursing, that she has been restrained in a wheelchair. At the desk outside my door, the nurses discuss Haldol. The drug is administered. Emma is quiet. At breakfast, Emma and her Haldol are subjects of discussion; everybody seems to know about it. After breakfast, I see her nodding in the wheelchair near the front desk. She's there all morning, for convenient watching from the desk, but it's cruel nonetheless . . . she's on display, visible proof that in the nursing-home you can't fight city hall. After lunch, Emma is banging her feet on her footrest and asking to get out of her wheelchair.

After lunch, there is a full-court press to search the food trays. Mrs. Parker has lost her dentures. After lunch, an aide tells me that on days like this, all you can do is laugh. By midafternoon, Emma is screaming for someone to come to her room. "Get me out of this goddamn thing!" Then, perhaps as a ploy, "I've got to go to the bathroom." She's weeping now, and it's heartbreaking. "I've got to go to the bathroom. I've got to go to the bathroom."

Emma's neighbor, Henry, is a usually polite, sometimes violent man who always says hello and apologizes if his wheelchair is in anyone's way. He has an alarm that sounds when he leaves the premises. He has escaped twice today, but he moves so slowly that he's easy to retrieve. A few minutes later he's trundling out the door again, answering freedom's call.

By now, Emma has made it to the hallway in her wheelchair. The nurse recruits Bea, another resident, to visit with Emma. "Bea, would you talk to this lady while I check on another patient?" "Emma, this is Bea. Would you like to visit with her for a while?" "I most certainly would," says Emma, her dignity restored. A perfectly rational conversation ensues and continues until dinnertime.

I wish today were an anomaly, but it isn't. As the days go by, there are reenactments. Emma is asleep up by the front desk almost every morning and, not surprisingly, fights with the aides who want to put her to bed right after dinner. Henry grabs an aide's arm and scared her enough that she sits sobbing at the front desk.

We Go to Lunch

Food arrives at 8:00 a.m., noon, and 5:00 p.m. every day. Each tray (is) a study in gray, brown, and white, with accents of shocking pink, pink sugar water, pink gelatin marshmallows bled on by other pinks. For my first ten days all meals arrive cold. The steam table isn't working. When hot food does start coming, it's manna from heaven, and it's still punishment. On a scale of bad to very bad, breakfast is the nursing-home's best meal. I eat in the small dining area near the rehab section. We're too good for the main dining room, used by the permanent residents in the long-term wings. After all, the rehab resident's median age is only about seventy-five. We're scared to death someone will think we're old enough to actually be living here.

Tablemates

We don't have much in common, but we don't need much to set ourselves apart. At the other two tables sit the older women and the people with cognitive problems. We've established a pecking order and seldom break ranks. The room is small, and we all use wheelchairs. With most of us pushed, not self-propelled, negotiating a workable seating arrangement is pure silliness and confusion. Wheelchairs are yanked and slid into place. Push rims and footrests clash. Portable oxygen tanks fall to the floor. When someone on the inside—always the inside—wants to leave, there's another round, an exaggerated version of the kid on his way to the bathroom making everyone in a theater row rise.

Today I sit with the ladies. It's not by choice or epiphany, some upstart has taken my place at the head table. Sitting at my new table is Phyllis, who is very old and has diabetes. "I control it," she says as she pours sugar into her coffee. "I don't hear the things I'm not supposed to." She sugars her porridge. "It doesn't give me a bit of trouble." She pockets packets of sugar to take to her room. Emma is back with us today. There's something impish about her smile that's winning. You can tell she wants to say funny things for us, and occasionally she does. She pours melted butter over her scrambled eggs, and dips her cinnamon roll in hot-pink sugar water.

Lana completes our foursome. She broke her hip three weeks ago. "Where are you going today?" Peggy asks Lana from the head table. "I'm not going anywhere," says Lana. "But you're all dressed up." Lana has presence. "Well, if I do go somewhere, I'll be ready."

Bob, a recent amputee whose manner is far beyond sardonic, invariably claims the high ground next to the microwave. He has the place sized up, has already visited the kitchen for coffee. When I first join his group, Bob turns from his newspaper and mutters his form of welcome, "We're not very friendly." Ward, a chemist who has diabetes and a heart condition, usually sits at this table, as does Peggy, who is recovering from a fall from her roof. She has appointed herself the den mother of grumpy old men, the upholder of conversation, but it's an uphill battle. I haven't learned why Don is here. He has eczema, which makes him scratch his face and bat at his head with both hands life a Dick Tracy villain: Fly Face! Carbuncle! Scratch! He's clearly miserable. We watch his health fall day by day.

Going Home

As the weeks go by, Ward goes home and our group is filled out by Tom, short for Thomasina, an energetic octogenarian who is all country talk and smart humor. Tom has a problem. She can't continue to live at her assisted-living facility, which she likes, unless she stops falling down unpredictably. If she can't find a fix, her known options are moving permanently to a nursing-home, nothing else. She's brave in the face of this injustice and uncertainty, but also scared. After she joins our rehab group, our breakfast club has genuine cohesion. Everyone loves Tom.

The "Not Now" Therapy

Outside my room, Emma dozes. Finally she starts to wheel into my room. "Emma," I say, "do you have the wrong room?" She recognizes me and backs out with the most comical 'silly me' gesture imaginable. Her grace has made it a charmed communication. Sedation robs grace. Soon she's asleep in her wheelchair, then awake again, saying that her back hurts. She calls for someone to take her to her room, her voice weak and desperate. She asks a passing aide. "Not now," the aide says, with no reason, no indication of when.

There is cohesion here, both subtle and obvious. Even in the rehab wing several people are kept in physical restraints. There are no ropes or handcuffs, for frail people in wheelchairs, an immovable lap tray is restraint enough. Combined with the infernal alarms, these restraints are effective and very public. Chemical restraints (drugs) are also common. Emma's not nodding at the front desk for her health. She's there for the convenience of the staff. Henry nods right next to her.

Medicare Rules? Resident Rights?

In my private room, I pull up the Medicare rules on the Internet. I learn that nursing-home residents are guaranteed "the right to be free from seclusion and physical restraints, as well as chemical restraints with psychoactive drugs, for any reason other than the treatment of a medical condition." But what is a medical condition? Mending bones would seem to quality. Does disorientation? Pure orneriness? As always, the devil is in the details.

In the broader sense, though, restraint is a constant condition for all of us here. It's not force majeure, not even staff obstinacy; it's conditioning, habit, insistent reminding that this is how we do things. We know how things go smoothly. Smoothness is greatly admired here. But when smooth operation is the paramount goal, subjugation follows. It's built into the institutional model.

Medicare Discharge

It's time to talk discharge, says a social worker employed by the nursing-home. Medicare pays for acute care, and at the moment I seem to be chronic. She proposes discharge in one week. It's up to me, not Medicare, to find some way to live alone, with one working limb. Of course, they're not kicking me out. I am reminded that I can self-pay $150 a day and stay indefinitely. Not an option.

In-home Assistance

I've become increasingly functional once I'm up in my chair, but I still need help at the beginning and end of every day. I'll need a team of helpers to cover those times and provide backup against no-shows. I don't want to end up spending the night in my wheelchair waiting for an aide who doesn't come. It is my responsibility to find these people.

The quest starts badly. I'm referred to Mary, a woman in her sixties who says she gives the best bed baths in the world and that both she and God loves me. Mary has two partners and she's sure

I'll just love "the girls," as she calls them. I imagine myself as an imprisoned companion to these three women. God help me. The girls charge $15 an hour and want uninterrupted eight-hour shifts. Even so, I arrange to meet Mary right after church. The night before, she calls. The girls don't want to risk the steep road to my home in the foothills. I feel delivered. Other candidates want a job different from the one I have to offer. After a week of cold-calling and dead-end leads, my luck improves. Lourdes wants only a few hours a day, a few days a week. Eve wants the same.

Dismissal

Two days before I go, the Breakfast Club has changed again. Bob is walking with his new prosthesis and is itching to get out. Peggy is walking on her own and will go home two days after me. Don has been ominously absent, and Tom is losing her options.

Meanwhile, the rehab wing has an influx of new residents. All these new faces, and our club's table has been usurped by perfect strangers. Pretenders! A palace putsch! Yes, it's time to leave.

Only "Institutions" Receive Government Monies?

The residents, myself included, are all here because we need care, temporarily or permanently. But that does not mean we need institutional care. If Medicare and Medicaid were willing to spend more on in-home help, wouldn't it keep us more active in the world, prevent unnecessary dependency, save taxpayers money? Since the 1999 Supreme Court decision in *Olmstead vs LC, (98-536) 527 U.S. 581 (1999)*, the law has recognized that disability services should be in the "most integrated setting." Yet the distribution of federal money continues to remain heavily biased in favor of institutional services. For many, the nursing-home is the only option.

What if I had to spend the rest of my life here? What if I had to live, as so many do, without any hope of release, without the unusual freedom of movement I have enjoyed roaming outdoors in my power chair and in cyberspace in my private room? What if I were trapped with this mindset that teaches all of us to tolerate endless cries for help, this unchanging gray existence, this total surround of people hoping for escape or waiting to die? If this happens, I see myself slipping away into passivity and dependency—better, I think, than cycling between obstreperousness (refusing to be controlled) and chemical restraint.

THE THOUGHT IS UNBEARABLE!
Utterly, unalterable unbearable!
It shouldn't happen to anybody.

Going home !

Barry Corbet, writer, editor, former mountaineer, filmmaker, the author of this article (previously entitled, "Embedded,"), did go home. Because his surgery results fell short of his hopes and his other shoulder deteriorated further, he did not regain the full physical independence he would have liked. As he discovered firsthand, however, personal independence doesn't always mean doing it all yourself. With in-home help, he regained control of his life. On good days he was able to take the steering wheel of his van and go anywhere he pleased. At other times he learned to enjoy being a passenger. Sometimes he worried about what would happen if he outlived his money. He didn't. He died on December 18, 2004, at the age of sixty-eight, after a graceful surrender to cancer. He was in his own bed, surrounded by people who loved him and who respected his wishes in things large and small.

Retyping this article was hard! I left the computer several times, weeping, as I saw myself in almost every instance. I am guilty of doing those very things Barry Corbet wrote about. I was a follower. I was blinded by rules and paperwork. My heart is heavy. This article reveals what is presently creating the psychological and spiritual dispassionate care of elders and disabled persons in a nursing-home setting . . . the medical modality and the lack of vision in providing activities and therapies developed on an individual and personal basis. Are not changes needed?

41

Paraguay, South America Home for the Elderly

Dr. Marie, Joe, and I were standing outside a lovely Spanish house surrounded by a tall, white stucco wall that surrounded the grounds. A large decorated wrought iron gate graced the entrance to keep its occupants safe and secure. Dr. Marie rang a gentle sounding bell. A young lady came running to the gate. Recognizing Dr. Marie, she unlocked the gate to let us in.

Gorgeous gardens with ample trees and flowing flowers in every color of the rainbow greeted us. We stepped through the front glass French doors.

The house had been purchased by Dr. Marie to care for "old people." The word "nursing-home" was as unknown as was the word "resident." There was nothing on the outside to denote this house was any different than that of the neighbors. There was just a house address.

Entering, I noted, again, French doors on the elder's bedroom doors. Inside the first room were two twin beds with lovely bedspreads (each different) and all the amenities of a home-like atmosphere. Another set of French doors in this room lead to the outside gardens. There were no locks on any doors except on the outside decorative wrought iron gate. Not one elder wore an alarm band. No alarms went off and no codes to punch in.

It was noon. Ten elders sat around a beautiful dining room table except for two elders in wheelchairs, who were being fed separately. There were no restraints of any kind. The kitchen was adjacent to the dining room so the tantalizing odors filled the dining room.

As I brought forward the question of training, all three staff looked at one another, not quite understanding what I meant when I said "training." None had any training in the care of the elderly. What I noted was a natural compassion and common sense in the care of the elders.

In speaking with the caretaker serving the meals, I discovered she was also the business manager and lived in the house. All food was prepared from "scratch."

And to prove the goodness of the menu (which was not posted) for that day, I sampled the food. To use the words of our youngsters, "It was awesome." The staff joined their elders, prayer was said, and the meal was enjoyed by all. No special diets nor portions mandated. Just simple, nutritious food. I noted none were overweight nor appeared exceptionally thin. The topic of conversation was this stranger in their midst who could not speak Spanish except one who spoke French with broken English and could answer my simple questions.

Walking into the kitchen, there was not a commercial dishwasher, nor stainless steel kitchen counter tops, nor a hood over the stove, nor two doors to the kitchen (in the States there is a regulation that one door is for the delivery of meals and the other to take the soiled dishes back). I had to remind myself, this is a *home* not a regulated institution.

The other two staff did all the duties required of caring for the elders as well as the housework and laundry (there were no dryers), so all linens and clothes were hung outside to dry. No names were written on clothes and personal items as staff knew each elder's clothes personally.

Each evening Dr. Marie and I went shopping for fresh fruits and vegetables for the Home. When Dr. Marie returned to the Home, she also paid the staff for the hours they worked *that day!* When I asked the reason, she said staff is quite poor and they needed the money to buy food/clothes/rent for the next day. Each staff was paid approximately $300 for one month's work.

As my mind was calculating the per hour rate, I was reminded that unemployment was exceedingly high. These young women were thankful to have a job to keep them off the streets begging for their food. Three hundred dollars per month was extraordinary pay. And they received free meals at the house during their work hours. In Paraguay there are no food pantries, welfare, or food stamps for the poor. If you did not work, you did not eat. Needless to say, staff turnover rate was almost zero.

Then calculating that it took three elders to pay just for staff wages, there was food, cleaning supplies, utilities, and upkeep of the house. There were no taxes levied against businesses or personal gain income taxes. Each home owner was expected to share in the upkeep of the street and sidewalks outside of the home.

Each elder paid for their own medications. There is no Medicaid, Medicare, or insurance to pay for elder care.

I asked where the medications were kept (as I was so brainwashed in the search for a "med" cart). A small white cupboard door was opened (not locked). Inside were twelve small shoe boxes. Each box had the elder's name on it and a notation as to when they were to receive the medication. The staff quietly closed the door and saw the look of amazement on my face. And then I thought back to the early seventies and said, "That's the way it used to be . . . simple. When did we think we had to have the rumbling, heavy, awkward medication carts! And now, all medications are in single, bubble packages that cost the taxpayer and private pay residents a fortune!

The elders were nicely dressed. Staff wore street clothes. In conversation, I was told there are no surveyors, just a yearly inspection, at which time the inspector talked with the elders to listen to any complaints. Actually, this inspector would be similar to an Ombudsman. There were no "consultants" to direct the staff, there were no resident rights posters, no activity directors, no social workers, no nurses, no medical director, no physical therapy, no maintenance department (they were called in when needed), no fire inspections, no MDS, or MSDS, or computers, or business managers, and no resident charts! There were no shelves piled high with policies and procedures. IT WAS A HOME!

It looked and smelled like A HOME! These elders, in this "home" will pass from this Earth amidst the gardens of flowers and trees, in a home-like environment with their families and familiar staff beside them.

I asked Dr. Marie how the elders paid their bills. She stated she sends out monthly bills to the family at $300 per month and for any extra charges such as medications, clothes, telephone usage, etc. Families come to the Home and take the elder to the doctor, or for a day of pleasure. The Home had no van.

I took pictures of the elders and several rooms (I did not have to obtain their permission to do so), gave hugs, and thanked them for their courtesies, thanked the staff and left, somewhat, again, awestruck as to how far we in the United States have permitted the caring of our elders to become big business for big profits and controlled and manipulated by government agencies.

Was everything perfect at the Asuncion home for elders? No, I would be amiss to say so. One iron bed was quite rusty around the frame, tiles were missing in the wash room, and a bedpan needed to be replaced. These would be deficiencies in the States. Of course just the method of medication distribution would close facilities down in United States. There's no profit in using shoe boxes. Overall, there was no odor (panty protectors were of washable cotton, not disposables), and the home was very clean.

Why Are United States Seniors Heading South to Mexican Nursing-Homes?

According to *USA Today*, there is a small but growing number of Americans who are moving across the border to nursing-homes in Mexico, where the sun is bright, the weather is warm, and the living is cheap.

Jean Douglas, an elder and U.S. citizen, has stated that nursing-home care cost her $300 per month for a studio apartment, which includes three meals a day, laundry and cleaning service and twenty-four hour care from attentive staff, many of whom speak English.

Richard Slater, another elder, has his own cottage (notice the word "cottage" rather than "room") receiving twenty-four-hour nursing care, three meals a day cooked in a homey kitchen and served in a sun washed dining room. His cottage has a living room, bedroom, kitchenette, bathroom, a patio, and a walk in closet plus room for his two dogs. For this Slater pays $550 a month. For another $140 a year, he receives full medical coverage from the Mexican government, including all his medicine and insulin for diabetes. Most elder care apartments are a section of private homes.

David Warner, a University of Texas public affairs professor is studying the phenomenon. He writes that there are an estimated 40,000 to 80,000 retirees already residing in Mexico.

Overall, the basic reasons for Americans to enter Mexican

nursing homes is lesser costs, good, natural foods, better care, warm weather, no governmental intrusion, and a home-like environment.

Can Nursing-Homes in the United States of America Change?

The following article written by Victor Hull appeared in the *Kansas Herald Tribune* in 2006:

Steve Shield's mother was in his nursing-home spending her last days on this earth. It was in this traumatic moment a movement began. Steve was the facility administrator. Steve remembers saying, as his mother was dying, "It's like I'd never seen anything before . . . the barrage of sounds, the beeping of medical equipment, clanging of meal carts, buzzing conversation. It seemed so unnatural and sick. This has to go." He asked himself if this is what we want for our parents and ourselves as we age and are in need of nursing-home care.

This facility was no different than any of the other 18,000 nursing-homes in United States, which house more than 1.7 million elders and handicapped persons.

At this moment, a personal transformation as well as a facility transformation was born in order to change the conventional, hospital-like facility into a different place that looks, smells, feels, and runs more like a home. Rather than being roused before dawn, herded to cafeteria meals, and bathed assembly-line style, the facility residents now make their own schedules, choose what they want to eat, and select activities. One resident gets up at nine or ten in the morning to have a muffin and tea, while another is permitted to stay up late to read, listen to music and write notes.

Have we, again, come full circle with the thirty-five active, innovative "Green House" communities now being developed across United States in which ten Elders live in cottages, eat in the kitchen, where they can smell the food cooking and the coffee brewing and are cared for by "family" called Shahboz. Can nursing-homes, built on the medical modality, make the transition? First, we must examine the metaphysical purpose of nursing-homes.

5

What Is the True Purpose of a Nursing Home?

Metaphysically, not one elder is in a nursing-home against his/her *subconscious / spiritual* will. No one forced an elder into a mental or physical disability. The elder chose to live a long life; every event that occurred in his/her life including disease or aged conditions of the body was brought into fruition by the elder person *alone*. Each chose his/her "lot" in life. Elders are completing their lives on this Earth exactly as they have chosen. Elders are working out their karma.

The Elder nursing-home residents have chosen their caretakers. And the caretakers have chosen to work in a nursing-home, *on a subconscious / spiritual level!*

The premise for this belief is that every human being has one life purpose and that is to return, perfected, to his/her creator. To become perfected, the human being needs many life experiences. There are those who need to understand and feel pain, loneliness, and loss of independence, and what better place than in a nursing-home environment. How the elder responds to his/her daily challenges is directly related to the "soul's" progression or regression toward perfection. Although every human being has free will, it is often forgotten that each of us has made a covenant with the Creator many eons ago.

If we are truthful within ourselves, we would accept the fact in our society we have relinquished our basic understanding of our societal purpose; our spirituality, our life ideals, goals, and morals. Most have lost the teachings of karma and reincarnation.

Thus, it should come as no surprise that one of the industries in the nation, nursing-home care, has lost its true purpose. Our nation, as a whole, is losing its way in thoughts, words, and deeds.

All thoughts are energies emitted into the universe. Each of us can and often do pick up energy thoughts of greed, egotism, perversion, hatred, manipulations, war with other nations and peoples on this Earth, the quest for power by financial institutions and corporations designing how to control and place the working class into slavery. All evil thoughts and words are emitted on a subconscious level to all humans.

If we insist on being with those on the dark side of life, we will take on that darkness. If we do not protect ourselves from these people, thoughts, and places, we, too, become unenlightened beings totally immersed in negativity. To combat these negative thoughts and behaviors, we must visualize ourselves wrapped in white light and use daily prayer, meditation, positive thoughts and words in our personal life, as well as during work hours. Daily prayer, positive thoughts, words, and deeds must be part of the elder's daily activities.

Both residents and staff have chosen to meet one another in a nursing-home setting to grow spiritually in this life. How well we do is coded in the Book of Life.

Consider not whether you are fed, clothed, or housed; but only whether you love and pray and serve others. When you work . . . think of God. When you rest . . . let him hold you . . . when you reach out . . . touch his hand . . . and then put your arm around a friend.
Hugh Lynn Cayce in **For These Times,** *1964*

The Meaning of "Home" Before Entering a Nursing-Home

During interviews with nursing-home residents I was provided the following definitions of what "home" meant to them prior to residency in a nursing-home:

"It was a sense of security and it was mine."

"I could call the day my own."
"I had my own things. And they were all my memories."
"I didn't need to worry that someone would steal my things."
"I owned everything in it."
"I had things that I was going to give to my children."
"I built this place."
"I worried about the bills and now I don't."
"I no longer could mend things."
"I have no strong feelings about the house."
"I don't miss the house, that's why I use to leave every holiday."
"A house is a house but I'm not going to make a god of it."
"The furniture is old. I am old. But I felt I needed to stay in my house because I needed to be faithful to it."

What statements hold the inner feelings of our elders?

6

Elders Entering Today's Nursing-Home

Elders are institutionalized into a nursing-home without ever committing a crime, except the crime of aging. With the relinquishment of financial, care-giving, and decision-making by the family, society, and religious organizations, the elder is placed under the control of an allopathic medical doctor being aware that an allopathic physician is one who treats diseases by using pharmaceutical medications that treat the symptoms, not the underlying cause of the illness.

An elder cannot be admitted to a nursing-home without allopathic physician orders. The elder cannot leave the facility, nor fold towels, sweep a floor, set tables, have an alcoholic beverage, smoke, or take a vitamin without the physician's approval. Elders are forced into dependency—anathema for many proud, independent American elders.

The majority of elders often seek refuge in a nursing-home setting due to limited vision, auditory, and/or dexterity, limited mobility, unidentified pain, memory decline, nutritional deficiency, loss of driver's license, financially not able to maintain house and utilities, fear of being alone, depression, gangs targeting the elder, or family members financially abusing the elder. My personal observation is that some elders seek nursing-home care with the sole intention of shortening their lives by refusing to eat, hiding medications to be taken all at one time, banging their head against a wall, falling, or cutting themselves.

All of the above reasons are not for medical need and can be alleviated by family responsibility, home health agencies, church, community, and the return of elder care in private homes, where governmental controls do not impact decision making in the type of care provided.

The mortality rate during the first year of admission to a nursing-home is significantly higher than the rate for those who stay in familiar and home-like environments.

By remaining in their own home, or in a more compassionate end of life natural health therapeutic facility, the elders avoid the exile, loneliness, and indignities that await them in most nursing-homes of today.

For more than fifty years, society has accepted the medical model nursing-home. Very few think there might be a more compassionate way to care for the elderly and disabled. Why is it that none of us reading these words want to go to a nursing-home? As I travel throughout the Midwest, I spot the typical nursing-home with its brick walls extending in opposite directions from the entrance way, a few flowers outside, and the American flag flying overhead. Inside the entrance door is always the nursing station and a myriad of offices, rarely a large, comfortable family room with fireplace, game tables, inviting tables and chairs for family visits. In the majority of facilities, soft music, fresh flowers and live plants are missing. Private family rooms are rare. In no nursing-home, do I find the sweet odor of fresh bread and cookies baking. How many "homes" have an overhead call system blaring day and night and the rumbling sounds of a medication cart? Certainly this environment is not a "home." By creating a compassionate end of life natural health therapeutic facility, the elders avoid the exile, loneliness, and indignities that may await them in most nursing-homes today.

The Allopathic Physician and the Newly Admitted Nursing-Home Resident

In my youth, the family doctor made house calls, delivered babies in a maternity home, was the community surgeon, family counselor, a friend, and a man who often carried a little black bag that consisted of a stethoscope, a bottle of castor oil, and a prayer book. The doctor was honest about Grandma when he knew her time was short. No miracle drugs, no life supports to prolong a tired body that was well prepared to enter another life.

Elders passed over in their own bed, in their own home, with their family at their side.

According to Dr. Robert D. Kennedy, geriatrician, geriatric medicine advocates that it seeks to *give* life to years, rather than years to life. "We do not advocate life-support systems as a twentieth century elixir. We are concerned with the quality of life with *dignity*."

Dr. Kennedy admits that medical practice is still often in the dark about what is appropriate treatment or management for elders in nursing-homes.

"We must remember," says Kennedy, "that elderly residents often have a different profile of illness and problems. Elderly residents have acute illnesses layered on chronic illnesses. They may have psychological problems as well as somatic and social problems and needs. They cling to long developed and fixed attitudes as a personal life-support system. Acute care hospitals with the mechanistic, macho, and all for this moment atmosphere . . . invade and often demolish the old person when admitted and cared for in an entirely different atmosphere."

The medical and nursing staff of a nursing-home are often only too ready and too eager to contribute to the alleged frailty and debility of their older residents not only by often mistaken diagnosis but by instantly placing elders in wheelchairs, assisting them in eating, and toileting, and delivering medications to their mouths because that is what staff is trained to do.

It is hard for an eighty-year-old resident to shake off the label "confused or "demented" once it has appeared in writing in the nursing and medical records. The stigma remains until the person passes away. The labeling begins with a mini-mental assessment. If the resident fails to identify the name of the last president (as if the resident really cared), or to determine today's date without glancing at a calendar (like the rest of us do many times in a day), or because of slow responses due to excessive benzodiazepine blood levels in the body.

Prior to entering a nursing-home, many elders had a spell of ill-health or fell in their own home. An emergency transfer by an ambulance, then a stay in a hospital setting, going through testing, and a change in medications often lead to confusion. The move to a nursing-home induces even more confusion, incontinency, and weakness, which often lead to an inaccurate diagnosis. This preadmission system of diagnosis often leads to being restrained either through medication or a physical restraint that only further confuses the thought processes, dampens responses, and increases incontinence. To be labeled "demented" all the resident needs to do is "be noisy" . . . get out of bed too often by her/him self . . . swear at the staff, slobber through his/her food, miss the toilet, repeat the same stories over and over, poop in the bed or pee in the tub while getting a bath—all due to the fact in one short week, life has been turned upside down.

Dr. Kennedy strongly states that the geriatric resident has little hope of escaping the labels given upon admission because, "we don't yet know how to cope with these difficulties."

Dr. Siegfried Kral, M.D., whose research states that the elderly, from age seventy to ninety-five, have the same brain chemistry. Only society labels the old as suffering a decline in intelligence and mental capacity.

In one facility I noted a gentleman playing classical music on the piano, reading *National Geographic* and he carried on a very professional conversation when I visited with him. Upon admission, he was labeled "MR." When I asked why, the response was, "that is what the physician documented, although his brother said he had a nervous breakdown." Speaking with his brother, I was told the resident had been a college professor.

How about this delightful mini-mental at the time of admission?

The Summer of Her Ninety-sixth Year

Did you ask where I am?
I'm in a very comfortable place, a hotel.
No, I don't know where it is
but they are very nice to you here.
You can do whatever you like, it's very nice.

What day is it you say? Oh, it's a summer day,
warm, I like it warm, it reminds me of my father.
He would smile when I sang.
It was so long ago, you know,
so many summer days.

The year? I always had trouble with numbers.
I remember the year my brother was born.
I was seven and I made believe he was my baby.
I wish my mother was here. Are you here, momma?
Are you my mother? Oh, I thought for a moment . . .

Did you say you are a doctor?
I've always admired the medical profession.
I knew many doctors years ago,
Most of them were kind.
Does the light fade early in the summer?

No. I can't eat anything. I'm not hungry.
I'm afraid of this food.
I'm sorry I can't hear. Did you say
I hurt my hip and had an operation?
Well, for heaven's sake. I didn't know that.

Hospital? No, this is a hotel. It's warm here.
God bless you doctor.
I'm glad we met but don't let me keep you.
You must have patients to take care of
and I'm all right.

—Conversation recorded by John Mann Astrachan MD,
New York

The Elder and Emotional Distress When in a Nursing-Home

The transformation in old age into a condition calling for total medical control has cast the elderly into a minority role that tends to makes them feel painfully deprived at any level of care.

Without compassionate and spiritual care offered primarily through the implementation of natural health therapies, elder residents exhibit pangs of anger, misery, depression, and bitterness often against family, staff, and society.

Unrelieved emotions evolve into demands for more and more services as residents feel they are a class who deserve any and all services available i.e. medications, surgery, dental and eye care, handicapped devices, and a myriad of other services paid for by Medicaid, Medicare, and insurances. These elders often become the "I demand" generation.

When not catered to, elders often tend to create a myriad of psychosomatic type illnesses, especially depression, which results in more medications. Elders, in this environment, thrive on any attention to compensate for their loss of independence and societal value.

One classic example was in a veterans facility, when I overheard a conversation between a member (resident) and a newly admitted member: "To get attention in this place, you make up symptoms."

The medical professionals respond, as they are trained, to do something. The allopathic physician discusses another possible diagnosis adding to the ever-growing polypharmaceutical regimen.

Depression is often seen in nursing-homes. Katz and Parmelee estimated that the rate of depression for nursing-home residents dramatically exceed those found in the general population. Depression involves 30 percent to 50 percent of the nursing-home population.

Remembering that residents in a long-term-care setting take approximately eight medications, double the amount of the older adult in the general population, the survey concluded that with this large number of medications, the central nervous system can be negatively affected.

Interestingly, society generally and the medical community specifically, think that nursing-home elders are supposed to be depressed due to the number of physical and mental impairments. The medical community seemingly disregards the fact that half of the prescribed medications for nursing-home elders are likely to have a depressant effect with adverse drug reactions occurring in 23 percent of nursing-home residents. (Garavaglia. "Avoiding Drug-Induced Depression in Nursing-Home Residents." Article, 2002).

The practice of polypharmaceuticals often creates a loss of appetite, increase in falls, anxiety, behavioral problems, incontinency, and confusion. My experience in over thirty years, more often than not, all mental and physical changes are, again, dealt with by prescribing additional medications.

Is There an Alternative?

Entering a nursing-home is traumatic for elders as they are often separated from families, personal possessions, neighbors, friends, and lifetime religious institutions.

And elders are well aware of reports of staff abuse, which have escalated due to a disorganized society struggling to make ends meet. Nursing-home elders see themselves as victims within that disorganized society.

Missing from most nursing-homes is the art of spirituality rarely introduced in today's nursing-homes. Spirituality offers an esoteric explanation as to the elder's existence and purpose in residing in a nursing-home. Plus elders suffer from a loss of touch and compassion. Elders know only boredom, illnesses, pain, and death.

Nursing-home medical staff, trained in the hospital model and medical modality, treat the site of pain but not the total (spiritual) being. Nursing-homes are even called institutions, though elders have committed no crime, other than the crime of becoming old and made to feel valueless.

According to Ivan Illich in his book, *Medical Nemesis* over 1,600,000 nursing-home residents in 18,000 nursing-homes, have been targeted by the pharmaceutical and medical industries as property to be converted into financial gain. Dr. Al Power states that for every dollar we spend on medications in nursing-homes, we spend $1.33 on the side effects of the medication (*Old Age in a New Age*, p. 165).

Nurses are trained only in medical nursing skills. Governmental entities and State Surveyors mandate paper compliance with more regulations than NASA. In my observation and research, for every hour of personal care, one hour is spent on paper compliance.

Therefore, elders continue to fear not only entering a dispassionate, government-regulated, medically controlled nursing-home, the thought of being there the rest of their life leads to depression and anger.

Nursing-homes can change with a vision to create compassionate and holistic care with the implementation of natural-health therapies that provide healing of the mind, body, and spirit. Natural therapies work to decrease pain, anxiety, and depression. Elders are taught to commune with God and Nature.

In the beginning the word "medicine" was derived from the Sanskrit root "ma" or "me," meaning balance (or holistic), connecting people and the natural world around them. Therefore, in the eyes of natural health therapists, society is seen "as human organisms, pulsating, vibrating, energetic, well-balanced, holistic spiritual beings."

The key to natural health care is *spirituality*. Without a strong, consistent spiritual attitude, all the natural food and therapies, will be for naught. Without a doubt, there is a growing acceptance and resurgence of holistic (natural or alternative) medicine (*Harvard Public Health Review*), except in the nursing-home industry. And how many facilities permit the entire staff to pray with the residents or talk about God or heavenly beings, the All in One, the Essence, the Energy Source, or Allah?

"One that fills the mind, the very being, with an expectancy of God, will see His movement, His manifestation, in the wind, the

sun, the earth, the flowers . . . —Edgar Cayce Reading 341-31
(Stevens, p. 23).

Their Purpose, Our Purpose

Society and families expect nursing-homes to correct a life-time (and past lives) of traumatic family and social situations. When the fact is only the resident has the power to make changes. However, the nursing-home staff and families can, with compassion and proper training, assist the resident to the next level of spirituality and understanding as to why life presented so many traumas. And in turn, nursing-home staff, when the opportunity comes their way to lift up another, they lift up their own soul.

On the other side of the coin, the resident who has come to the nursing-home owes much to the staff. Here is an elder's opportunity to change spiritually and uplift the staff with their prayers, meditations, positive thoughts, and words. Nursing-home elders have chosen their caretakers on a spiritual level. How the elders treat the staff is part of their karma.

The elder woman has much to contribute as her energy is often turned towards spirituality. She is to be a mentor, a teacher, a counselor for the younger woman whose energy is directed toward the family. The elder woman must lift up the younger woman in daily prayer. This is the primary reason why most nursing-homes have a majority of female residents and female staff.

Society and families see only the more obvious reasons for elders being admitted to a nursing-home such as:

1. The abuse of over-the-counter and prescribed drugs.
2. Depression and loneliness.
3. Malnutrition.
4. Financial manipulation by family/relevant others.
5. Physical, emotional, financial, sexual abuse.
6. Personal hygiene.
7. Alcoholism.

Whether for esoteric or the more socially acceptable reason for admittance, all nursing-home staff and residents have their spiritual work cut out for them. The only way to heal souls is to heal oneself first by beginning the long and mysterious journey into the world of touch, love, positive thoughts and words, meditation, prayers, introduction to reincarnation, and the practice of natural-health therapies. But what are natural-health therapies?

7
What Are Natural Health Therapies?

Natural-health therapies date back to the creation of man with the use of herbs, the healing energy of the sun and fresh air, and being in touch with nature; dance, Native American drumming, prayer, color, music, mantras, meditation, reflexology, massage, dowsing, homeopathy, and the recognition of each human as a spiritual, vital force being.

Man knew instinctively that mind was the builder (H. Reilly and R. Brod, p. xiv). What man thought, so it was. Reincarnation and karma was the philosophy of many cultures including Old Testament peoples and the first three hundred years of Christianity.

Up to the turn of the twentieth century, medical books (one written by M. Melendy) were abundant with natural therapies and homeopathic remedies. The country doctor and family physician utilizing natural therapies was respected and well-known for his dedication, knowledge, and adherence to the Hippocratic Oath . . . (M. Bealle, p.13), which states that the physician will prescribe regimens for the good of patients according to his/her ability and judgment, and first, *do no harm.*

Natural-health therapies in the care of the elderly continue to be practiced throughout many nations with the exception of the United States. Natural health therapy is sometimes known as:

- Complementary/integrative care
- Alternative medicine
- Drugless therapy
- (W)Holistic therapy

In Sweden there are Health Homes, Health Farms, and Health Ranches with the primary aim of promoting good health. Seventy percent of Swedes utilize alternative methods, with 20 percent of the Dutch selecting alternative methods. Alternative means other than the use of prescribed medications or surgery. Fifty percent of the Belgian population uses one or more natural remedies (J. Carter, p. 233). Germans spend $4 billion every year on herbs alone (R. Strand, p. 79). In Asuncion, Paraguay, I observed herbs being sold on every street corner and used in the Homes for the Elderly.

England's Royal Family endorses alternative therapies, consuming only organic foods grown on their farms. Prince Charles, as President of the British Medical Association, appointed a homeopathic physician to introduce alternative methods in all colleges and underwrite alternative research (J. Carter, p. 244).

Data indicates that in Europe medical facilities utilizing drug free techniques are known as Biologic Clinics or Sanatoriums (J. Carter, p. 233), with fresh air and daily sun baths as part of the healing regimen. European and South American countries endorse alternative therapies because they work and are cost effective (J. Carter, p. 244).

In 1997 noninstitutionalized Americans spent $27 billion out of pocket on natural therapies, according to a study by researchers at the Beth Israel Deaconess Center for Alternative Medicine Research and Education—comparable to the amount spent out of pocket for all physician services in the same year. The Beth Israel Deaconess researchers also estimated that U.S. adults made a total of 629 million visits to alternative therapists in this same year (Nutritional Health Profiler).

Seventy-seven million aging baby boomers are entering retirement. These baby boomers are well versed in natural remedies and what it means to have good health. If nursing-home care is needed, they will demand holistic care. Despite the handwringing by allopathic physicians and pharmaceutical companies, the time has come for change.

The primary focus of natural-health therapies in nursing-homes would be on positive thoughts, understanding the purpose of life, one's spirituality, a continual uplifting of each resident, energy work, keeping the body in alignment, use of homeopathies (herbals and minerals), and a diet of wholesome, nutritional meals using only fresh organic products.

Alternative therapies are at the genesis of holistic health being utilized by many in the general populace; however, the nursing-home industry is at this time, offering few, if any alternative therapies for the elderly in nursing-homes.

Who Are Natural Health Professionals?

Even with severe shortages in the allopathic medical field and nurses, excluded from nursing-homes in the care of the elderly are osteopaths, chiropractors, massage therapists, natural health dietary counselors, homeopaths, naturopaths, herbalists, tai chi and yoga teachers, acupuncturists, colonists, chelation therapists, aromatherapists, music, art, color and dream therapists, holistic dentists, spiritual and energy professionals. The majority of natural-health care professionals are licensed, certified, and/or holding college degrees with annual training workshops mandated. Most natural-health practitioners possess life experiences in spiritual development (with a strong prayer life) and implement natural therapies in their own lives.

At times, osteopaths and chiropractors who work on nursing-home elders do collect from insurance companies; however, nursing-homes would not be reimbursed by Medicaid, Medicare, nor insurance companies in the utilization of natural health care professionals.

And then there are those courageous medical doctors and pharmacists who implement or encourage natural therapies and products and find that doing so risks losing their license. An all-too-familiar case is of the nationally known physician William A. McGarey, who served his country in the Navy in World War II and as a flight surgeon in the Air Force during the Korean War. He opened a practice in Phoenix, AZ and the Oak House in service to clients for over forty years. Dr. McGarey was forced into retirement when the Arizona state medical board ruled that his reliance on alternative measures was "inappropriate." Dr. McGarey was ordered to take an exam to determine his knowledge of the latest prescription drugs. He chose to retire. However, the authoring of many books and articles on alternative therapies reached an even wider audience.

With the utilization of natural-health therapists, it is my earnest belief, there will be a decrease in the care level simply because of the contentment of the elders, a decrease in the need for medications with partial homeopathic remedies, which are much less expensive, and as family sees their loved one more content and on less medications, the relationships between family and staff would improve. There would be a decrease in lawsuits and just as important would be the elders loss of fear of nursing-homes. Most importantly, well-trained natural-health professionals and staff would provide a higher level of compassion in the training of staff because spiritually, the staff would understand who they are, what their purpose is in life, and the philosophy of karma.

Why Are Natural Health Professionals Not In Nursing-Homes?

The questions must be asked: Why would the government, supported by the taxpayers, not want elders in nursing-homes to have better health at lower costs? Why does society not want elder care at a lower cost? Perhaps Portia Nelson has the answer in five short chapters:

There's a Hole In My Sidewalk
Autobiography in Five Short Chapters
by Portia Nelson

Chapter One
I walk down the street
There is a deep hole in the
  sidewalk
I fall in.
I am lost . . . I am helpless.
It isn't my fault.
It takes forever to find a way
  out.

Chapter Two
I walk down the street
There is a deep hole in the
  sidewalk
I pretend that I don't see it.
I fall in again.
I can't believe I am in the
  same place.
But, it isn't my fault.
It still takes a long time to
  get out.

Chapter Three
I walk down the same street
There is a deep hole in the
  sidewalk.
I see it is there.
I still fall in . . . it's a habit
  . . . but,
My eyes are open
I know where I am
It IS MY fault!
I get out immediately.

Chapter Four
I walk down the same street.
There is a deep hole in the
  sidewalk.
I walk around it.

Chapter Five
I walk down another street.

Could walking down another street lead us to a natural health care facility that is different from today's traditional nursing-home? Can natural-health professionals help alleviate the problems associated with the shortage of allopathic physicians and nursing staff?

Let us enter a nursing-home that has made simple changes by implementing natural health therapies. Which therapy would your nursing-home like to implement first?

8

Admission To a Natural Health Care Facility

To begin, the facility would eliminate the word "nursing-home or nursing center." For a suggestion, we will call the facility "The Healing Place," and each room would be a "cottage." A resident is called "family" on a first-name basis, just like in their own home.

Secondly, the facility will take down all signs on the outside designating the building as a nursing-home. An attractive sign with the facility address is all that is needed.

The Healing Place will have a beautiful wrought iron and brick-walled area surrounding the facility and a beautiful wrought iron gate with a bell for visitors to ring when they wish to enter. The walled in area provides adequate protection for all residents to roam as they wish, summer and winter. There will be no wrist or ankle bracelets to set off alarms and no nurses running through hallways to "capture" the runaway.

Do we agree that bracelets are hospital/institutional based and are a degradation to our elders? With no need for an alarm system, there would be a tremendous savings for the facility and the taxpayer!

The walled-in area will be full of trees, flowering shrubs and flower gardens with bird feeders, bird baths, a stream flowing gently through the garden, plenty of benches, walking paths wide enough for wheelchairs and a *labyrinth*, which is a circular path one follows slowly and meditatively to calm the body of earthly concerns, to be walked by elders and staff. Elders must spend time in this garden on a daily basis, regardless of the weather. A resident or staff with allergies, due to the outdoor environment, would be treated by a homeopathic physician.

Admission to the Healing Place would begin with a *suggestion* (no allopathic physician's order!) After all, no one should ORDER a respected elder into any facility. Doctors are NOT judges! ANY health-care professional may provide a thorough medical history. The elder and family would make the decision to move to a new "apartment" or cottage. The allopathic and naturopathic physician will be working with a myriad of natural health care professionals in their initial assessment of the elder. The allopathic and the naturopathic physician would receive a quarterly summary of therapies implemented in the resident's plan of care. Suggestions would include vitamins, homeopathic remedies, herbs and prescribed medications that would not be harmful to the elder. Professionals would meet on a quarterly basis with the resident.

A conference would be held prior to admission with the elder and/or family/guardian/relevant others so all would understand and be accepting of natural therapies.

Holistic Health Begins in the Mouth

Prior to admission, the elder would be asked to have a dental exam by a holistic dentist as holistic health begins in the mouth. If the elder has silver amalgams, they would be removed and replaced by a substance nonharmful to the body. The elder or family would underwrite the cost. Why remove silver amalgams?

In 1988, the EPA declared scrap dental amalgams a hazardous material more toxic than arsenic. Multiple sclerosis patients have been found to have eight times higher levels of mercury in the cerebral spinal fluid compared to neurologically healthy controls.

Other requirements to admission would be:

- Family involvement. Family would agree to come to the facility no less than once a week to assist in the cares of the elder . . . from assisting with a bath, hair care, taking clothes and linens home to wash (or making arrangements to do the wash in the facility), cleaning out the bedside table and closet, making sure the elder has proper clothes, taking unused clothing and items home, assisting with feeding, dressing, and dental care, and assisting with natural therapies, i.e., back and foot rubs and use of the Chi machine and the massage chair.

- Family care would be documented by the family for the medical record. What the nursing-home industry has done is to take away family responsibility. Up to this point in time, families have been indoctrinated that the nursing-home is totally responsible for their elder. NOT SO! If the family lives a distance away, they must be responsible for paying an off-duty nurse aide or a friend to come in and assist with the cares. Families will be responsible for all transportation to doctor's appointments, etc. Sadly, Medicaid mandates that the nursing-home provide and pays for all transportation for a Medicaid resident, which takes away family responsibility. However, with this rule changed, the family must be responsible.
- The elder must have a colonic upon admission or must go through a colon cleanse using a herbal remedy. Then at least annually. Colonic treatments or the cleanse would be the financial responsibility of the family.
- Chelation therapy within the first month of admission and annually, if needed. Chelation treatments would be paid by the family.
- Chiropractic treatments upon admission and at least four times a year. Treatments are the financial responsibility of the elder or the family.
- Complete body massage at least one time a month, paid for privately.
- A full body lymphatic drainage massage as needed.
- Agreement to a complete nutritional change.
- An understanding there will be all-faiths daily prayers, affirmations, meditations and positive thoughts, and words. There would be no proselytizing of one faith, but the use of universal teachings.

Medicare, Medicaid, nursing-home insurances, veterans,

and private-pay elders would be accepted. Medicaid elders receive $50 per month for personal items such as hair care. At $600 per year and with the family and community and religious organizations supporting the elders, natural therapies would be possible with no extra cost to the nursing-home and the taxpayers.

These positive changes make society directly responsible for elder care, not just the nursing-home industry, the allopathic physician, and the pharmaceutical conglomerates.

With personal involvement by family, complaints and lawsuits would lessen, which in turn would create less cost to nursing-homes and the taxpayer. Elders without any family at all would be supported by religious organizations.

Religious organizations build mammoth religious buildings and spend billions of dollars each year on supporting foreign countries in missionary work and providing food and clothing to the poor overseas. The churches need to look around their own communities at the number of nursing-homes and what it is costing the taxpayer and private-pay families. For each religious institution, taking one nursing-home and a small number of elders would cost pennies in comparison to what is spent for overseas missions.

Without a doubt, the first remark to be heard would be that religious organizations do not wish to support a large corporation that would put more money into their already bloated coffers. Corporate officers must agree to make changes. And it starts with petitions by each nursing-home to the Department of Health and Human Services in demanding reimbursements for alternative therapies. At the present time nursing-homes are reimbursed at a high rate as the resident's care level increases, i.e., more medications and more nursing hours. DHHS pays considerably less for "wellness." Alternative therapies, at this time, are not reimbursable. With the reimbursement for alternative therapies, the facility would gain, not only financially, but see staff turnover decrease and the overall improvement of elder care.

9

How Do We Generate Necessary Dollars for Alternative Therapies?

First, mandates for consultants must be revoked. Has anyone ever asked why a nursing-home has this army of consultants? It has been said that corporations send out consultants to make sure the facility is running appropriately. And the taxpayer pays. Then the government stepped in with a mandate for Medical Directors and pharmacy consultants. And the taxpayer pays. If the truth is revealed, consultants add very little to the personal care of the elder. If corporations, private, or public-owned nursing-homes choose to have consultants, so be it. However, the taxpayer should not have to pay the price for consultants who just add to the overall cost of elder care. Without federal and state reimbursements, one would see consultants and management firms fade away without any ill effects on elder care.

Henceforth, I make a motion, as a taxpayer and family member, to petition the Department of Health and Human Services to not reimburse facilities for the tremendous cost of regional managers, dietary consultants, social service consultants, activity consultants, nurse consultants, housekeeping consultants, management firms, medical directors, attorney fees, and pharmacy consultants.

I believe the majority of department heads have the ability to run their department without a consultant. If a department head has an issue, a competent administrator will intervene. Nursing-home administrators need to stop being indolent and do their job without a consultant standing beside them.

Secondly, the mandate for degreed social service workers would be revoked as well as the fifty CEU workshop for nursing-home administrators.

Not last by any means, would be the demand for reimbursement for alternative therapies. Nursing-homes must be paid for wellness, not just for the degree of ill health. And nursing-homes must receive a higher reimbursement for the implementation of nutritional, organic foods.

10
Nutrition and Dietary Managers

Changes in nutrition have to come about on the state level as well. According to state regulation a certain portion MUST be served to every resident. Anyone who has worked in a nursing-home is appalled at the 50 percent waste at every meal. Portions must be smaller and rich in nutrition. Nursing-home residents have often stated that the large plate of food turns off their appetite. In one nursing-home, the resident enjoyed her breakfast; however, she made it very clear she did not want the noon meal. The state came in and said that she was to be brought to the dining table and a plate of food set in front of her, "just in case she was hungry." In six months I saw this lady just sit disgustedly in front of a full plate of food without every touching it. The food was thrown away. I ask, "isn't this abuse by the surveyors?" Where were HER rights?

Organic foods must be slowly implemented. The optimal would be fresh organic vegetables and fruits, whole grain breads, organic pasteurized milk (not homogenized), less meat and more fish, poultry, and fresh eggs. The public needs to be aware that the state does not permit fresh fried eggs served to elders in a nursing-home due to a *possibility* of salmonella poisoning.

I do not endorse meat unless it is organic meat or grass-fed animals. With mad cow disease plus contaminated meats brought in from foreign countries, meats could possibly add to the lowering of the already compromised immune systems in our elders.

If you believe that our food products are safe and healthy, I ask of each reader to watch the video, *The World According to Monsanto*, a documentary that Americans won't ever see, shown

71

in France on March 11, 2008. The filmmaker was Marie-Monique Robin.

Not one consultant nutritionist, in my thirty years, has even come close to designing nutritional meals through no fault of her/him. Licensed nutritionists are following orders from their organization.

Meals in a nursing-home are full of pesticides, colorings, chemicals; are overprocessed, and are cooked to high temperatures, destroying any sign of a nutritious meal. Is it a wonder that many elders are obese and sick? The body is constantly calling for life-giving nutrition and receiving very little. White bread, white flour, white sugar, candy, overprocessed, instant, hybridized, and pasteurized foods must be banned from nursing-homes as part of total holistic health care. If states really have altruistic compassion for elders, they will mandate nutritional organic foods.

Nutritional foods must include heavy nonprocessed grains and raw honey or Agave as natural sweeteners. *All snacks will be fresh fruits*. Water replaces the state requirement for milk at every meal. Milk tends to be constipating. I was informed by one allopathic physician to not serve milk products to any elder with a cold or lung congestion.

Dr. William Campbell Douglass II, MD says that raw milk is nature's most perfect food and considers that ultrapasteurization has turned a great food into a white "milk flavored" drink because the heating during the pasteurization process has destructive effects on the immune system. My opinion is that homogenization is far more destructive.

Microwave ovens are also destructive to the value of food. The Soviet Union and other countries have banned the use of microwave ovens, as they found carcinogens were formed in virtually all foods tested after being heated in a microwave oven. Russian research calls microwave ovens no more than radiation waves causing a myriad of illnesses such as cancers, heart diseases, irritability, inability to concentrate and sleeplessness (Wayne and Newell, p. 32). I noted all of these symptoms are rampant in nursing-homes. It is my personal observation that microwave ovens are used daily in most nursing-homes.

I can see the eyes of dietary supervisors seeing their budget going out of control. However, what the facility saves in not throwing away 50 percent of the less nutritional food, savings would go directly into a more nutritious dietary budget.

Most Dietary Managers are excellent cooks, hard working and well organized. Dietary Managers must do all the ordering of food and supplies, keep inventory, schedule staff, replace staff as needed, assist in the cleaning of the kitchen, monitor dishwater temperatures, train new staff, counsel staff, discipline and be prepared to release an errant employee, prepare and deliver dietary in-services, meet with surveyors, the fire marshal, OSHA, attend all plan-of-care and MDS meetings, assess the needs of the residents, listen to complaints, and still smile at the end of the day. What the public needs to know, and help to correct, is that dietary managers must follow the menus designed only by a college-degreed licensed nutritionist with the knowledge that college nutrition classes are supported by food processing corporations and pharmaceutical companies.

Surveyors check two weeks of menus with what the dietitian has written. One surveyor wrote a deficiency because she counted the number of pieces of wieners in a meat and bean dish and found there were not enough wieners to satisfy the meat requirement.

What makes a dynamic Dietary Manager? Bob and Irene were not just cooks. Neither was my mother as a school Dietary Manager. They are chefs! They had flare. They improvised food to make each dish tasty and attractive. Good Dietary Managers do not need consultants. I remember one cook asked me if he could put a little celery leaf on the plate to make the meal more attractive. Why did he have to ask? Cooks should have the freedom to prepare foods for the enjoyment of the residents, not follow a menu to the letter of the law. Following recipes to the inch is why many nursing-home residents say the food tastes the same every day.

Not all Dietary Managers have the calling to work in a nursing-home. I brought my juicer to one nursing-home for the dietary staff to juice raw vegetables rather than cooking the vitamins out of the vegetables. The juiced vegetables were to be for those who were on liquid meals. A week later I walked into the kitchen to see the juicer wrapped in a plastic bag, sitting on a shelf. The Dietary Manager said they did not have the time to use it.

This was the same facility where I saw the most vomitous (new word) looking white pureed bread that looked like snot (sorry about the description, however, I have promised you to tell all) being placed before a resident on this same liquid diet. I told the dietary manager that if the bread was placed in a bowl with warmed milk, a bit of sugar, and cinnamon, it would at least look edible and taste much better.

One dietary department would dish up a full meal and then throw a piece of buttered bread on top of the entire meal. I asked the dietary manager if she served her husband in the same way? I requested that the main dish (such as meatballs and spaghetti) be served in special baking cups to make room for the vegetables and bread on the plate. I heard nothing but complaints because now there would be additional dishes to do.

I witnessed cooks throwing away chicken backs prior to baking chicken. I asked why they did not put the backs in a stewing pot for chicken broth. I was told they didn't have time. Interestingly, later in the day a resident with the flu requested a cup of chicken broth. Dietary opened up a package of very salty chicken powder, added hot water, and took that "mixture" to the resident.

In another facility, there were no knives on the table. Even the staff said they had to go to the kitchen and ask for knives to cut the meat. I asked for knives to be put on the tables and for that dietary did not speak to me for a month because now they had extra silverware to do.

Not all dietary managers should be managers. One manager sat in her office all day, never scheduled herself in to cook, nor checked the kitchen for cleanliness. When I surveyed the kitchen, I found the kitchen range in deplorable condition. Asking why, I was told that maintenance cleaned the stove. Really? That was a first! I looked under the refrigerator and in the storage closet and found months of greasy dirt and a plastic bag full of cockroaches. A hometown dietary manager, she kept her position for years after I left.

Sad to say not all good cooks are in the dietary department for the purpose of serving elders. One young lady was pilfering foodstuffs to take home to feed her day-care children.

Those who prepare foods for others should do so with a feeling of love and goodwill. As food is prepared, dietary managers, cooks, and those who assist should hold the following thoughts: "This food is divine and spiritual substance and it will be greatly enjoyed by all who partakes of it."

Dr. Siegfried Kra has written that nursing-home residents need 1,200 mg of calcium in the diet on a daily basis to prevent the loss of bone strength. This amount is equivalent to a quart of milk a day. However, I endorse the taking of "Calcios," a product that can be spread on crackers and served as an afternoon snack. It is very easily digested. Calcios can be purchased at the Association for Research and Enlightenment located in Virginia Beach, Virginia.

In Dr. Richard Torack's study it was found that poor nutrition was found among most residents confined to nursing-homes primarily due to poor eating habits. The most common deficiencies are those in iron, vitamins B-1, B-2, B-9, C and D and potassium. In the elderly, a deficiency of thiamin coupled with an onset of fever can cause confusion. A niacin deficiency has been associated with neurological abnormalities. Vitamins can be suggested by both the allopathic physician and a naturopathic physician. The reader needs to be reminded that Medicaid and Medicare do not pay for vitamins, so the cost, at this time, would be the resident, family, or those supporting the resident's needs.

At one facility for the mentally handicapped, surveyors threatened to close the facility down if they did not do away with the long institutional tables. The facility purchased round tables and tablecloths and placed fresh flowers on each table. What a pleasant change! I made this change each time I worked in any facility. However, one facility continues to have the fold-down long tables and uses the old green trays. I tried the china dishes only to see the owners return to using the trays for whatever reason.

In several facilities rooms for those who need assistance were adjacent to the main dining rooms. One dietary manager had the assist room painted an earthy green and placed pictures of flowers down low so residents could see them; plants were hung around the room and an attractive tie back curtain was hung between the rooms to decrease the noise from the main dining room. I shopped every week for fresh flowers (on sale) at local stores and flower shops. Many funeral bouquets were broken down, with residents dividing them and placing them on the tables. I placed a radio in one assist room to provide calming music only to have the owners take it out. No one ever promised me it would be easy.

Obesity reigns in nursing-homes. (Lapane and Resnik, *Journal of the American Geriatrics Society*). Obesity is deadly in a nursing-home. Not only is placing a resident on a diet an impossible method in which to lose weight, but the staff is often placed in jeopardy during personal cares such as bathing and lifting. With the majority of elders receiving little or no exercise, could it possibly be if elders were provided a nutritional meal with plenty of raw fruits and vegetables, their weight would normalize? Are we providing another avenue in the compassionate care of obese residents with the change over to nutritional meal plus a daily dose of vitamins and minerals?

Let Us Chit-Chat about Organics

Organic products are everywhere, from health food stores to farmers' markets, supermarkets, health food stores and entire shopping centers like Wholefoods, located throughout the United States. United Natural Foods, Inc. delivers organic foods and products to co-ops located throughout the nation.

Organic products comprise one of the fastest-growing segments of the food industry with growth rates of at least 20 percent annually for a total of $6.6 billion in the year 2006. And the organic industry is still growing.

Certified organic farmland in the United States more than doubled during the 1990s. Throughout Europe and Japan the market for organic products has risen to over $22 billion annually. The country of Austria has over 8 percent of the farmland under organic cultivation.

Organic has gone global due to concerns about the chemicals used in the soil, waters, and air plus the use of genetically modified ingredients in the food supply and the repeated food recalls coming out of China.

Around the world and especially in the United States with medical costs rising beyond the reach of most Americans, citizens are demanding products that are healthy, wholesome, flavorful, and grown and produced in a way that protects and restores the environment for a sustainable future.

What does "organic" mean? Organic is a process by which foods and fibers are grown and processed. The soil is healthy and rich, producing strong plants that resist pests and diseases. The key to organics is in the soil. Organic farming and gardening prohibits the use of toxic and persistent chemicals in favor of more Earth-friendly practices that work in harmony with nature.

Organic standards require that land on which organic food and fibers are grown must now be treated without any prohibited substances, both chemical and fertilizers, for three years prior to certification. Detailed records are kept and products are audited annually.

Organic farmers and gardeners use a variety of techniques to build healthy soil and grow a diversity of crops, including crop rotation and the planting of cover crops that prevent weeds and increase the organic matter, which in turn prevents erosion and holds the water in the soil, with the outcome being less irrigation.

Organic cattle feeders use H_2O_2 or diatomaceous earth to control cattle worms and infections. Both H_2O_2 and diatomaceous earth are nonharmful to humans and other animals. In turn, organic composted manure is a natural fertilizer, enriching the soil on a yearly basis.

Gardeners take advantage of newspapers for weed control plus cayenne and tobacco juice for pests. Organic growers entice the toothless garter snake and the bat to diminish pests plus permit tall grasses to grow outside the gardens and crops for grasshoppers to feed on rather than coming onto the crops. Healthy poultry is raised on organic feed, running free with plenty of sunshine.

Farming organic is usually labor intensive and adds to the cost of organic food products. Nursing-homes would do well to contract with small organic gardeners to supply the basic garden vegetables in order to curb costs.

I recommend the following organic processors: Hain, Barbara's, Food for Life, Seeds of Change, Natural Sea, Lundberg Family Farms, Organic Valley, Walnut Acres, Alta Dena, and Earth Balance, to name a few of many good brands.

And then we must remember to fold the hands over the food as it is served and thank God for the blessing of nutritional food and pure water.

Why are nutritional foods not being served? A young mother of two developed a home industry of grinding organic wheat and baking bread for customers in the area. I contracted with her for bread one time a week much to the delight of the residents. When my successor took over, she was so fearful of surveyors, that she cancelled the home baked bread. Who lost?

I brought in organic squash to one facility and when they did not appear on the menu, I asked where they were. The dietary manager said the dietary staff did not want to bother with them so they all took one home. Who lost?

A health food outlet was moving to another location and was selling fifty pounds of flour for half price, so I asked the dietary manager if I should purchase a bag or two. She said her staff would not know what to do with it as everything comes out of a box or is precooked. So much for homemade food. Who lost?

Pie was served almost weekly in one facility. I asked why the pie was not homemade. The manager said she purchased pies by the case for ninety cents a piece and absolutely did not have the staff to make pies in-house. This is a manager who sat in her office all day long. Who lost?

What Organics Are Not

Pesticides are pervasive, traveling via wind and water and accumulating in the fat tissues of fish and wildlife, which in turn transfers up the food chain. Researchers have found residues of toxic agriculture chemicals thousands of miles from the place of their original use and in some cases these chemicals persists for decades. DDT residues remain in North American cities and on the land, though it's been banned in the United States for nearly forty years.

Henceforth, "organic" cannot be 100 percent free of pesticides. Tests have proven that most organic foods have consistently been found to have minimal or nonexistent pesticide residue.

Another misconception is that "natural" equals "organic." Natural usually means foods without *added* artificial ingredients, preservatives, and dyes, it does not address the way the food is grown.

Organics

In June 2003, Heinz, known for its slow growth, bought 19.5 percent stock in Hain Food Group for nearly $100 million. Hain is the leading producer of organic foods in the country with annual sales, at that time, of $206 million.

Why? Why? Why?

Why are organic foods and natural health therapies not in nursing-homes? The answer is very simple. They threaten the livelihood of pharmaceutical companies and the medical profession. We sicken a nation with chemicalized foods and by the practice of polypharmacy. Ill health means financial gains and control. Financial gains mean control by the government and our Congress, the medical colleges, and allopathic physicians. Financial gains mean control of our state colleges who teach nutrition courses.

Let's Talk about Eggs

Soft fried eggs are not permitted in nursing-homes with the exception of veterans' facilities. The powers that be have ruled against the egg due to the fear of salmonella.

Animal rights organizations are on the hunt for "cage-free" eggs with the thought those eggs are better. The answer is "no." All it means is that the chickens aren't kept in pint-size cages, but it doesn't mean the chicken is any better off, nor the eggs nutritious. "Natural" means nothing.

The only label to look for is USDA Certified Organic. This label means that the hens are fed organic feed, that they have access to the outdoors and sunlight. Farmers that raise chickens for meat and eggs must have a rooster on the place in order that the eggs have the proper protein in them. If a nursing-home can obtain farm fresh, clean and candled eggs, the residents would receive a healthier, a wonderful protein source and a better-tasting egg.

The "no fresh eggs" regulation must be annulled for nursing-homes that wish to purchase organic or farm fresh eggs.

Let's Talk about Unsafe Water

Hydrotherapy in any form is very healthful, *if* the water is not chlorinated or fluoridated or an ammonia mix. All are chemicals toxic to the residents and staff. Nursing-homes will need to purchase reverse-osmosis filters for drinking, showers, and tubs or add hydrogen peroxide to tub water. It has been reported by the *Douglass Report* that the water people are now playing around with choloramines, a cholorine/ammonia mix that may be three hundred times more toxic than the chloroform you are now drinking and using for cooking and bathing.

The year 2008 brought forward the issue of drinking water being contaminated by human urination dumped into water systems The urine is excreting excesses of psychotrophic drugs, birth control pills, and a myriad of prescribed medications. Water treatment plants are not able to remove such chemicals from the system. And water in bottles is often taken out of polluted rivers.

Eustace Mullins, researcher and writer, boldly declares that the chemical sodium chloride, a by-product of aluminum, has been put in the water in many cities in United States for the sole purpose of making humans passive. The name was changed to "fluoride" with no proof whatsoever that it would prevent tooth decay.

Let's Talk about Raw Milk

In the *Milk Book*, William Campbell Douglass II, MD, states one of our greatest losses today is the destruction of fresh milk through pasteurization, ultrapasteurization, and the homogenization. Through the process of high heat, Dr. Douglass, believes the nutritional values of milk is lost, devitalized; Vitamin C and calcium, antibodies, and hormones are destroyed, which diminishes the overall value of milk.

Douglass contends the propaganda that pasteurized milk is safer than fresh raw certified milk can be easily put to rest as case after case has been documented that one could consume over six million more quarts of raw milk than pasteurized without getting sick.

Moreover, illnesses such as heart attacks have only become common since the advent of homogenized, pasteurized milk, oleo margarine, and the increased consumption of polyunsaturated vegetable oils.

It must be said that if one is to drink raw certified milk, one must be aware that the cows are raised on green grasses rich in nutritional value. Green grass contains twenty-three times as much Vitamin A as carrots, twenty-two times as much Vitamin B-2 as lettuce, nine times more thiamin than green leafy vegetables, and fourteen times more Vitamin C than citrus fruits. The humble blade also contains niacin, Vitamin E, minerals, and enzymes.

Green grasses are the closest things to a perfect food. Pasteurized, homogenized commercial milk destroys all nutritional value, causing more harm than good. Even organic milk is ultrapasteurized; however, it is one step better than commercial milk.

Dr. Lorraine Day, diagnosed with cancer, was on her deathbed. She made the decision to try an alternative nutritional diet using only fresh vegetable juices and fresh fruit. Dr. Day not only survived but today is an advocate of alternative medicine, which she implements into her practice. Dr. Day says, "There are no incurable diseases." Dr. Day's website is www.drday.com.

A German doctor uses a similar dietary protocol for detoxification using only raw vegetables and fruit juices, low sodium and high potassium foods (J. Carter, p. 30). Dr. Warren Levin and Dr. Michael Davidson promote the use of omega-3 fatty acids as a daily dietary supplement or suggest eating salmon or tuna or fish dishes on a weekly basis. Dr. Davidson believes that the lack of seafood and excess of pork and beef in American diets results in the prevalence of such degenerative diseases as arteriosclerosis, cancer, and arthritis (J. Carter, p. 260).

A nursing-home menu should contain limited meat, limited pork (crisp organic bacon only), limited dairy products, and no processed foods, as the milling and refining of food products removes vitamins and minerals often causing the three "Ds" found in nursing-homes . . . dermatitis, diarrhea, and dementia (J. Carter, p. 21).

The highly nutritional menu must consist of 80 percent alkaline producing food such as organic raw fruits and steamed or raw vegetables except cranberries, plums, olives, prunes, and blueberries and 20 percent acid producing foods such as meats and grains, except buttermilk, yogurt, raw milk, peanuts, pecans, and walnuts. Elders need sixty grams of protein a day, which can be obtained from beef, poultry, fish, eggs, dairy products, nuts, seeds, or legumes.

The alkaline balance is checked by measuring the pH balance in saliva or urine. An appropriate pH balance is 7.0.

Edgar Cayce repeatedly insisted that viruses such as colds do not thrive in an alkaline environment. Too much meat, dairy, and processed grains produce acidity, lowering the immune system.

With low rates of coronary heart disease and certain cancers, the traditional Mediterranean diet has an abundance of vegetables, legumes, fruits, nuts, unrefined cereals, and olive oil. Moderate amounts of fish, dairy (yogurt and cheese), and wine at meals are consumed. Only small amounts of red meat and poultry are eaten.

A Menu of Prayer and Nonprocessed Food

A typical menu in a natural health care facility would be the following:

Morning neck exercises followed by prayer One raw fruit for energy Glass of water with flavored chondrotin, glucosamine and Vit. C. or a tsp. of cod liver oil and a tsp. of coconut oil. Organic coffee ½ c. oat groats with raw honey plus flaxseed and raw milk Ezekiel 4:9 toast/butter Vitamins/homeopathies/medications Prayer of Thanksgiving Exercises with music	Noon exercises followed by prayer. Blackboard mind stimulation game. Music played during the meal. Water and green tea Fresh vegetable juice Homemade fish chowder Blueberry spelt muffin/butter Brown rice dessert with fruit to sweeten, 1/4 c. yogurt. Prayer of Thanksgiving	Evening exercises with prayer. Soft music to calm the body and soul in preparation for the evening's rest. Water and chamomile tea with natural agave sweetener Fresh lettuce salad with pieces of chicken, beef, or fish. Whole grain crackers Fresh fruit such as sweet cherries, strawberries, peaches, pears, kiwi. Prayer of Thanksgiving No dairy products	Morning snacks Fresh juiced oranges Afternoon snacks Popcorn or a fig cookie or mummy food Evening snacks Nonsweetened fruit juice with black walnut tincture or a piece of fruit or crackers or a cup of Dr. Miller's Holy tea. No diary products.

Following the evening meal, an activity or visits with family and friends and, upon request, a small glass of wine, residents are prepared for bed with a five-minute back and neck massage, dental care, hair brushed, prayers said, soft music from the resident's satellite radio, dream journals placed by the bedside, hug therapy, and "I love you" by each staff as a goodnight memory. Cherokee people do not say I love you. They say, "You dance in my heart." Can you imagine the smile on each resident's face just hearing this Cherokee good night?

Hugs Heal

The Touch Research Institute at the University of Miami Medical School has led the way in documenting the favorable outcomes of loving touch. Gentle, caring touch and a fifteen-minute gentle massage has been shown to boost the immune system. The recipients showed greater sociability and exhibited fewer signs of stress. A dose of touch is as critical as the right exercise and a healthy diet. All must work together for the good of the ALL.

However, the power of touch was nothing new, as in the late 1920s research was implemented in an orphanage with babies. One half was held, talked to, and cuddled while feeding. The other half had their bottles propped up in the basket and touched only to bathe and change clothing.

After one year, the "cuddled" babies were thriving. The babies not held were not only weaker and fussier, but many had expired with no known cause. These babies were called the marasmic babies. The word "marasmic" means a gradual wasting away of the body, generally associated with severe malnutrition or inadequate absorption of food. It is my observation that in most nursing-homes we have marasmic elders.

Prayers

In only one nursing-home were prayers said before all meals by either a resident or staff. Prayers are of utmost importance as they create an environment of thanksgiving.

When one folds the hands together in prayer over the food, it is said to energize the food so that food provides the necessary sustenance for the body.

Prayers can be universal or specific.

Mealtime Prayers

For each new morning with its light,
For rest and shelter of the night
For health and food,
For love and friends
For everything Thy goodness sends.
—Ralph Waldo Emerson (1803-1882)

O God, when I have food
Help me to remember the hungry;
When I have work
Help me remember the jobless;
When I have a home,
Help me to remember those who have no home at all;
When I am without pain,
Help me to remember those who suffer;
And remembering,
Help me to destroy my complacency;
Bestir my compassion,
And be concerned enough to help,
By word and deed, those who cry out
For what we take for granted.
—Samuel F. Pugh

Blessed are You, O Lord God, Eternal King,
Who feeds the whole world with Your goodness,
With grace, with loving kindness
And with tender mercy.
You give food to all flesh, for Your loving kindness
Endures forever. Through Your great goodness, food has never
failed us.
O may it not fail us forever, for Your name's sake,
Since You nourish and sustain all living things,
And do good to all, and provide food for all Your creatures
whom You have created.

Blessed are You, O Lord, Who gives food to all.
—A Hebrew blessing
(The above prayers credited to the *Omaha World Herald*,
Omaha, Nebraska 12/2/07)

Bless us, O Lord
And these thy gifts
For which we are about to receive
From thy bounty
Through Christ our Lord.
Amen
—Roman Catholic

Grandfather, Great Spirit,
Once more behold me on earth and lean to hear my feeble
voice.
You lived first and you are older than all need;
Older than all prayer.
All things belong to you . . .
The two-legged, the four-legged, the wings of the air,
And all green things that live.
You have set the powers of the four quarters of the earth to
cross one another.
You have made me cross the good road and the road of
difficulties.
And where they cross, the place is holy.
Day in and day out, forevermore,
You are the life of things.
—Black Elk, Holy Man of the Oglala Sioux.

11

The Psychology of Food

If one is overweight, the overeating is thought to desensitize the self, so that you will not feel so deeply about things bothering you. If you allow yourself the full pleasure of eating what you like, without criticism, then you will not overeat, nor will you need to eat the food that you crave every day.

When your weight is acceptable, you do not like to eat food because the food causes you to accept your body in this physical world (and in which you do not wish to be because this world has caused you much pain). And by now perfect weight causes one to be grounded.

The full feeling makes you feel as if you are going too slow. Then you will not have all the information you need to protect yourself from hurts. These hurts may be from past lives or the present in the fact that you were punished for something and did not understand why.

You will discover that if you eat less, you will stay totally aware, more alert, and be prepared to learn whatever it is that you are to learn.

Listen to your body . . . thin, overweight, or appropriate weight. Hear when you are full. Have no thoughts reprimanding yourself. Take pleasure in every bite. You are not eating for emptiness of the physical body. You are eating because of your emptiness of emotions. This is the reason for prayer before meals.

Say, "I love, nurture and care for me as I am Christ within."

Why We Crave Certain Foods

- When eating chocolate, it tends to create a momentary euphoria and then grounds your energy.
- When eating lots of butter or greasy foods, it tends to slow down your sensitivity, so that you can have a little freedom from feeling every emotion.
- The result of eating or drinking sugar products tend to expand you, so you temporarily feel free of things that are coming at you too fast and of situations that seem out of control.
- You eat meat when you have the need to drown your emotions. Meat tends to direct the body toward the lowered emotional animal instinct.
- Salads are eaten when you want your thinking to be clear and when you do not wish to feel "bogged" down.
- Vegetables are eaten for energy and endurance and when you do not want any drain on your emotional or spiritual energy. For every vegetable grown underground, one is to eat three vegetables grown on top of the soil. Dr. Oz , TV and radio personality, says to eat five servings every day the size of your fist.
- Eat fish for grounding, moving through a situation gently.
- Whole grains are eaten to feel in touch with Mother Earth herself.
- Fruits are eaten for energy and vitality. And to clear the body of toxins.

Non-forgiveness creates acid in the system. To gain perfect health is in forgiveness.

Daily meditation and speaking these words: "All that has offended me, I forgive. Whatever had made me bitter, resentful, unhappy, I forgive. Within and without, I forgive. Things past, things present, things future, I forgive."
—*The Dynamic Laws of healing by Catherine Ponder, p. 47.*

From the savings in serving nutritious foods and the revocation of consultants, we turn to another savings when the high turnover of nursing-home administrators is decreased.

12

Nursing-Home Administrator Turnover

According to Nicholas G. Castle, Ph.D., a researcher for the Agency for Health Care Policy and Research, the average annual turnover rate for nursing-home administrators is 43 percent. Dr. Castle also reports nursing-home chain administrator turnover is correlated with a higher than average proportion of residents who were catheterized, had pressure ulcers, and were given psychoactive drugs. These facilities had a higher than average number of quality of care deficiencies.

In nonchain facilities, the turnover of administrators is associated with a higher than average proportion of residents who were restrained, were catheterized, had pressure ulcers, and were given psychoactive drugs.

Dr. Castle believes his survey of 420 nursing-homes provide evidence that the turnover of administrators has a direct impact on the quality of care in nursing-homes.

Why the High Turnover?

To reveal the truth of why there is high nursing-home administration turnover, one must approach the educational factors, preceptorships, and morals and ethics of nursing-home boards and corporate officers as well as the politics played.

To begin, most states require a four-year degree in which few hours are spent in gerontological studies. Education requirements should be no more than a two-year college degree, recognizing the program as a specialty. Those two years must be spent in study of rules, regulations, policies, procedures, state and federal mandates, employee rights, unemployment, workers compensation, gerontology, communication with the public, staff, and residents, proper filing, how to apply for grants, resources available, budgets, and sex, age, race, and religious discrimination, with all courses enveloped with one's own level of spirituality, morals, and ethics.

During this two-year course, there must be a mandated nurse aide and medication course, an activity director course, social services course, a course in nutrition, organic foods, and a business management course including MDS training.

If the student has never worked in a nursing-home, there must be a four month administrator-in-training program in which the college professor/preceptor will oversee. These four months will be part of the two-year program. The administrator will keep a weekly report, signed by the AIT and sent to the college.

If the student has worked in a nursing-home, regardless of what position held, the student must serve no less than three months in an AIT program under the auspices of the college professor/preceptor. The AIT will work in every department except the one department in which he/she has expertise. Weekly reports will be sent to the college.

An AIT, who is with a corporation, is paid a stipend during the four-month internship and is usually hired by the corporation.

AITs who enter a city, county, state, or privately owned facility are rarely paid, thus the AIT internship is not only costly, but time-consuming as AITs are expected to work a forty-hour week. These federal and state nursing-home administrator exams are difficult. Two AITs failed the first time. Both admitted they did not study.

Who and Where Are Administrators in Training?

I have trained nine administrators-in-training. One woman came in to ask if I would be her preceptor. I asked why she wanted to become a nursing-home administrator. She said she was presently a teacher and wanted something easier. I denied her request.

One young AIT had his wife bring him in on the first day as a "new admission." I was the only one who knew of his scheme as he wanted to know the intimate details as to how the staff would treat him as a new resident. He told the staff he had been in a bad accident, was crippled, and unable to care for himself at home, as his wife worked.

The AIT told me later that the staff were really kind, but a bit puzzled as to his injury, but answered his light in an appropriate time, was introduced to his tablemates, given a shower, and dressed for the night. His main complaint was the bed was very hard and he had difficulty sleeping with all the noise in the hallway and lights on all night. I rejoiced with this AIT as I felt he would be an excellent nursing-home administrator; however, his first position was in a city-owned facility. Less than one year later, he resigned. The reason given was the interference by the nursing-home board. He later gave up his license for a position not so political.

A second AIT was also very good. Tall and with a delightful air of a businessman, he, too, successfully passed his nursing-home administrator's test and began his career only to resign under pressure by a city-owned facility run by a board of directors.

One AIT was an LPN. Smart, hard working, passing her exams, she was immediately hired by a city-owned facility in which she had worked as a nurse. I warned her that she needed to get rid of all her relatives who were working there as this would, sooner or later, cause her trouble. She did not listen. She was fired within the year.

Two wonderful, intelligent young ladies, both RNs were trained as nursing-home administrators in a Native American facility. One left because the tribe was making an overall sweep of the medical facility and everyone who was not of their tribal ancestry was asked to resign. She did. The second young lady left because the tribe did not offer her retirement and medical benefits.

One business manager who was the best of the best in common sense and hard work is still an administrator of an assisted-living complex. However, she resigned from a large nursing home because she was asked to falsify information. Bless her for her strong morals and ethics.

Another AIT was the worst of the worst, refusing to comply with training as required of all AITs. He was extremely egotistical, controlling, and manipulative. He did not pass the exam the first time and blamed me, although he admitted he did not study. He is out there somewhere. I release him from all the hurt he caused me and those around him.

The next AIT I trained was another LPN. She passed her exam and then proceeded to undermine me to the board, and you guessed it. The city board said I was not "operating the facility the way they thought it should be run," although the facility was running full, with a more than adequate balance sheet. Raises had been given, the facility was undergoing remodeling, a pet program had been started. She was hired and I was let go. Interestingly, she was fired a year later. You reap what you sow, sooner or later.

The last AIT was young, pretty, with a four-year degree. Her interest was in her upcoming marriage and having a family. She soon discovered that being a nursing-home administrator required fifty hours a week, many weekends, a multitude of telephone calls at night and being on call twenty-four hours a day, seven days a week.

When a position opened up for a manager of an assisted-living facility, which does not require a license, she went to work there. This was a wise move for her.

Politics and need for power and control over others and just plain not being knowledgeable about the importance of working issues out with an administrator are the primary cause of nursing-home administration turnover. How many administrators are fired or not hired because of age is unknown. One large corporation has an unwritten rule not to hire any administrator over the age of fifty. This same corporation hires administrators who have no vision, no ambition to do well, and will not challenge corporate officers or owners when poor elder care occurs. These administrators want the prestige of being an administrator and are willing to sell their morals and ethics to remain in that position. This is how large corporate officers make themselves feel important.

Then we have persons who may be very competent in their positions, such as a business manager or social worker, or a nurse and when offered the position as administrator, they see, again, the prestige and the money. None are necessarily attributes of a competent, compassionate administrator. The Peter Principle adds to the turnover of nursing-home administrators: "One rises to the level of incompetency."

I worked for a large corporation not knowing that it was a set up for several months while they were grooming a business manager to take my place. The business manager did pass her administrators test. I resigned when I saw what was happening. She became the administrator. Interestingly, several years later she was fired. I saw karma in this one, too. You really do reap what you sow.

I was offered an administrator's position in an adjoining state only to discover the State Nursing-Home Administrator Board was adamant on providing jobs for their own people. They did not want "outsiders" to take jobs in their state. I fought for six months to obtain permission to take the state test. My application was sent back twice. Then I was told the board was not meeting for several months and lastly, I did not hear from them at all until the CEO received a letter that I had better not be in that facility after my six months of interim period was over. I was forced to resign. Several weeks later, at home, I received a personal call from one of the board members saying that I could now take the state test. When I replied that it was a bit late as I was out of a job, the board member said, "Oh, well, you will find a job somewhere."

In one community, the postmaster said, "Oh, what next! Hiring a woman?" In another community, I was harassed as the first woman administrator and never accepted, especially as the males in the community saw the advancements made at the nursing-home. Interestingly, 50 percent of all nursing-home administrators in United States are women.

I worked for a small county-owned facility, which, after examining the books, I found to be totally broke. A new and wonderful Director of Nursing came on board the same time I did. Changes had to be made quickly. The DON and I worked feverishly to correct the financial problem and that meant we would be stepping on a few toes. A longtime LPN was placed as a charge nurse instead of doing paperwork. We actually had a visit by the husband—both were so mad at the transition. I explained that it was either making unpopular changes or the facility would close and there would be no jobs for anyone.

Next in line was to survey hours used in the laundry department plus I had been told that one laundry aide was going home several hours every day and not checking out. I also noted the department head of laundry was bringing her handiwork to work with her. I asked her about this, and she said she had free time between loads of laundry. We revamped the entire schedule and cut hours for all laundry staff. Hours were cut in dietary, and then there was the activity director, who was the sweetheart of the community, refusing to do her job and spent most of her time calling staff to her house and undermining what I was trying to do to save the facility.

I created the first budget for the facility and presented it to the County commissioners. I received a call at 10 p.m. at my home by an angry commissioner who yelled at me saying, "how dare you give yourself a $20,000 raise." I inquired as to what he was reading. Then I explained that in the administrative cost column there was my wage (with no raise) of $30,000 and $15,000 for the secretary, plus the administrative column included facility insurance, workers compensation insurance, unemployment insurance, and office supplies, which was $5,000, for a total of $50,000. He said, "Oh" and hung up. No apologies, ever. So much for county commissioners knowledge of a nursing-home spreadsheet.

When I fired a secretary when she and her husband broke into my office and went through the files, this was my doom. In a small community, regardless of a financially troubled facility, you do not tamper with hometown people. I resigned after nine months. Since that time, the facility has had no less than five administrators. The nursing-home board and the county commissioners, of which none had ever worked in a nursing home, just could not keep their noses out of the work that needed to be done. They were not open to new ways. They simply lived as things were fifty years ago. "My people perish who have no vision," sayeth the Lord God.

For the reader, does it not become obvious why there is a high turnover of nursing-home administrators? To stabilize a nursing-home, the facility needs a long-term director of nursing and administrator. That is not happening in the nursing-home industry. The basic reasons are:

1. Administrators are poorly trained by their preceptors.
2. No direct oversight by the colleges.
3. Administrators-in-training not being told the truth about job duties and their responsibilities. Morals and ethics not being taught.
4. The majority of college classes do not address the compassionate needs of elders in a nursing-home setting.
5. The nursing-home administrator program does not discourage those who are not administrator material.

Changes Necessary

1. States need to negate the mandated four-year college degree to permit more suitable people into the field who have shown great compassion for the elderly and have proven leadership qualities.
2. And shame on nursing-home owners who advertise for an administrator who has a masters degree in business administration. Corporations control the budget, the purchases, and staff wages. So, why the degree in business? More appropriately is the administrator whose ministry is in caring for the elderly.
3. The two-year nursing-home administrator program must be intense, with instructors and preceptors working together to discourage those who are not administrator material.

4. All board members must receive one six-hour workshop every year to maintain their position on the board. Morals and ethics must be strongly emphasized.
5. No AIT should be permitted to usurp her/his preceptor in the facility in which he/she was trained.
6. Sixty percent of every nursing-home board must be former nursing-home employees. Board members must be paid, at least a stipend.
7. All nursing-homes must be required to report to the state the reasons for an administrator dismissal and the state ombudsman will then investigate the issues.
8. State licensing boards must give permission to take the state exam within a two-month period from the time of application.
9. If owners and board members do not support the administrator with their guidance, wisdom, prayers, positive thoughts and words, there will be a continuation of high administrator turnover. My mentor told me that it takes one year for an administrator to get a firm grasp on the dynamics that occur in a nursing-home. With every turnover, there is bound to be confusion and chaos.
10. Board members and corporate officers must be charged with elder abuse and fined by the state for inappropriate firing of administrators.
11. Most states mandate fifty CEUs every two years and offer workshops that are usually irrelevant and boring. Nursing-home administrators would do just as well with one six-hour workshop every year that is intense and worthwhile. The costs of fifty CEUs for nursing-home administrator's recertification license is approximately $5,000.00. But who is profiting from worthless workshops? The state associations, colleges, teachers, online classes and creators of CDs and manuals. All training costs are reimbursable on the nursing-home cost report. When Health and Human Services do not reimburse for workshops and convention expenses, worthless workshops will cease.

Who Wants to Be a Nursing-Home Administrator?

As a nursing-home administrator, I have worked the trenches, scrubbed floors, painted, wallpapered, cleaned up vomit, wiped butts, been sworn at and fondled, hired, fired, manipulated, loved, hated, lied about, called a witch, bitch, and asked, "Who made you God?, held the hands of the lonely and dying, wept, lost hundreds of hours of sleep, worked holidays and weekends, spent months away from home, took calls in the middle of the night, made beds, dusted, cleaned closets and toilets, did laundry, attended numerous and boring meetings, mediated family disputes, protected the rights of the elderly, spent hundreds of hours traveling, lived in boarding houses, trailers, and apartments without furniture, pleaded cases with judges, family, and board members, developed first-time budgets, brought facilities out of the red into the black financially, and then was blackballed by a State Health Care Association because I elected to spend monies to pay bills rather than belong to the Association; attended resident weddings and funerals, was threatened by a gang of hoodlums, had my car soaped, gravel dumped in the gas tank, car rims, personal computer, tape recorder and a precious ring stolen, lent money to staff, paid for medication and hospital costs for needy staff, paid for school meals for staff children, counseled a possessed resident, stopped a tornado from hitting a nursing-home by calling on the name of Jesus, witnessed suicides, prayed, had dreams and visions to give me encouragement to continue on and keep my eyes on my calling. The benefits were no insurance, no retirement, and always the expectation to be on call twenty-four-hours-a day, seven days a week.

And the end result was that I was no longer hirable because I was too old. Who should be more aware of getting older than an older, wiser, competent, compassionate nursing-home administrator? Only those who are "called" become dedicated, compassionate nursing-home administrators regardless of their age, gender, race, disability, or belief system.

The wage for a nursing-home administrator depends on the size of the facility. For a first-year administrator in a seventy-five-bed facility, it may average from $40,000 to $50,000 per year plus benefits.

13

The Director of Nursing

The following research from the Duke University School of Nursing was published in the June 2004 issue of *The Gerontologist* stating that the chronic staffing turnover common in many nursing-homes in the United States is lower in facilities that have stable nursing leadership. The study surveyed the staff of 164 nursing-homes in Texas.

The researchers found lower turnover rates for registered and licensed practical nurses directly related to a longer tenure for the Director of Nursing. Nurses need their DON to create the right work environment so they feel comfortable at the facility and want to stay. For each year the DON remained in her/his position, the RN turnover decreased by 16 percent and LPN turnover decreased by 11 percent. The longer the DON remained at the facility, the more stable the nurses perceived their work environment to be.

When DON turnover is high in any facility, there is a major shake-up in the nursing department and throughout the facility.

In many nursing-homes, if something happens, blame often lands squarely on the shoulders of the DON, said Ruth Anderson, Ph.D., RN. who is on staff at Duke University School of Nursing. Dr. Anderson says that often the DON is fired rather than using the error as a moment of learning and growing.

Connie J. Rowles, in the November-December 1995 edition of *Nursing-Homes*, writes of an all too familiar situation:

> You are the DON of a 250-bed skilled nursing facility. On Monday morning—at a time when surveyors are expected—you arrive in your office to find that six of your nursing staff have called in ill for the day, two more of your nurse aides have quit, and your

charge nurse on the subacute unit has just had "words" with a resident's daughter, who now wants to remove her mother from your facility.

On the way to the administrator's office to discuss staffing problems, (he/she has always given you good advice), you are called into a meeting and informed that last Friday was the administrator's last day and his/her replacement will begin tomorrow.

Here we find again, the dismissal of an administrator without the input or knowledge of the DON. The DON's position is critical to the quality of care and day to day operation of the nursing-home. The knowledge that she/he must now make another major adjustment involving a new administrator often leads to days of confusion and stress.

Rowles' article plainly states the myriad of duties required of the DON: resident care, budgets, knowledge of regulations, staffing, purchasing, training, being a mentor for professional nurses, communication and interpersonal relationships, attending plans of care with families, the MDS conferences, inventory, and planning twelve staff in-services. The demands on a DON are tremendous and facility management must take all into account to keep a good DON, regardless of errors that may be made, knowing that the errors were not harmful to the residents.

As a Consultant Social Worker and Administrator, I offer this simple Welcome letter to the new Director of Nursing and a few old Directors of Nursing:

Welcome to the wonderful world as Director of Nursing!

You have been chosen by a higher power for the opportunity to grow spiritually, mature in your abilities and be life challenged.
Each day is to be cherished.
Each day you will receive new teachings offered to you and grow by doing.
Each day brings to you special persons to mentor and to assist you on your path.
Each day will bring tremendous challenges in your relationship with God.
You and only you are in control of your actions.

There will be moral and ethical decisions.
You will evolve or devolve dependent on how you handle each day.
You will fail, at times.
You will grow with each failure as failures make one humble.
You will celebrate your successes.
You will quickly know if you love your position
by the excitement you feel each day
as you walk through the door.
You laugh easily and pray often.

Welcome to the world as a Director of Nursing!

A Director of Nursing from the Perspective of an Administrator

To begin, all DONs must have a cell phone and an answering machine to stay in contact with nursing-home staff in time of an emergency. The DON must communicate to professional nurses that they (as professionals) are to make decisions relevant for a professional and not to call the DON for every decision. However, the DON must realize that she/he is subject to be called twenty-four hours a day, seven days a week.

The dependable DON is expected to arrive at the facility on time and on the days posted on her/his door. The administrator and the staff need to know whether or not the DON is coming in.

The DON must carry a small notebook and pen at all times. DONs can not be expected to remember every little conversation up and down the hallways. Writing on toilet paper or the hand is okay, too.

A DON needs to immediately go to the nurse's stations to:

- Check the twenty-four hour reports.
- Check daily assignment sheets and reassign as needed.
- Pick up all incident reports, review, sign, and take to the Administrator's office.
- Analyze incident reports, track and prepare for the monthly Quality Assurance meeting.
- Attend the daily department head meeting.

- Check where rehabilitation aides are. If they have been pulled to work as CNAs, the facility will not be properly reimbursed by Medicare for five days of rehab as mandated by regulation.
- Talk with all nursing staff, especially the CNAs to get their input for the day's work.
- Pick up the previous day's bath aides comments on skin assessments.
- Do treatments one time a week with the treatment nurse to assess the degree of healing.
- Conference daily with charge nurses to see to it that the charge nurse is properly directing CNAs and answer any of their questions.
- Oversee nursing mediation of complaints/grievances. The best DON sees a potential problem, brings all parties together for a bit of "chit-chat." The DON is usually amazed as to what comes out of a short meeting, why the problem exists and when the staff comes up with a solution.
- Track medication errors on a daily basis. Ask why, who, when, and what time it occurred.
- Prepare the medication error report for the monthly Quality Assurance meeting.
- On a weekly basis, put away nursing supplies and check inventory of nursing needs (unless you have a Director of Supplies, and then lucky you).
- In smaller facilities, the Director of Nursing handles the nursing schedule. This is a tremendous job and very time and energy consuming. Again, thank your heavenly Father if you have a scheduler.
- One time a month, check all nursing equipment, such as the suction machine, lifts, bath belts, shower chairs, etc. Report your findings to the Administrator and during the Quality Assurance meeting.
- Audit charts for errors. This takes months of training. A semiretired nurse often can be hired to assist or one can take on-line training or workshops. In this era of information, one can learn anything in a short amount of time. Learn to ask for assistance. When speaking to any older,

experienced DON, they will tell you they are still learning.

- Attend all Care Plans. Get to know the residents and the family. Nothing is worse when a family walks into your office to ask how their loved one is getting along and you know nothing about that resident.
- All MDSs must be checked thoroughly as this is the facility's reimbursement data.
- One time a month, work as a CNA.
- One time a month, work the two to ten shift and the ten to six shift.
- Know and implement HIPAA regulations.
- Be in the dining room for one meal a day to assess resident needs for special eating equipment, if residents can easily reach their plates, behaviors by both residents and staff, and if residents are being transferred from their wheelchair to a table chair.
- And this is most important . . . if short-staffed, you must be more than willing to help feed, bathe, transport, or do CNA work. This is how you develop rapport with all staff. It is an eye-opener as to what you will discover. May I share a short story with you?

Short-staffed means ALL auxiliary staff (this includes the administrator, too) jumps in to help.

I was assisting a CNA in the changing the disposable on a female resident. The feces was hard and sticky (she needed more water plus a high fiber diet). The CNA used paper towels to clean the area. I went to the DON and asked her if she had ever wiped her bottom with a brown, harsh paper towel? The DON was shocked! The error was corrected that day with a short meeting with all the CNAs, at which time they were shown where all the soft wipes were located. This situation was alleviated by the Administrator working beside the CNA.

- Have a basic understanding of Medicare, Medicaid, skilled care, long-term care insurance paper work; the MARS, TARS, Care Plans, nursing-home regulations, fire regulations, MSDS manuals, OBRA, and the daily posting of nurse hours per shift.

- Attend all admission conferences to meet with residents and family (at the hospital or in the home), to know the dynamics and medical needs. Do you have the staff to handle heavy care residents, those with Alzheimer's, behavior problems, runaways, the alcoholic, the smoker, or a resident who weighs 390 pounds when you know the facility scale will only weigh up to 300 pounds and the lift will tolerate only 290 pounds. Think carefully when accepting a resident even though the owners may be pushing to fill the place. You are responsible for resident care. You and only you. Never forget that one fact. It is your license and your reputation on the line.
- Do rounds with the physicians and health care professionals. Talk with pharmacists about any issue when medications are delivered.
- Have a drawer full of thank you's and warm fuzzy's. Use them daily.
- If a nursing staff member resigns, be sure to have a short exit interview on his/her last day of work.
- Document and track if there is a high turnover in the nursing department.

Don't forget to take care of yourself. You are making good money. Spend a bit on yourself for a massage, hair care, colonics, chiropractor, take vitamins, or homeopathics. Have a personal counselor whom you trust and can talk to easily (a former DON or an empathetic Administrator is a perfect counselor). For the female DON, remember you may unwittingly have a hormonal imbalance. Get this checked out. For both the male and female DON, when under stress or you have mood swings, check out serotonin imbalance. Serotonin is depleted in stressful situations. There are many good medications and homeopathics to bring the serotonin back in balance.

- Have living plants in your office
- Use aromatherapy in your office

- Play soft and soothing music in your office
- Walk outside every day and talk to Mother Nature; walk the peace path
- Memorize positive affirmations
- Post positive affirmations in your office and on your office door
- Always be kind and respectful
- Love what you do
- Celebrate each day as you come to work and as you leave your work
- Thank God for the opportunity to serve our elders!

The wage scale for a Director of Nursing depending on years of experience and size of the facility and geographical location would range from $50,000 to $150,000 plus benefits.

14

The Nursing Departments

Certified Nurse Aides

Nationwide, there is more than 950,000 nursing staff working in nursing-homes. Nursing staff includes Registered Nurses, Licensed Practical Nurses, Certified Med Aides, and Certified Nurse Aides.

Certified Nurse Aides hold 65 percent of all nursing positions in nursing-homes. Although CNAs are not required to have a high school diploma or prior work experience, federal law requires that CNAs in Medicaid/Medicare certified nursing-homes complete a minimum of seventy-five hours in class and practical experience plus pass a competency exam within four months of employment to become a Certified Nurse Aide.

All the basics are taught, such as lifting, feeding, toileting, cleaning of teeth, washing, bathing, combing the hair, dressing, transporting, making a proper bed, changing of linens, proper changing of disposables, cleaning of the private areas, preparing the body for the undertaker, communication, documentation, HIPAA regulations, taking blood pressures, and understanding infection control measures. If nurse aides work in a natural health facility, training would include basic massage, reflexology, touch therapy, music, and color therapy plus affirmations and to feel comfortable in the leading of prayers.

In today's nursing-homes, the position as a CNA can be difficult, psychologically devastating, and hard physical work. They can be exposed to infections, diseases, physical violence, and name calling by rude and callous residents and verbal attacks by families. Back injuries are frequent, often occurring when preventing a resident from falling.

According to the Injury Fact Sheet for Healthcare, 291 nursing-home workers were seriously injured in falls in the years 2002–2004 resulting in over 3,000 days off work. In several cases, the worker was permanently disabled. Not only was there a loss of an employee, but it affected the rate of workers compensation insurance. The facility pays a base rate of 0.84 to 1.03 per hour for each staff member.

To view the full cost, if the facility had ten full-time nursing-home employees, and had an average number of claims for injuries, the facility would pay almost $20,700 in premiums per year. In conversation with a workers compensation insurance adjuster, I was informed that even if the facility had no injuries for a period of five years, our premiums would not go down. Where is the incentive to control injuries with the exception that no facility wants an employee to suffer injury and pain and lost time within the work force.

Injuries can occur when the nurse aide is transferring a resident, slips on water or urine, falls over a wheelchair, bed cranks, and items on the floor. One nurse aide was injured by an out-of-control Alzheimer resident who struck her. I, as an administrator, was hit so hard by an Alzheimer's resident that I sustained a back and shoulder injury when I tried to stop him from running into the street.

In an assisted-living complex, poor carpet installation resulted in three- to four-inch bumps in the carpet. Residents and staff could trip and be injured. I contacted a carpet layer to cut and pull the carpets to get rid of the ridges, and then was "called on the carpet" by the owner as I was spending too much money for repairs. The owner was oblivious of the fact of not only possible resident but staff injuries and lawsuits, and I could have lost my license. This owner and its corporate officers should have been charged with neglect and abuse by the residents and families.

Accidents do occur. Staff teachings are to check for nonskid waxes, wipe up spills immediately, replace worn out nonslip mats in the shower rooms and in dietary, keeping hallways free of equipment, and checking for lighting needs in every room. Transfer belts are mandatory for all CNAs to wear when on duty.

Proper lifting is taught by physical therapists. The use of lifts are mandated.

Because they are the assigned caregivers, CNAs are often the brunt of abuse cases, even though, many times, they are totally innocent. Many, and I say many, CNAs are injured when preventing a resident from falling, and are kicked, bitten, and have fingers twisted and hair pulled. Because of this type of resident behavior we ask that no one wear dangling ear rings, large finger rings, and for infection control, no tongue piercings.

Because nursing-homes must provide care on a twenty-four-hour basis, CNAs are often required to be available to work extra shifts, evenings, holidays and weekends. With the extra hours, exhaustion sets in, which often leads to an accident. According to the Hospital Compensation Service, the average hourly earnings for CNAs in nursing-homes is $8.25. Annual turnover rates for CNAs are often over 100 percent due to higher pay in other medical facilities and in home health, which offer better benefits and a less stressful work environment. The following is a chart to review direct care minutes spent on each nursing-home resident.

*HCFA, a federal program, is an acronym for Health Care Financing Administration, now known as the Center for Medicare and Medicaid, which creates and enforces policy and finances the health care industry through your tax dollars.

Let us compare a 1999 average nursing hours per resident day to the 2002 HCFA mandate, keeping in mind today's (2009) nursing-home residents are older and sicker.

According to HCFA, as of October 1, 2002, an updated policy was set into motion with aggregate licensed nursing and nurse aides staffing levels being maintained at or above the following standards for nursing facilities licensed by the Department of Public health as chronic and convalescent nursing-homes and rest homes with nursing supervision: One will note very little change from the 1999 chart of staffing hours and the mandate of 2002. Of utmost importance is the policy that facilities cannot count DON hours nor ADON hours in the direct care and services of residents. Does this mean HCFA sees two highly skilled

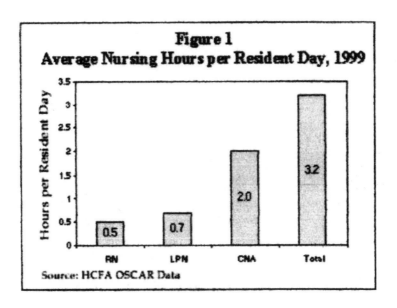

Figure 1
Average Nursing Hours per Resident Day, 1999

Source: HCFA OSCAR Data

professional nurses doing paperwork only?? The 2002 HCFA mandate is as follows:

*Over a twenty-four-hour period, each facility shall provide:

- At least 2.0 hours of direct care and services given by nurse aides per resident; and
- At least 0.75 hours of care and services given by licensed nurses, of which 0.2 hours shall be provided by a registered nurse. (Forty-five minutes in a twenty-four-hour day for direct care by professional licensed nurses? What is HCFA saying here?) In defense of HCFA's nursing quotas, if they increase the minutes per day, with the nursing shortage, the nursing industry could not meet the quota required.
- The Director of Nursing shall not be included in satisfying the licensed nursing staff requirement for facilities with a licensed bed capacity of sixty-one or greater. Facilities with a capacity of 121 licensed beds or greater shall employ a full-time assistant director of nursing who shall

not be included in satisfying the licensed nursing staffing requirement.

As principle caregivers in nursing-homes, CNAs averaged 2.0 hours direct resident care in a twenty-four hour period, which equates to forty minutes per resident during an eight hour shift. The key here is "direct care." This is three to four times the number of minutes averaged by LPNs and RNs, which were fourteen and ten minutes per resident per shift, respectively. The average total for all nursing staff combined is sixty-four minutes per resident per shift in direct cares. Direct cares, according to HCFA, means hands-on care provided to residents, including, but not limited to, feeding, bathing, toileting, dressing, dental cares, lifting, and transporting residents, changing disposables, delivering medications, medical cares such as eye drops, critical cares such as treatments for bed sores, rashes, cuts, bruises, IVs, oxygen needs, and transporting to and from activities and therapies. Direct care does not include food preparation, housekeeping, or laundry services, except when such services are required to meet the needs of a resident on any given occasion.

If the facility can take from the CNAs the bedmaking duties, picking up the room, cleaning closets, transporting to and from therapies, activities, and meals, cleaning of wheelchairs and equipment, filling of bottles of shampoo and lotions, and clothes inventory, the direct care hours would increase over and above HCFA requirements. To assist the shortage of CNAs, alternative health care workers could be on staff, who would count as direct care staff, as residents are involved in natural health therapies. And it is my belief that natural health therapists are waiting in the wings to be called into the care of our elders in a nursing-home setting. However, HCFA must be prepared to reimburse the facility for natural health care therapists.

Mermaids

Bath aides are a must in every facility. Bath aides do most all whirlpool baths and showers during the day shift, documenting any skin abnormalities, need for podiatry, clean fingernails, shampoo the hair, cut hairs from the nose and heavy eyebrows, lotion the body, and give a short massage on the back and neck areas. The CNAs are responsible for undressing the resident, transporting the resident to the whirlpool room, and again transferring the resident back after the shower and redressing.

Residents are usually transported on portable "potty" chairs, with residents covered by a large wraparound cover. CNAs are warned not to expose the resident during transport. To avert this method of preparing for a whirlpool or shower, the resident could be undressed and again dressed in a special room adjacent to the whirlpool room called the "dressing" room. Then both the CNA and shower aide would be present to assist the resident, preventing falls (and CNA injuries), and alleviate the sometimes embarrassing transfer on the potty chair.

In one facility, a daughter came in twice a week to give her mother a bath. The daughter was the primary caregiver prior to her mother's entering the nursing-home. This is how the daughter kept the bond between the two.

One facility had a whirlpool bath tub, but when I asked why it was not used, I was told that "whirlpool" tubs are filthy, and it was better to give all residents a shower. The truth in this situation is that showers can be given faster, which meant less staff hours needed. And the residents lost by not being provided with a very therapeutic mineral salt whirlpool bath.

My personal physician was opposed to the one bath, one shower every week because he felt it dried out the already very thin skin. If a nursing-home decided to provide one bath a week, the whirlpool is the therapeutic bath of choice.

Whirlpool tubs, with their jets are a necessity in natural healing therapies not only for stimulation but, with Queen Helene mineral salts and oils added to the water, they are extremely therapeutic for aches and pains.

Families assisting with baths and personal care are not only allowable but encouraged.

Mermaids wage average $12 per hour.

The Licensed Nurse

To provide more time in personal, compassionate, and spiritual care, the nursing-home industry must petition the state and federal governments to decrease the enormous amount of paperwork required of the professional nurses. To this date, professional nurses are behind the desk filling out repetitive forms and documenting in medical charts. The mantra is "if it is not documented, it did not occur, thus it is not reimbursable."

In the 1970s, one would see not only the Director of Nursing working the floor beside her staff, but all RNs and LPNs were passing medications, doing treatments, and assisting with personal cares. Today, due to the immense amount of paperwork, the skilled professional nurse is used for paper compliance.

In one facility, a state surveyor came to me and said that in one eight-hour day, she did not see the charge nurse leave the desk, except for breaks and lunch. This is inexcusable from both sides of the story. Was the nurse a bit lazy or was she so immersed in paperwork that she could not be of assistance to the residents?

One LPN in a small facility spent the entire day, every day, documenting for the physical therapy aide. And on the other side of the picture are the LPNs passing medications, completing paperwork, working intimately with the residents, talking with families, answering the phone, and directing the CNAs. One RN could not get anything done, leaving paperwork for the next shift. When I made a night shift call, I found the night shift watching TV and one nurse was studying for her RN tests. Most professionals are excellent and have heavy responsibilities as charge nurses. And they, too, must remain on duty until their replacement arrives. If that does not occur, they will be working another shift, which causes concern for her/his family and babysitting situations, plus the quality of resident care suffers. Working in a nursing-home is not easy. That is why nurses must be "called." It is a ministry, not a job.

The Licensed Practical Nurse average wage scale is $15 to $20 per hour.

The Registered Nurse average wage is $18 to $30 per hour.

Nurse wages are dependent on locality and experience. Hire on bonuses and benefits are a plus.

Pool Nurses

The pool nurse industry has grown exponentially in the last decade due to the requirement of nursing-homes to maintain proper nurse staffing.

I drafted a white paper in one nursing-home to find that paying facility nurses double time when the facility calls them back to work would be a savings to the facility. Known facts in hiring pool nurses are:

- They do not know the residents as well.
- Upsetting to residents who do not recognize the nurse caring for them.
- There is an increase in medication errors.
- Poor documentation or no documentation.
- Treatments and the delivery of medications not completed in a timely manner.
- Treatments not completed at all.
- Facility staff must show the pool nurses daily assignments and duties, which takes time away from personal resident cares.
- Facility nurse aides have stated they would rather work short than have a pool nurse to train.

Positive results of paying double time for facility nurses or a bonus rather than pool nurses:

- Residents feel secure with nurses they know.
- Less medication errors.
- Better documentation.
- Quicker response in an emergency.
- A reduction in cost vs. pool nurse costs.
- Increasing wages of facility nurses who are willing to work extra hours.

- Provides an attractive incentive for facility nurses.

The opposing view to paying double time is the manipulation for a fill-in nurse with the knowledge the next shift is short. A nurse may choose to return home, wait for a call, and be paid double time rather than staying on for an extra four or eight hours at the regular rate of pay. Volunteering for extra hours for double-time pay often results in burn out. Paying double time when in crisis often creates discontent among nonnursing staff.

We must recognize the fact pool nurses can not be totally eliminated as there will always be extreme emergencies when there are no facility nurses available. And at times the Director of Nursing, the Assistant Director of Nursing, and the RN-MDS coordinator can step in and receive incentive pay according to her/his contract.

Professional Pool Nurses can cost up to $50 per hour. A pool CNA or a CMA cost is an average of $25 per hour.

Medication Aides

Changes that must be made in all nursing-homes are in the utilization of the certified medication aide who delivers medications to the residents. I have found that the well-trained med aide, given proper time and without interference, makes few med errors and does an excellent job in completing any treatments needed. With the severe RN and LPN shortage forecasted, med aides must be granted their proper place as a caregiver.

In the February 2007 issue of *Clinical Nursing Research*, an article titled, "Nursing-Home Error(s) and Level of Staff Credentials," described an exploratory study of Certified Medication Aides vs. the professional nurses relating to the administration of medications.

In this study, when medication errors were considered by level of credential(s), RNs had an error rate of 34.6%, LPNs had an error rate of 40.1%, and CMAs had error rates of 34.2%.

However, when wrong time errors were removed, RNs had the largest percentage of error (7.4%), but the highest rate of interruptions (39.9%). Both the complexity of the medications being delivered and the competing demands on the RNs time explain both the interruptions and medication error rates.

The conclusion reached was, "this study provides some initial evidence to suggest that CMAs can be effectively used for routine medication administration." This study also suggests that minimizing interruptions would improve the safety of medication administration.

In one facility, it was a house rule that the CMA passing medications could not be interrupted for any reason . . . no telephone calls, no messages, no good mornings! The eyes of the CMA were focused on the right resident, the right dosage, the right time, the right method of delivery, the right documentation and his/her signature. Errors were minimal. I agree with this house rule as I worked as a medication aide and wanted no interruptions in order to concentrate on the job at hand and at that moment.

The Lumber Wagons, i.e., Medication Carts

Medication carts appeared in the late 1970s for the sole purpose of preventing the loss or pilfering of medications. Medication carts do not prevent either. The cart is not only expensive but the pharmaceutical firms created the single "bubble" pack, which is very costly to the private pay residents and the taxpayer.

Newly admitted residents have come in with medications that cannot be relabeled or used by the nursing-home. All new medications must be ordered via the bubble pack. And who is profiting from this system?

All nursing-homes have a medication cart with the bubble packs, so a change in delivery would not be feasible at the moment. However, for the interest of the public, prior to the 1970s medications were delivered in the bulk (less expensive) with pills for each resident placed in small medication cups. Families bringing in medications from home were relabeled by the pharmacist. This method was just as safe and sanitary and considerably less expensive and the nurses were not worn out pushing and tugging a medication cart as heavy as the old lumber wagon.

However, in one large facility, the in-house pharmacist sent medications to each unit via a nurse, who carried them in a pretty basket with a ribbon on top.

Medical Records

Medical records personnel do a myriad of duties. They are usually underappreciated and underpaid. With prolific governmental paper mandates, medical records must be well organized and perused by personnel checking for inconsistencies and lack of documentation by all staff. The Medical Records director is the "hounddog" who obtains signatures, checks proper dates, gleans out medical charts, puts forms in proper order, must prove through progress notes the authenticity for billing, is knowledgeable what can be billed and shares information with the Director of Nursing, files and is prepared to resurrect information needed by surveyors and sometimes for the Courts.

Medical records serve as a tool in litigation, either for the plaintiff or the defendant. In recent years, the resident's chart has become the determining factor in 80%–85% of all malpractice lawsuits involving resident cares. Nursing-homes may run into a problem if medical records are vague, inconsistent or missing data.

Medical records personnel attends monthly staff meetings, resident care planning and peruses the MDS sheets prior to be transmitted. Medical records is a two year program in community colleges, however, a proficient nurse aide who works the floor no less than one time a week, could easily serve in medical records. This is a position for a physically handicapped person or an older staff person proven to be well organized. The average wage is $25,000 per year.

Career Advances in Nursing

With the severe shortage of nurses, I have always encouraged Certified Nurse Aides to further their education. Most nursing-homes pay for classes. The average pay scale for CNAs is $8 to $10 per hour. To advance to a Medication Aide is to increase the pay scale to $12 to $13 per hour. Licensed Practical Nurses are paid from $15 to $17 per hour and have gone to school for approximately one year. I prefer to hire an LPN who has a good background as a Certified Nurse Aide and as a Medication Aide, as they understand the care level needed, are more understanding toward CNAs, and can take over easily for the Medication Aide. RNs pay scale range from $18 to $25 per hour, depending on years of experience. RN school takes approximately one year, depending on nursing background. I have noted, in today's computer world, some nursing classes are available over the Internet and can be taken at the person's leisure.

Administrators and Director of Nursing must always encourage CNAs to continue their education in nursing, to advance to a med aide, then on to no less than an LPN. It is my personal opinion that those who have come up through the ranks are usually the best as charge nurses.

Most nursing-homes will pay for advanced education, especially for those who have a high work ethic and have proven their compassion and common sense in decision-making involving the care of the elderly.

Selected facilities that have not been cited for serious deficiencies may offer CNA training in house. Facilities are mandated to pay for all books and supplies, plus minimum wage when in class and when working as nurse aide interns.

However, not all is well when those who enter the nursing field are not sincerely interested. It was known throughout one area that there were those persons who hit one nursing-home after another to take classes (free), were paid to tag along with certified nurse aides, and then not take the test. Then on they go to the next facility to start the charade all over. And at what cost to the industry? Research states that it cost $1,200 to train one CNA. The Red Cross organization of Greater Boston charges

$850 for CNA training. The facility pays the new CNA for three days' work as she/he shadows a mentor.

Nursing-homes often assist those who wish to go on for their LPN license. They sign a promise to work at least one year at the sponsoring facility. I do not ever remember any staff working more than a month or two at the facility that paid for their license. They are off and running where they could make more money. The promise meant nothing.

Fortunately, as wages increased for nursing staff, I have noted an influx of male certified nurse aides, medications aides, and licensed nurses, plus male Directors of Nursing.

Nursing-homes need the masculine energy due to the fact there are 90 percent female residents and 95 percent female staff. It is my belief and observation that when a facility has a more balanced female-male energy, there is less friction and better camaraderie. In a Veterans facility the gender was turned around with 95 percent male veterans and 75 percent female staff. With a somewhat balanced energy, again, my opinion, the facility seemingly operated more efficiently and calmly. Overall, nursing is an excellent profession to enter where age is no factor and the need will always be there.

Not All Are Called to Be Nurses

During my career, I believe that over 75 percent of CNAs are well above average caregivers often working extra hours to cover when short-staffed and going the extra mile for residents who are often not the easiest to cope with. Then there are the 25 percent that includes professional nurses who were never called to be a nurse. One CNA came to work bragging about her new ring that she had taken off the body of a deceased resident. Her nurse aide career ended that day. Another CNA worked three days, just long enough to steal a new pair of expensive shoes from a resident.

Two CNAs decided they would look elsewhere for work one evening as I was leaving work at 5:30. All residents were in the dining room when I noted a table of residents had their trays in front of them with no staff visible to assist them. I put my purse and attaché down and slid inside the horseshoe table and began to feed the residents. There was no intent on my part except there was a possibility their food would be cold before a staff person arrived. I noted two CNAs talking loudly across the room from one to another. One staff said, "I can hardly wait to get out of here, go to the bar, get drunk, and get laid." At that moment they both saw me. When a staff came to relieve me I quietly went to the both of them and said I wanted to see them in my office following the meal. Both were very red faced. One resigned immediately and the other within the week. Are morals and ethics taught in CNA courses?

An RN "squirreled" psychotrophic drugs away in the trunk of her car and gave them to the residents in her wing. The only way we discovered this was the Activity Director came to me and said she noticed that on the east wing, all the residents were always sleeping and she couldn't get them involved in any activities. An investigation ensued, with the RN eventually admitting she was overmedicating residents so they would not cause her any problems on her shift. The RN resigned under the guise of retiring.

Once a surveyor came to me and said they were in sight of a nurse's station where they noted an LPN Charge Nurse had not moved all day to answer lights. This is a frequent challenge, especially if the charge nurse is not passing meds. The charge nurse is just as responsible for direct care as the CNAs.

I have walked into facilities many times about 6:30 in the evening to find 90 percent of residents in bed and CNAs hanging around the nurses station or reading newspapers. In talking with the residents in their beds I asked if they had wanted to go to bed. They usually said, no. So, I walked to the CNAs and told them to get the residents back up, and remake all the beds. Then I check for dental care. Nothing had been done as food from the evening meal was still on the teeth and dentures were still in residents' mouths. So dental cares were completed, diapers changed, faces and hands washed, and hair brushed. Residents were taken to the lounge to watch TV or play a game of ball or cards or do puzzles or just visit. When the clock struck 8:30, I then told the CNAs to start putting those who asked to go to bed, back to bed, permitting others to stay up later.

What possesses CNAs to think it is okay to put elders to bed so early? Is this issue discussed in classes? This is elder abuse! Regardless of the facility, this problem seems to permeate the evening shift. Change comes with a hard-nosed Charge Nurse who gives orders and assists the CNAs, not sitting behind the desk with paperwork.

Families can assist by visiting in the evening hours, informing nurse aides that they cannot put their loved one to bed so early. Family is encouraged to bring a musical instrument, pets, grandchildren, games to entertain not only your loved one but two or three others.

In one of Edgar Cayce's readings, it said that we receive double the hours of sleep after midnight because of the deep sleep entered into. If that is so, putting residents to bed at 7 p.m. and getting them up at 6 a.m. would be a total of seventeen hours of sleep. And then nursing staff wonders why so many residents are restless during the night. They want to get up!

Working the night shift (as an administrator), I enjoyed residents who wanted up. We played checkers, or cards, or just talked.

We had $100 donated to one facility to spend for something the residents would enjoy. I purchased several large wall pictures with animals and birds and was hanging them where residents liked to sit. A nurse aide came by and said very belligerently, "I think you should be giving raises rather than buying pictures."

I have often witnessed TVs turned on to a nurse's favorite soap opera as they are doing personal cares for the residents; hard rock music played on a residents' radio; and nurse aides have brought their boyfriends in the nursing-home to visit or watch TV together.

I have found nursing staff studying, reading, or sleeping during the night shift and then the morning shift would find residents' beds soaked from urine, snacks never given, and paperwork not done. The charts from night nursing often read, "Resident quiet, slept all night." Nurses seem to do in a nursing-home what they would never do in their own home nor with their own children. Or do they?

In 1977, nursing was the dominant department in the delivering of most services to elders in a nursing-home setting. Today social services, activities, and administrators have taken on the role of all but nursing cares. One day a director of nursing stopped to talk for a moment and said, "I don't know what we would do without social services. Do you know who bought resident clothes, opened and read their mail to them, cleaned closets, mended clothes, and helped them make telephone calls? Yes, it was nursing. I remember shopping for them after I got off work. Thanks for all you do for nursing!"

And then there are those unenlightened beings who destroy any camaraderie among the staff, such as a director of nursing who thought nothing of chastising and humiliating nurse aides in the hallway where all could hear. One director of nursing refused to leave her office to assist her charge nurses and certainly would not lower herself to help a nurse aide. This same director of nursing was rude to families as well as other staff.

One day a family member stopped me in the hallway and said that he thought I needed to do a better job when hiring nurses. What this family member did not know is that not only do applicants fabricate their abilities but we are not allowed to call former employers concerning why they left. This is just another regulation that needs to be changed. A county attorney told me to never permit three-month trial periods for new employees so we changed the policy to six months. His theory was that negative behaviors tend to show up in a lengthened period of time. And he was correct. With a combination of poor work ethics in a difficult job, those not called will leave, which again adds to the high turnover and cost to the facility. Those not called are no more than "thieves" in the industry, costing the taxpayer millions and an insult to the elderly.

Could an answer be in alternative therapies not only taught to nursing staff for the residents but also for the staff to implement in their own lives?

All nursing staff must be open to alternative teachings to work in a facility that endorses positive thinking, meditation, and affirmations that create an environment of well-being for both elders and staff. It is not unprofessional to give hugs, to laugh, and to bring joy into the workplace.

In one facility in which I noted no music, no talking, no hugs, no laughter, I finally asked why. The charge nurse told me the last Director of Nursing told them it was unprofessional to joke and laugh. That directive ended in that moment, that day. It was hard for nursing to make that change. However, when I visited their wing, they heard me laugh, hug, and giggle, so after a few months, the entire wing changed . . . happily.

The majority of today's nursing staff is female . . . female with a multitude of life challenges. Each day, facilities receive calls from moms who have sick children, or sick elder parents, have no gas money for the car in which they rely on to get to work, car problems, housing problems, abusive husbands or live-ins, financial problems, no food in the house, no medication for children or for themselves, no clean uniform, or they have a drug or alcohol problem and have been arrested, are in jail, or in court for child abuse.

A trusted Medication Aide was found to be taking pain medication from the med cart. The Director of Nursing and I counseled her as to why she would do this. In tears, she said her husband had been diagnosed with cancer and with a new baby in the house, they could not afford the prescribed pain medication for him. A call was made to the pharmacist. Her case was investigated with no charges. The DON and I took turns paying for the medication needed.

One of the best of the best CNAs came to work very upset. When I inquired, I was told she, being a very proud person, refused to have her children on free school lunches. Their lunch tickets had run out and the school refused to feed the children. I was so angry I called the school superintendent and told him that under no circumstances was a school system receiving government commodities to refuse to feed children. I asked what the lunch's cost and sent the school a check with the warning that this was never to happen again to any children of nursing-home staff.

A CNA came to my office in tears as payroll checks (two days before Christmas) were not to arrive on time. She had no money to purchase any gifts for her children. I asked her what the amount she would need to cover a few gifts. Would you believe $20? I advanced her the money. It was paid back with a beautiful hankie enclosed in an envelope. I cherish that hankie and think of her many times.

Another Christmas when the checks did not arrive until December 24 late in the day, panic ensued. When the corporate office was called, the comptroller said, "What difference does it make?" Only a very self serving person could respond in that manner. A motto for all nursing-homes: "Don't tamper with payroll checks!"

I applauded one facility that was open to advancing monies to staff in need. In this manner staff avoided a stressful situation, was usually appreciative of the advance, and thus a more dedicated employee.

Most nursing-home employees live on the edge of financial disaster. Many private corporations today are offering employee financial counseling. However, I will go one step further. All nursing-homes must incorporate spiritual/financial counselors available not only for the elders, their family members, but also for the staff.

Work Ethic

In most nursing-homes there is adequate nursing staff. I learned quickly, as an administrator that to be overstaffed promotes laziness and irresponsibility. One of my facilities was overstaffed on a daily basis. Less was done for the residents than in a lower-staffed facility. I found with overstaffing, the staff tended to stand around, talking more with peers, took longer breaks, was more prone to not show up for work, and left the facility for long periods of time and was found watching television with the residents in the lounge for lack of anything to do. The overstaffed shift of nurses did not find work for themselves, such as cleaning drawers, files, closets, straightening up residents rooms, or simply focusing on the needs of the residents.

There has been a drastic change in morals, attitudes, and work ethic since the 1970s. What makes for a negative work environment? Gossip, backbiting, unprofessional behavior, foolish words, thoughts and actions, and the lack of responsibility.

Think on this one from *The Alchemist's Handbook to Homeopathy.*

"Soon after polio vaccinations were given, strange behavior was noticed in some of the children who received it. In the 1960s, after the polio epidemic, the United States had a whole era of 'flower children' or hippies. These young people who had received the polio vaccine began taking drugs to ease the emotional and physical pain they were experiencing as a side effect of this vaccination. They lived together in communes because they lived in fear instead of trusting life. This fear comes from being cut off from their higher spiritual self."

As I read this, I began to understand the difficulty many young people have with authority and responsibility.

How can we help in this situation? Could prayer or meditation be the answer? Does the facility have full-spectrum lights in offices and over the nurses' stations to prevent undue tiredness and irritation? Should facilities implement color therapy, music therapy, massages just for the staff? Are in-services geared towards staff self-esteem? Is a counselor available for staff to vent their frustrations and cope with personal problems? Does the facility provide exercise equipment and nutritious snacks? Is there a day-care center for staff children? Does the community pay tribute to the staff through Chamber recognition? Or at Christmas time? Does the administrator recognize staff on their birthdays or special days? How many staff are encouraged to further their education? Is the staff taught preventive health measures especially homeopathy.

Poor work ethic and negative behaviors and remarks are not acceptable in a facility that promotes a more spiritual setting. In a therapeutic, spiritual setting, nurse turnover would most certainly decrease. With the implementation of natural therapies, nursing staff would enjoy taking part in the therapies not only in the residents' behalf but for their own professional growth. How many other simple, inexpensive changes can be made in order to lighten the load for nursing?

The Value of Bedmakers

It is essential that nursing-homes hire the older worker for bedmakers, which, again, would relieve the nursing staff from mundane duties such as bedmaking, cleaning beds, changing of linens, and picking up the residents' rooms. Bedmakers are usually paid minimum wage and are hired part time and with no benefits.

Another, usually unsung value of bed makers is their compassion. Elders find them easy to converse with. Bedmakers are another set of eyes for the elder who may need assistance.

Bedmakers are the first to notice a mattress that needs to be replaced or closets that need cleaning or a cubicle curtain that needs to be taken down and washed.

If one facility had bedmakers they would have saved thousands of dollars. Because no one had taken the responsibility to clean closets, termites had seriously invaded the walls. It took pest control services many trips to rid the facility of the unwanted creatures.

Bedmakers, as part of the nursing staff, are usually trained to transfer residents and assist with feeding during dining hours. And it is the bedmakers that I encourage to open each resident window as they make the beds so outside air can freshen up the room.

The Gero-Teen Program

In one facility, I implemented the Gero-Teen program visiting the local high school to request credits for any teenager who wished to volunteer an hour or so daily working beside any staff person they choose. Special uniforms were given to the teenagers to wear while on duty. The teenagers were permitted to assist in any department. Out of this program, the community brought back nurse aides who went on and obtained professional licenses.

I tried this program again in another community and was told by the school counselor that he would not permit any student to ever work at the nursing-home without pay and was not interested in a Gero-Teen program.

What did I expect? After all, my own alma mater refused my efforts to acknowledge the need to teach gerontology or classes in nursing-home administration. One professor actually said to me, laughing, "Who would want to take those classes?"

I find it interesting when a community or a college has a job fair. How often has anyone noticed nursing-home staff at the fair? I have never been called to be part of a job fair. How many professions in a nursing-home? Let us count: the administrator, social service directors, activity directors, dietary managers, business managers, nurses, maintenance, schedulers, housekeepers, and laundry workers. Ten or more positions available. And yet, the colleges seem to be oblivious of the nursing-home industry.

Family Involvement

How can family assist in the nursing crisis? Family members, instead of just paying a visit, can comb hair, clean and polish finger nails, wash the face, put makeup on, put on a clean shirt or blouse, lotion the arms, hands, and legs, make the bed, change the linens, if needed, clean the closet and drawers, water the plants, and mop the floor if there has been a spill.

Family members are welcome to take part in meals and assist their loved one; assist with bathing, dental care, and most importantly take their resident out to lunch, a ballgame, a musical, for hair care, a massage, the chiropractor, or just for fresh air on a sunny day or better yet, take the resident's shoes off and run through the grass or a puddle of mud, touch the trees, the flowers, smell the good earth; play music, sing, dance! Show old family movies, hold a family reunion at the facility, take your loved one to church every Sunday (or Saturday and on Holy Days).

126

Take them to the activities kitchen and bake favorite meals and desserts. Brew a pot of coffee. Our elders are with us for such a short time and when gone, there should be no regrets as to quality time spent with them. Ask yourself what you would do for him/her if your elder was in their own home? Go fishing? Play checkers? Drive into the country to see the old farm place?

It is of utmost importance that the family speak in a positive manner, assist in prayers of thankfulness, and encourage the elder to pray for others or be of assistance in small ways, even if it is encouragement or a smile or a wave of the hand.

When families are directly involved in personal care, hopefully they will be more understanding of the degree of difficulty in caring for their loved one, especially those residents who constantly complain and demand.

It is imperative that grandchildren come in as often as possible to assist a grandparent, due to the fact the family unit is fractured when grandparents are placed in a nursing-home. There needs to be a bonding between the two generations. What a wonderful opportunity for the grandchildren.

Now, we have discussed many issues and challenges. What changes are you willing to make in order to overcome the nurse shortage?

Keys to Unlocking the Nursing Crisis In Nursing-Homes

1. Hire bedmakers so Nurse Aides spend their time completing resident cares.
2. Hire Medication Aides to deliver medications and do treatments so professional nurses can assist with resident cares and oversee CNAs.
3. Demand less paperwork of the professional nurse so the professional has the time to provide personal cares and assist the Nurse Aides.
4. Hire nonnursing staff as nurse schedulers.
5. Hire nonnursing staff to do nursing inventory.

6. Complete medical chart gleaning by well-trained nonnursing staff.
7. Numbers 4, 5, 6, and 8 can be accomplished by physically handicapped persons who need work.
8. Nonnursing staff prepare for nurse interviews, check references and licenses, and inform the nurse scheduler of new hires and dismissals. The DON always does the interviewing. This will free the DON to assist with residents cares and oversee CNAs and the professional nurses.
9. Nonnursing staff fill bottles of lotion, soap, check oxygen bottles, etc., and keep the nursing supply rooms clean. These duties could be completed by the bedmakers.
10. Train all nonnursing staff to transport residents to and from meals and assist with feeding. Nonnursing staff equates to activity directors, social workers, counselors, housekeepers, bedmakers, office workers, maintenance, and administrators.
11. Upon admission, families must understand their part in elder care, such as assisting with personal care, transporting, and feeding.
12. Religious organizations must be approached to take their share of responsibilities in elder care with such simple duties as keeping closets free of excess clothing, calling families to take unused clothing home, and contacting families for any needs. Volunteers, with a bit of training could transfer residents to and from meals and assist with feeding.
13. Hire older, compassionate nondegreed trained hospice workers to relieve nursing from the time needed to be with a dying resident.
14. Nursing-homes and the schools work together to develop Gero-Teen programs to interest students in the field of nursing and other nursing-home professions.
15. Implement natural health therapists into the total care plan for each elder, which would decrease the need for the overworked nursing staff.

16. Release of consultants, who at the present time have very little personal contact with residents, to generate the dollars needed to raise CNA hourly rate to a livable wage.
17. As the medication carts need to be replaced, consider a less institutional method of delivery which in turn would take less time to deliver medications.
18. Health and Human Services must count the Director of Nursing and the Assistant Director of Nursing into personal care time when working directly with residents.

15

Unemployment Judges as Elder Abusers?

Society is led to believe that only nursing-home staff abuse residents. However, as an insider, I believe differently. Here are several examples: an aide once slapped a confused male resident diagnosed with Alzheimer's. The CNA reported that he pinched her in the backside as she walked by. She was fired immediately. We were challenged by the unemployment court due to the fact we did not suspend her for three days during an investigation, although we told the judge her action was witnessed by the director of nursing. But to no avail. We were found guilty of not investigating the incident and not training the nursing staff that this behavior occurred in nursing-homes. The aide was awarded full unemployment benefits. I turned to the judge with my final words, "Someday, when you become a resident in my nursing-home I will make sure to hire this nurse aide to care for you."

Another unemployment hearing brought this story to the forefront. A nurse aide was overheard to say to a resident, "If you don't lay still, I'll stick this up your ass." This particular situation was reported, and the nurse fired. And to unemployment court we went. The nurse won her case because according to the judge, "The incident did not happen the day the nurse was fired, henceforth, I had no reason to fire her." I presented the nurse aide's personal file with no less than ten occurrences that had been reported over the past five years involving abuse of residents. The judge said the file was irrelevant, as they were all in the past.

These are two of many unemployment hearings in which I took part. I believe there are unemployment judges who fear/hate nursing-homes, thus, they take their fear and hatred out on them by rewarding staff that are abusive. Instead of assisting us in ridding the system of those who should never work again in a nursing home, unemployment judges reward the abusers. In essence this makes unemployment judges abusers of the nursing-home elderly. But, then, who has ever charged unemployment judges of abuse?

16

The Ombudsman

Almost all nursing-home facilities participate in Medicare and Medicaid. Therefore they are subject to "Conditions of Participation," which includes the Resident Bill of Rights, the forbidding of verbal, sexual, physical, mental, and financial abuse.

Under the Older Americans Act each state provides an Ombudsman program, which, if contacted, must investigate any issues that the facility may have. The Ombudsman must then report the conclusions of the investigation to the state health department. The Ombudsman is an advocate for those who reside in a nursing-home.

I have found that if an Ombudsman is called, many times the issues can be resolved and is far better than having disgruntled residents or family calling the state with a complaint.

According to Attorney Dana Shilling, in her book *Legal Issues of Dependent and Incapacitated People*, she utilized the 2005 annual report of the South Carolina complaint process, which recorded 1,333 skilled care, intermediate care for the mentally handicapped, residential, and community training homes that are covered by the Ombudsman programs.

The report broke down the number and type of complaints investigated. The program received about 5,000 complaints, slightly more than half from skilled nursing facilities. There were 1,650 from residential care facilities and about 700 from other facilities.

In skilled nursing facilities, there were 303 complaints for physical abuse, 192 for verbal abuse, and 128 for gross neglect. In the residential facilities, the complaints were very similar to the skilled-care facilities. There were 88 complaints about denial of access to information about rights and benefits and 132 complaints involving discharges and evictions. There were 101 complaints about staff attitudes and failure to grant respect to residents, 62 complaints about personal property stolen or used improperly and in all facilities, 571 incidents involving improper handling of residents. There was a small number of complaints in categories such as rehabilitation, improper use of restraints, social services, activities, food, environment and staff levels.

Of the 2,982 total nursing-home complaints, 2,302 were resolved to satisfaction; 1,416 were verified, no action was deemed necessary in 164 cases; 143 were referred without a final report; 86 were withdrawn; 45 were not resolved; 99 partially resolved, and 10 would have required a regulation change. Interestingly, I did not note that Ombudsmans were called. These statistics are deplorable when read by the public.

Outsider Abusers

However, the statistics do not reflect who other abusers are because these abusers are never held accountable, such as:

- A family came to visit their uncle. After they left, the uncle reported his antique collection of little wooden trains was gone.
- A daughter visited her mother and reported an expensive ring missing. The facility reimbursed the mother for the ring. Several months later another daughter came into my office and told me her sister was wearing her mother's ring.
- A son visited his dad once a week and had his dad sign a check for "farm repairs or equipment." A neighbor came into my office and told me there were no buildings nor equipment on this farm. It took a court order to get the conservatorship away from the son, who was bleeding his dad out of the last of his money.
- An alcoholic mother came to visit her handicapped son. After she left, the staff noted that the son's new coat and clothes were missing from his closet.

- A son came to his mother's room and had her sign a new will, with all her assets willed to him. There were five other children in the family.
- An attorney refused to relinquish any funds for a wealthy resident even for personal care. The lady had no known relatives. Her will left everything to the attorney.
- A physician told a family, who were in the room with their mother, that he would not transfer their mother to a hospital because, "she was going to die anyway."
- In one facility Walmart stores donated a blanket to every resident for Christmas. When I returned to work the next day, most of the blankets were gone. Families had come in to visit and took the blankets home with them.
- Spouses who come to visit often are found eating the residents meals served in the room. Family fills their purses with fresh fruit left in the room by staff for the residents' snack.
- A husband reported his wife's teeth were missing again so he called the state. The facility paid for another set of dentures. Maintenance was suspicious as he had often seen the resident "play" with her dentures so he pulled up the toilet in her room and found the dentures. The husband never returned the money.
- Clothes were frequently missing. Upon investigation, it was found prisoners who were doing the laundry for the facility were the thieves.
- And even more frequently is the family's personal use of the resident's Social Security check. Only when the facility reports financial abuse are Social Security checks transferred directly to the facility.
- The husband who took his very confused wife home with him for weekend sex.
- The group of hippies who took grandma out for a ride every Sunday and made sure she had her checkbook with her to pay for needed car repairs, etc.
- A group of young men (one was the sheriff's son) who got the key to an elder's house, broke in, and stole a gun col-

lection. No charges were ever brought against any of the group.

- How about the elderly farmer, with no family, who was a resident in our facility for twenty years. In comes a promoter for the neighboring facility and gets the resident to sign a paper donating all his land to that facility. Moral? Ethical? Or financially abusive? You be the judge.
- Unemployment judges who grant abusive employees full unemployment benefits.
- Workers compensation courts that refuse to accept the truth about an alleged injury and grants months of benefits that are costly to the facility and eventually for the taxpayer and the elders who reside in the nursing-home.
- A guardian (son) who left orders to the staff not to permit any other family member to visit their dad. The dad told the staff he wanted to see all his family.
- The mortician who treated a body of a resident with such disdain, saying, "It's only a body."
- Allopathic physicians who refuse to make rounds for the bedridden, who then have to be transported via ambulance or facility van, creating physical and emotional stress to the resident and excessive cost to the facility which is passed on to the taxpayer.
- Allopathic physicians who insist all nursing-home residents receive flu vaccinations and continue to practice polypharmacy.
- A family and their physician who sent their elderly mother to a psych ward because she said she wanted to die.
- Families who rarely or never visit their parents. Is that not abuse?
- A guardian who sold his dad's herd of cattle over his dad's objection and with the knowledge of the judge who overrode the elder's wishes for another guardian.
- A religious organization that told a member (our resident) that he would not be one of the 144,000 saved now that he was in a nursing-home and was not able to go out

into the world and preach the truth to others. The resident was in deep distress over their comments.

- A priest who refused to come and minister the last rites to a dying elder because the elder had not been to mass for several years. He really meant she had not contributed any money.
- The allopathic physician who would not permit the nursing staff to take off bandages after a leg amputation. The odor told us that something was wrong. Against the physicians orders, bandages were taken off only to find a deep infection and maggots. The resident was taken immediately to the hospital, where she later passed over. An investigation ensued. The nursing-home was blamed. The physician took no responsibility.

And I am only one administrator/social worker who has worked in a dozen facilities and know intimately about the abuse that occurs from "outsiders." Ask why only nursing-home staff abuse statistics are made public?

Today, with my strong belief in Karma (you reap what you sow), I forgive all those who abused elders and the disabled in any way and send my love and peace their way. Not taught in churches today is that Karma is set up during negative behaviors and those person(s) will suffer the same treatment they have bestowed on others, in this life or the next life.

Let us now enter the wonderful world of Social Services.

17

Social Services

I was employed for five years as a Consultant Social Worker in four nursing-homes meeting over 300 elders every week. I was thirty-nine years of age with three necessary attributes . . . common sense, a sense of morals and ethics, and the ability to work hard. I was not welcomed by administrators, as they saw me as nothing more than another expense.

However, as time passed, each facility recognized the need for a hard working Social Services Director. To assist me was a forty hours a week Social Services Director in every facility. The SSDs knew the residents and their families intimately, were exceptionally compassionate, and possessed all the attributes essential for a good SSD.

My master's research paper investigated the characteristics necessary for social services workers in nursing-homes. Research found that the middle-aged woman, whose family had left the nest, possessing high nurturing traits, work ethics, and morals proved to be the best choice to work with elders in a nursing-home setting.

My expectations for SSDs or social workers is that they visit with every resident every day in some way. This can be in a very covert way by making a bed, cleaning a drawer or closet, taking wilted flowers and plants out of the room or watering a plant, arranging bedside items, or more openly by reading to residents and writing a letter, assisting with finances, and sometimes transporting residents or assisting during meals. A Social Services Director is a mediator, advocate, interviewer, counselor, and overall friend of the resident. Social Service Directors must have a tremendous sense of humor and the patience of Job. All of the above are absolutely essential for the SWs or SSDs in order to witness behaviors, emotions, and family dynamics. The SW or SSD must have no fear of confrontations.

The social worker has a four-year degree. Social Services Directors may be a high school or GED graduate and hold a thirty-six hour training certificate. SSDs and SWs must be present during admissions, as well as during the dying process and death of a resident, must have a myriad of resources, be knowledgeable in medications, rights of the resident, attend Care Planning meetings, review the MDS sheets, and do no less than monthly charting on each resident plus charting any changes in behaviors and any family dynamics. Social workers and SSDs often are van drivers to appointments. Social workers or SSDs attend all resident funerals.

SWs and SSDs spend their time working the floor, sometimes with the Activity Director, visitors, families, ministers, and health-care professionals. Those who work in the Social Services department must be emotionally and spiritually resilient, having the necessary emotional and spiritual qualities to deal with stress, grief, loss, risk and other difficulties that may arise.

Overall, in over thirty years, there have been two degreed social workers that I deeply respected. The other degreed social workers sat in their offices, rarely interacted with residents, and didn't seem to have a clue as to what a social worker was to do. Mentoring did not seem to work as most thought the degree made them above mundane duties. I asked, "Why?" And the answer is these degreed social workers did not possess compassion for elders and saw their position as a job not a calling.

Colleges need to teach what is expected of social workers and counselors when they accept a position in a nursing-home. Personally, I do not see the need for a degreed social worker or counselor nor a consultant in nursing-homes. Consultants have difficulty in knowing all the dynamics that have occurred and usually are in the nursing-home (by regulation) to undersign what the SSD has documented. Nursing-homes would do much better to have two SSDs than the cost of one consultant or one degreed social worker. Are all SSDs wonderful? No. For example, one full-time Social Service Director really stopped me in my tracks when she told surveyors that she didn't have time to work with a resident who had threatened suicide (I was never informed of the situation). The nurse had documented the issue, but social services had not called in a counselor, a minister, and had not addressed the threat to anyone. Big-time deficiency! And then went on to tell surveyors that the facility had no business taking severely handicapped residents. Well, I went looking for another SSD.

Another SSD sat in her office all day and had the idea that she could tell all the staff what to do. The Administrator permitted her the power to make decisions that he should have been doing. She ate in her office, which smelled like old potato chips, and her office was dirty. As an interim administrator, I simply reported back to corporate office that this facility needed to search for another SSD. Eventually, they did.

What does a social worker or Social Service Director do all day? Here are several examples.

At the request of an administrator, I worked with a Nurse Aide and a DON when they tangled in the hallway, providing them coping skills when in a high-anxiety situation.

I counseled a long-term and hard-working CNA after she gave her two-week notice. I asked the administration to put her on a leave of absence rather than accepting her resignation. The CNA came back after six months of working in a factory. I knew this CNA was too precious to let go.

I assisted and investigated abuse cases and sexual abuse cases. One case involved a husband who insisted on taking his very confused wife home every weekend. Again and again the nurse aides came to me as they cleaned up the wife after every home visit. They convinced me that the husband's reason for taking his wife home was for sex. I talked with her physician with the conclusion that the wife was being abused. The physician wrote an order that she was not to be taken from the facility by the husband. A first and second talk with the husband failed, so the third time, I suggested that he just cruise the red-light district for his sexual needs. For whatever reason, he never came back to the facility to visit. However, when the Administrator found out what I had suggested, he was not very pleased.

An elder received severe injuries to her fingers, not once but twice. In my investigation, I found that her injuries had never been documented in the nurse's notes, not even an entry that she had been taken to the doctor's office. Visiting with her personal physician, we both came to the conclusion that there was abuse. The elder was able to wheel herself in her wheelchair. When one CNA wanted to take her to her room and the elder did not want to go, the elder would put her fingers in the spokes of the wheelchair. The CNA would evidently continue to push, which broke the fingers, in two episodes. Why the DON would hide the episodes is still a mystery to me. When I reported the events to the administrator, I was amazed to be taken off my job for several weeks "as the entire staff" was upset with me (for telling?). When I returned to this facility, I felt the coolness, and then had a visit from the dad of the CNA, who told me that his daughter would never injure anyone. However, the physician was the one who informed me that this area had many reports of spousal abuse with females working the fields and being treated just like a hired hand. With this information I simply implied where there is lack of love and respect for wives and daughters, there will be anger and resentment. Staff anger and resentment, uncontrolled, is often the reason for elder abuse in nursing-homes.

When a group of physicians were boycotting the local hospital, one of my facilities was affected, as critically ill residents could not be transferred to the hospital. I counseled a distraught family to simply transfer their family member to another out-of-town physician and hospital. This is one time I nearly lost my job when one of the boycotting physicians came to the administrator and asked who was running the nursing-home, her or the social worker. Social workers often are in trouble, especially if they take a stand on behalf of the residents. Politics are part of the game.

When one administrator did not like to speak in public, I was assigned to make public speeches in behalf of the nursing-home.

I developed and taught a portion of the thirty-six-hour Social Services workshops and traveled the state of South Dakota teaching workshops on Elder Abuse.

I usually presented Resident Rights in-services and held

Family Councils in all the nursing-homes in which I was employed. Social Services staff attend most evening activities and always help during special events like Christmas, New Year's celebrations, Fourth of July picnics, Veterans Day, etc. I also did preadmissions in homes and in hospitals.

As a Social Worker, I was asked by the Police Department to investigate an elder abuse situation. The night before, an elderly man was brought to the facility, disoriented and in filthy rags. His neighbors had reported strangers going in and out of his house. Police found the man in a state of malnutrition, suspecting that a group of hippies had been taking his Social Security check and physically abusing him. Nursing gave him a whirlpool bath, bandaged his wounds, found clean pajamas, gave him a hot meal, and put him to bed. I purchased clothes for him at the Salvation Army store. What a wonderful little man he was. His house was eventually sold, and he remained as a resident in our nursing-home. Social Security was called, but the hippies were never identified.

A police van was involved in a wreck near our facility. The police were transporting a sex molester to a nearby city hospital. The molester had suffered a stroke and was brought into our facility. Nurses came to me to say they would not provide nursing cares because he grabbed at their breasts, and would I please go in and talk with him?

I entered the room to be almost blown backward by the negative energy in the room. I took his hand, looking him straight in the eye, never raising my voice, I said, "In the name of Jesus, let this demon pass from you." I shared with him that I cared for him and would be there for him if he needed anything, however, no more grabbing at the nurses. In the days forward, the nurses told me they did not like to care for him, but his behavior was much improved.

A lifetime farmer was admitted to a nursing-home at his only son's insistence. The son said the farmhouse was no longer livable, with no running water and an outhouse. Two weeks of hell ensued with me being hit with his cane, him calling the sheriff and telling him we were keeping him prisoner, and rolling his wheelchair outside, yelling for all the neighbors to hear that we were poisoning him. I asked the administrator if she would call his physician and have him released to go home. All were in agreement. The son was shocked, but agreed to take him back to his home. We all hugged and wished Ed well. I have never seen a man so happy. He just couldn't get out of that nursing-home fast enough. How he would manage, we did not know, but Ed was happy. And that seemed to overcome all our fears for him.

Several days went by. Then a telephone call from Ed's son. The son had stopped by early in the morning to check on his dad. Life on this Earth was over for Ed.

Without a doubt in my mind Ed was a happy farmer when he took his last breath. He was in his own home, a place where he had spent his lifetime . . . the family farmhouse, the old wooden, grayed barns; the little crooked outhouse; his faithful shepherd dog; the comfortable old iron post bed with all the memories of wife and child; and those special earth smells that were all too familiar. The narrow, winding cowpaths among half-fallen trees giving birth to baby catnip; the browning rows of corn heavy with life-giving seeds; blue-green waves of prairie grasses and patches of green nettles under every bush and canyon. The rusty but ever faithful water pump and its towering windmill quietly forecasting a weather change; each sunrise bringing in the distant crow of a cock rooster and a roadway of beaming yellow sunflowers to welcome Ed home . . . his eternal home.

Here are three human entities that God placed in the care of nursing-home staff. Three very different and unique individuals. Each was a spirit living out their karma, making positive and negative karma for themselves and the staff. How blessed we were to touch their lives in such a small way!

As a social worker I rarely took fifteen-minute breaks. Not only did I not have the time, but I felt my "breaks" were being with the residents. I never had an office. I worked on a table in a barber's room, in the activity room, in a sunroom, and at the nurses station. Perhaps that encouraged me to work on a one-to-one in the resident's rooms.

Social Services administer minimentals, which are state mandated, for all new admissions. To begin with, I am offended by the term, "minimental," which are usually given only a day or two after admission. However, according to Dr. Kra, standardized tests (similar to the minimental) stress speed rather than experience and discretion, almost invariably present a depressed, distorted, and misleading picture of an older person's intelligence. Dr. Kra argues that such testing can be worse than useless in dealing with the older population (especially elders who have just been released from the hospital). Test scores always improve when these same tests are given at a leisurely pace in an unstressful environment—several weeks after settling in.

Nursing-home staff must acknowledge that older people do function differently from younger people, but this is certainly no reason to conclude that they are less intelligent, senile, or incompetent. Dr. Kra states that those over the age of sixty-five who are suffering from mild brain failure may suffer from causes whose conditions may be reversed with better nutrition, change in medications, or an illness not recognized and treated appropriately. Minimentals need to be given much later than mandated or not at all. When the resident is relaxed in his/her environment, how about just a simple visit documented in the Social Services progress notes?

When I came on duty at 8 a.m., the first duty of the day was to ask the Administrator if there was anything special I could do for her/him. In this way, I could go to work on projects Administrators felt were priority. At the end of the day, I turned in a short report of what I had accomplished.

Changes to Be Made in the Social Services Department

Changes that must be made in the Social Services department are to strongly and forcefully petition the State and Federal regulators that no nursing-home needs a four-year-degreed Social Worker. Four years of college plus the license does not guarantee compassion, a high level of spirituality, nor a good work ethic.

Psychologically, if nursing-home residents need a counselor, such as when they overeat to keep their bodies stimulated, a counselor should be contacted as this is a subconscious desire to continue life and not face death. These residents need professional counseling by a gerontological-experienced counselor who is comfortable and knowledgeable in the death process. Serving the aged, who are, for the most part, religious beings (and spiritual beings), social services must understand and practice similar concepts in their personal life, or should not apply for a social services position in a nursing-home setting. Social Services Directors are paid an average of $8 to $10 per hour. A degreed social worker can make up to $20 per hour.

The nondegreed Social Service Director must be supported by the families, the churches and community volunteers. With this support, plus the advent of alternative therapies, compassion and lack of nursing staff would no longer be an issue.

And who but a compassionate social worker or Social Services Director would understand the emotions of nursing-home elders that are heightened during special holidays such as Christmas? Christmas brings not only excitement but often depression.

A Christmas That Once Was

My heart is heavy at a time when the world is celebrating the birth of a baby named Jesus of Nazareth. It is Christmas season again.

I work in a nursing-home and have seen the sadness in the eyes of many of our elders during the Christmas season. As we talk, I hold the hands of those dear elderly people and see the deep blue veins from hard work; the arthritic knurls caused by the washing and ironing of thousands of shirts, baby clothes, underpants, socks, diapers, long legged underwear, and heavy bib overalls.

I see the hands that hoed and weeded, nurtured, gathered, and canned hundreds of jars of vegetables and fruits in preparation for the winter months.

Arms, now flabby and wrinkled, once held a loved one, a new baby, a crying child with a scraped knee, or the sick child with croup, mumps, or chicken pox.

144

Those arms encircled a child setting off for kindergarten, or the child, now adult, heading off for college or to serve in the military.

Sitting so close, our legs touch and I feel the wobbly legs that no longer can hold their weakened body that once ran after a passel of children, worked in the field, stood for hours cooking, cleaning, feeding the chickens and slopping the hogs, or standing for twelve hours working in a WWII plant or teaching country school, or working in coal mines.

The now-dimmed eyes that once looked over at a tall, young handsome boy or girl, knowing their heart had just been stolen. The eyes that saw a newborn calf, a litter of kittens or puppies; the eyes that read Bible scriptures to the children; or read *Little Red Riding Hood* or *Three Bears* to wide-eyed children; the eyes that wept when a child lay critically ill; the eyes that saw Death come walking through the door; eyes that saw marriages and divorces; eyes that lifted up to God in prayer and supplication for the warmth of the hearth, food on the table, and clothes to cover the children. And eyes that saw a bountiful crop that would pay another payment on the farm or house or that new Model A Ford or tractor. Oh, what those eyes have seen.

I feel the heart beating that has beat millions of times in the raising of a family, of the love shared, the bitter tears, and agony the heart felt at the loss of a spouse, a child, a parent, a brother, a sister, a neighbor.

Elders did not expect much in their day. They worked. They laughed. They wept. They prayed. They wanted no more than love and respect from their family, to remain in their own beloved home with their memories, to live out their days in the joy of grandchildren and reap the benefits of their hard labor.

However, ill-health brought the elder to a nursing-home. Nothing is familiar. Their possessions are gone. Their little space is shared by a stranger. A single bed, a bedside table, a dresser and a mirror above that which is hung so high the elder cannot see herself to comb her once thick and long, shiny, brunette hair. This is all that is left.

Oh, they say they are grateful for a warm place to stay and staff who care for them. But their eyes say, "Is this my reward for all that I gave to life, to family, to my church, to my community?"

You can see elders in every nursing-home . . . sitting close to the door . . . hoping, hoping for a visit from family or friends . . . thinking, remembering.

145

There is plenty of time to think and remember, now. The elder looks down at her hands . . . and remembers. The memories are very fresh. Memories are all that are private. Memories are secret to her or him only. Especially at Christmas time. Eyes close to see, in the mind, happier times . . . decorating the tree, secretly making or buying gifts for each child, heating up water for baths and washing and ironing each set of clothes, polishing that row of shoes, preparing tins of Christmas cookies, cakes, and pies, setting the table with special dishes that once belonged to her parents and pulling out of the oven the butter-browned turkey with all the trimmings. This day was special. It meant family.

Now, the family is gone. They are busy with their own families and jobs. As the dimmed eyes open ever so slowly, the memories disappear for the moment. I whisper in her ear, "It's time for dinner or to go to the bathroom or to take a nap."

"That's okay," she says, "I'll just go to my room for a little nap." She knows that sleeping is where dreams and memories appear again. Dreams of that first young love, the first child, a life fulfilled and once needed.

Sleep precious one. Dream of family and a Christmas that once was.

Written by S. Kraemer so many years ago.

18

The Activity Director

Activity Directors are the core of happiness for most residents. Usually full of prunes, promises, and pink panther suits, activities in a nursing-home are quite good. Directors must have a multitude of talents . . . from ceramics, to crafts, popping corn, baking pies, making jellies, snapping beans, arranging parties, bands, and church choirs, scheduling library days, shopping days, and van rides. Then squeeze in the weekly news articles for the local paper and the monthly newsletter which goes out to the families; peeling potatoes, planning picnics and fishing outings, masterminding volunteer groups, blackboard games, bingo, bowling, reading stories, setting up cassette players for talking books, planting flowers. Blessed is the facility that has an activity director who sings and plays the guitar, piano, or accordion. Days are not long enough, especially in the summer, when I insisted that all residents be taken for a walk through the gardens after breakfast.

I loved the rainy, warm summer day when I took residents out in the rain to walk in the water running down the street. All were barefoot, including me. What a good time we had, except the housekeepers who were mad because we "puddled" all over the floor when we came in. The day the AD and I collected snowballs, took them inside and had a snowball fight with the residents. This time the both of us mopped up. A touch with nature and our childhood is a healing touch. I ask, "Why not?"

My favorite was on a St. Pat's day when the AD and I put on green gremlin costumes and with painted faces appeared outside dining room windows jumping up and down to see the residents breaking out in peals of laughter. And that's what it is all about!

The best of the best are those Activity Directors who are

middle-aged, with children gone from the nest. Focus is on the residents. They must have a willingness to work holidays and weekends or an evening or two. The Activity Director must have a natural ability to communicate with families, volunteers, and the staff.

Activity Directors must possess a high level of creativeness, open to new ideas; possess intimate knowledge of residents' past so programs can be developed on an individual basis. Each resident is a very unique human/spiritual being. From reading spiritual material to responding to spiritual needs is imperative.

Sharon played the guitar and sang. I asked her to go to every bedridden resident to play and sing. One day, she said she was plucking that ol geetar in a room where the resident was considered totally nonresponsive. The toes started to keep time to the music. What right do we have, as nursing-home staff to document that a resident is nonresponsive?

Taking male residents to the community airport to watch the planes come in and out was a weekly event for Sharon. I wondered why the residents always came back to the facility so happy until Sharon confessed she stopped at the local bar and bought (out of her own meager wages) a six-pack of beer. So, they all spent an hour at the airport watching for planes to come in and out and drank their favorite can of beer.

And, of course, we had the weekly shopping at the local shopping center until I lost a resident. I was a bit embarrassed to ask the clerk to announce the name of the "lost" resident. When we found her, she wanted to know where I was as she thought I was lost.

After a New Year's Eve party, I was visited by a group of Lutheran ladies who were very concerned about liquor being served in our facility. I shared with them that most of the drinks were grape fizzies and the others were served liquor or wine at their request. Then I quoted a passage from the Bible, Proverbs 31:6–7: "Give strong drink unto him that is ready to perish and wine unto those that be of heavy hearts. Let him drink and forget his poverty, and remember his misery no more." And I Timothy 5:23: "Drink no longer water, but use a little wine for thy stomach's sake and thine infirmities."

The ladies (bless their hearts), looked at me with such a surprise that I surmised they had never read those passages. They thanked me and left. I often wondered what their next Bible study passages were about. The most interesting part of this story about this New Year's Eve party was that those who drank "grape fizzies" (alcohol-free) said they were "very dizzy" from the drinks and wanted to go back to their rooms! Halleluiah! Praise the Lord!

The Activity Director can be thwarted by owners and administration. In one facility, social services set up therapeutic towel folding only to have an owner yell that the facility was overstaffed and did not want any staff to be in the room when the towel folding was being done.

In another facility, no dancing was allowed, no clapping of hands, no joy! At Christmastime, the Activity Director and evening staff requested to bring residents around the tree and all would decorate. The owner said, "No, nursing is paid to do nursing, not decorate trees." Oh, woe is me!

One Activity Director was so filled with animosity that it spilled over unto the elders. She refused to do much of anything, regardless of the suggestions brought her way. Another Activity Director catered to the "wealthy" and the alert residents. One Activity Director falsified the MDS billing, stating she had provided activities for this resident and that resident; however, I never saw her do those activities. I eventually fired her and, of course, it went to court because she claimed I was discriminating against her because she had a mild case of multiple sclerosis. Oh, woe is me! If ever staff wants to bring karma down upon their heads, just don't do your job, tell untruths, and then run for a lawyer. You will, in this life or the next life, reap what you have sown. I send my love and peace to these Activity Directors.

I saw an Activity Director clocking out at 1 p.m. She said that was all the hours allowed her for the number of residents we had in house. I walked to the Activity calendar and noted all the activities for the afternoon. I asked who was going to take care this. She said she did not know, and it was not her problem. Not only were there no afternoon activities, but the activities were falsified as they were not being carried out. Do I need to tell you

149

that within a week, this Activity Director was back as a nurse aide and I was advertising for another Activity Director? I hired a middle-aged woman with many creative talents who not only loved the residents but found volunteers to take a few hours plus the nurses accepted simple activities such as ball, cards, checkers, and music. It takes a little creative thought, a little work, a love of the residents, and a "calling" to be the best of the best.

Fortunately, OBRA is not overly demanding concerning the paperwork. However, the activity director must attend MDS and plan-of-care meetings, do her own admission and dismissal paperwork, and the charting on each resident as to the degree of participation in planned activities. The Activity Director is usually in charge of the scrapbook, taking pictures during special occasions, and setting up for family gatherings held at the nursing-home. It is not unusual to see the director in costume for the holidays much to the delight of the residents and staff. She/he encourages staff participation and operates on a very limited budget, so is also a beggar of supplies for her cache. Her voice can be heard over the intercom in the morning and afternoon, announcing activities and is the familiar voice saying the noon meal prayer.

Every resident must have an activity plan and the plan must be carried out. The Activity Director must communicate well with volunteers and must be respected by her peers and community.

Activity directors hold a thirty-six-hour certificate of training and need yearly CEUs. A college degree is not mandated at this time . . . just lots of talent, a sense of humor, a good pair of feet, and the desire to bring a smile to the faces of our elders. Activity Directors are paid from $8 to $15 per hour.

Last but not least is the Activity Director who is aware of what residents *really* would like to do or have. A letter like the following may be sent to all families, printed in the local newspapers or copies provided for religious organizations. Who said, "Seek and you shall find. Ask and you shall receive"?

Grandma and Grandpa's Letter to Santa

Dear Santa,

We cannot say whether or not we have been naughty or nice. We live in a nursing-home. It is like a home without a Mom or Dad. Anything can happen. However, we, like you, Santa, are seen to be somewhat the same . . . old, popular once a year, bellies that shake like jelly when we laugh, a head full of fluffy white hair, and a few, long scrubby, scratchy beards when the barber doesn't show. We skip the red flannel long johns with the buttoned flap in back 'cause we just don't know if we can make it in time. Besides, the laundry gals say they fade in the wash. However we like to stick with the tall black angora lined boots to keep our ever cold feet warm. Babies love us, children are hesitant until they get to know us, teenagers don't believe in us, and sometimes our children don't know what to do with us.

Santa, we confess that sometimes we show off by playing Russian roulette with our dentures (this really freaks out the nurses) and the other day we threw doughy pieces of underbaked buns at the administrator. Ned and Nell are engaged, but we are keeping it a secret until they elope. When social workers are on the prowl for beer in our rooms, we just relabel the bottles to say "Mouthwash." The guys love to pinch the gals in the bottom and hear them scream.

The administrator told Rollie to stop smoking in his room. So Rollie just took the screen off his window, leaned out, and puffed away. When the administrator asked him what he thought he was doing, Rollie said, "You said I was to never smoke *in* my room and I'm not. I'm smoking *outside* my room."

One day we were all very bored, so Phil revved up his electric scooter, telling all of us in wheelchairs, to just hang onto the rope to make a train. So over the snow banks we flew, just like you, Santa. The staff followed those tracks and found us at the local pub whooping it up. Honest, Santa, we try to be good!

Well, for better or for worse, here is our list. We sure go for bright and colorful clothes, hats, and suspenders. No black or dreary colors. Right, Santa? We like cotton pj's, stockings, and underwear as cotton keeps us warm and cozy. A real joy would be candy striped or flowered sheets and pillowcases. While you are looking over our list, could your elves remember to sew our names on our clothes? We do not appreciate wearing Ehhir and Addie's underpants when there is fifty pounds difference in our weights.

Add a computer to the list so we can email all the grandchildren and a comfortable electric chair to lift us out with ease. Ooh, yes, lest we forget, we would really appreciate a satellite radio so we can listen to all those old songs and radio programs every day. Hi Ho Silver! And Awwway!

Gift certificates are nice, too, for a perm, to a special restaurant, a musical, or tickets to a sports event, a massage, or a chiropractor treatment.

Santa, we have worn out catalogs looking at neat foot massagers, talking clocks that not only tell us the time but the day. Add a green plant for our rooms, please, and an electric toothbrush or a pretty bed throw. Guys love a large outdoor thermometer and ladies love to watch the birds who come to the birdfeeders outside their windows.

Since our neighbor is an old spinster who keeps a rolled up newspaper handy for "wanderers," an attractive door decoration with our names in big bold letters would be great so we get into the right room without getting walloped.

On the other hand, how about classes in Tai Chi! Yep, Santa, we are neoagers with style! None of this necktie and booties thing. We said BOOTIES, not booze, which wouldn't be a bad idea either. Santa, turn up the hearing aid that is hiding under your red stocking cap!

For residents who have family across the nation, they would like a video of all the grandkids, the old schoolhouse they attended, the old hometown, and even a shot of any old cronies that are left.

Fruit baskets that come every month would sure be nice. No candy, please, as the nurses weigh us in every Wednesday.

Well, Santa, as you are well aware, there are elders here who do not have family or visitors and are very lonely. The KIT (Keeping in Touch) program can be subscribed to. The KIT program sends a letter weekly and a gift or card on special days like birthdays and holidays. Could you make a special list and count it twice for some elders who would like to receive cards, letters, and a gift once in a while. Mail is so important to all of us, but especially to those without anyone.

For our stockings hanging by the fireplace, just stuff them with stamps, envelopes, music boxes, costume jewelry, cosmetics, small purses with a dollar or two inside.

There is one gift that costs nothing and is more precious than all the rest. Gifts of a visit, a hug, play the guitar, be silly, just talk with us and hold our hands, tell us we are loved.

Thank you, Santa. Remember, we believe in you! Martha! Do you hear what I hear? Go back to sleep, it's just Rollie taking the screen off his window again!

Good night, Joe. Good night, Eddie. Good night, Betty. God bless Santa and all the good staff who care for us and all us guys and gals who live in nursing-homes.

The Activity Calendar

State regulations mandate activities seven days a week and in the evening. If not for volunteers and the creativity of the nursing staff, this would be impossible. Monthly schedules must be posted for all residents to read and the daily schedule is written on the Activity Calendar Board. It is sad to see the same activities over and over, which are usually bingo and church.

In the Healing Place facility, Activity Directors will have on their calendars many new and exciting activities with the assistance of volunteers and staff:

1. "Homemaker" duties to prepare vegetables for meals or baking or folding linens.
2. Residents "giving" to others at Christmastime. In one facility residents decorated the facility tree with small gifts of pencils, little books, ribbons, crayons, children's purses, billfolds, etc., to give to needy children.
3. Following a tornado, the residents gave a "shower" for the couple who lost all their belongings.
4. Residents operating a "shopping center" within the facility with profits controlled by the Resident Council to spend for what they want.
5. Select a competent resident to become the mail carrier in delivering mail to other residents. Mail call is on the daily activity calendar.
6. A "council of voters" who encourage the setting up of

voting booths at election time and pin on the "I have voted" ribbons.

7. Residents invite candidates to the facility and put up candidate posters.

8. Residents plan "candlelight" meals and entertainment once a month.

9. Residents taken on snowmobile, golf cart, old buggy, or antique car rides.

10. Sports persons asked to display their guns, bows, fishing equipment.

11. Recital students asked to play their pieces at the facility.

12. Student sports teams asked to come into the home in full gear. Nebraska football coach Osborne was asked to come to one nursing-home in which I was administrator. I will tell you that all work stopped and every resident was so excited, they were literally speechless. The home received news media attention. Sad to say, corporate officers severely chastised me for not "clearing" with them when the news media walked in . . . so much for little corporate minds . . . And hats off to Coach Osborne!

13. Community leaders invited to the facility to tour the facility and speak with residents.

14. Residents encouraged to say a prayer before meals. The resident's name would be on the Activity calendar.

15. Residents take part in community activities, such as coloring Easter eggs, filling Christmas sacks, folding church bulletins, hosting and judging art contests, hosting Boy and Girl Scout/Campfire Girl meetings/4-H demonstrations, and an annual Chamber/Rotary/Womans'club/Lions club meetings.

16. Inviting visiting evangelical groups to sing at the facility.

17. Residents have a column written by them in the monthly newsletter.

18. Residents become speakers at the colleges that teach classes in gerontology.

19. GED classes offered in the facility.
20. Art, music, sculpture classes offered.
21. Computer classes offered.
22. Meditation classes offered.
23. Natural Health care professionals invited to speak to the residents.
24. Style shows held on an annual basis.
25. Hair stylist, cosmologists, and color analysts invited to the facility to work with residents.
26. The resident's handmade articles displayed and sold and taken to the county fair.
27. Residents "rearrange" funeral bouquets for table decorations and resident rooms.
28. Residents fold towels, etc., assist with clearing tables, sweeping floors, dusting.
29. If a resident has a specialty, like that of a school teacher, they are encouraged to read to other residents or hold Saturday reading sessions for children? Farmers or gardeners permitted to work the soil in the spring? In every facility, there is usually one or more who enjoy "mowing" the yard. I bought an old, workable nonmotorized mower at an auction and just set it in the yard. It was amazing how well the yard was kept manicured!
30. One day a week to water plants, inside and out.
31. Residents announce activities over the intercom and change the activity board and the menu board.
32. Mind stimulation games played while waiting for the noon meal.
33. Parades of children with their trikes, babies, pets.
34. Brown Bag day in which each resident has a "little brown bag" with the word *God* on it, as a place to throw in their concerns, prayers, needs.
35. Have a sunshine day on a cloudy day. All residents spend at least fifteen minutes under a full spectrum light as calm music plays. Hand out a sunshine sticker for all those taking part.

36. Have a checker game tournament. Invite others from neighboring nursing-homes.

There is no reason to have an activity board with few monthly changes. This is why elders become bored, and depressed, and angry.

Activities must be supported by volunteers from all walks of life and all ages. The calendar needs to be full of stimulating activities developed for each individual resident.

Owners must provide large and well-equipped activity rooms. Even in this age, I still find Activity Directors without a room or an office conducive to providing stimulating activities.

Pet Therapy

Years prior to pet therapy being introduced into nursing-homes, I accidentally discovered a man who desperately needed nursing-home care. He refused to come without his faithful dog. I more than approved, although I was fully aware that the state surveyors would give us a deficiency if the dog was seen in the facility.

The dog was well-behaved, lying at the feet of his master during meals and in the resident's room. When surveyors came, the dog was simply taken to a nephew's house. The staff went around smiling about our little secret. Happy was the man who just wanted to be with his dog.

A second instance was when an elderly lady with Alzheimer's refused to come without her poodle. The poodle came. And the complaints started. Housekeeping said they were not hired to clean up after a dog, and nurses said they were not hired to feed and water the dog . . . that they had enough to do just caring for the Alzheimer's residents.

The poodle stayed. We billed the attorney for veterinarian fees, dog food, and a leash and heard the attorney complain about the bills. The poodle stayed until the resident no longer noticed the dog. I ask the compassionate reader to judge this staff and this attorney for themselves.

In one facility, again, pet therapy appeared on my doorstep. The county sheriff stopped by to ask if the residents would like a cockatoo, a parakeet, and several canaries. I welcomed the pretty birds, their cages, and sacks of seeds. The birds had been confiscated during a drug bust. The facility had a staff person who loved animals and did a terrific job of caring for them, moving the cages from room to room, cleaning the cages and taking them to the veterinarian for check-ups (state requirements). And the residents loved them.

One bird flew into rooms and sat on the shoulders of residents to their utmost delight. One male resident said, "If I had to choose between humans and birds, I would take the birds." Animals and birds evoked responses in every resident regardless of their physical condition.

When dogs come into a facility, notice how many residents reach out to touch and pat and smile. A dietitian brought her very large, beautiful and well-behaved dog with her as she worked. And the dog returned home as one very spoiled dog with all the hugs and pats on the head.

Spring brought in the new litter of kittens, baby chicks, a baby brown bear, a newborn lamb, and summer brought the ponies and a llama.

The therapeutic effects of pets on nursing-home residents have been documented in scientific studies to show animals can decrease blood pressure, reduce stress, and anxiety, lower the need for medication, and even prolong life. Can we say that it is the altruistic love by the animals and birds? They don't care if someone is missing a part of their face or are wrinkled and bent over or have wet their pants or spilled food all over their clothes. The animals and birds are totally accepting and in return nursing-home residents give and give of their love for them.

Sadly, when I left one facility, my replacement did not see the relationship between animals and the birds and nursing-home residents. She rid the facility of all birds and animals.

In another facility, the owners posted a sign on the door that all animals were to be kept in the arms of their owners. The owners made it clear they did not want any pet therapy in their nursing-home. What a loss to the residents! And what karma was being set up for these owners!

Activity directors, administrators, and staff not believing in the power of healing through prayer, meditation, animals, birds, plants, sunshine, hugs, music, personal possessions in resident rooms, affirmations, and positive thoughts will no longer be hired in any capacity in an innovative "Healing Place" of today.

Music for the Soul

Music is one of the most powerful therapies in the healing of the soul. Music is known to have healed the physical man, the psychological mind, and spiritual soul. Music can assist in the healing of any illness, i.e., a mental illness, a mental handicap, suicidal tendencies, the depressed, seasonal affective disorders, and the emotionally distressed.

Music is instrumental in times of prayer, meditation, praise and thanksgiving, joy and celebration, patriotism and cultural tales, myths, and history.

Music has the power to energize, tranquillize, soothe, and lift the soul into a higher dimension. Music is food for the soul.

Thaguas (500 B.C.) said that everything is music or vibration. All humans, plants, and animals respond to vibrations (music).

According to the Edgar Cayce readings, the vibration of stringed instruments has the highest vibration for the highest level of consciousness. The readings mention the cello, specifically. It has been recorded that David and Jesus of Nazareth played the harp.

A harpist volunteered to play her instrument in a unit for babies whose mothers were drug addicts. The staff noted that after one performance, the babies were calmer. Today, a music therapist has been hired on a full-time basis to perform in such hospital units.

In a nursing-home setting, it is imperative that music is provided on a daily basis according to the resident's physical, psychological, or spiritual need or mood. All residents must be taken to music programs, have a tape player and tapes in their rooms, or a satellite radio which provides a myriad of music.

All staff are involved in music therapy. A variety of tapes are made available in the facility library. Music and color for the personality are suggested as follows:

To stimulate and energize, use the key of "C" music such as The Sousa marches.

The key of C denotes the color red for the resident to wear on this day.

For those who need courage, confidence, are introverts, lack energy, has repressed anxieties and fears, and need daily stimulation, the key of D music should be played such as The William Tell Overture.

The key of D is represented by the color orange, which stimulates the mental forces.

Aged residents who have low I.Qs or need mental stimulation should listen to music in the key of E such as Chopin's Etudes (Polonaise).

The key of E corresponds to the color yellow, which is to be worn by residents on a frequent basis . . . yellow is the sunny side of life.

For the resident who is restless and has difficulty relaxing, "green" music should be played, which is in the key of F. This resident should also have ample green plants in her/his room, work in the garden, mow the lawn, walk barefoot in the grass, feeling and touching the leaves, flowers and trees. Music that would benefit this resident includes Clair de Lune and Images by Debussy.

Green music is a great balancer and when in doubt as to what music to play, use music in the key of F. The resident is to wear green clothing.

For residents who do not tell the truth, are not calm, have little inner peace, are cool, aloof, feel irritated, frustrated, and apathetic, play music in the key of G which is the color blue. These residents frequently have the "blues." The key of G may also be used for those who wish to meditate: Air on a "G" string by Bach.

159

Every staff member is responsible for music therapy, especially those who prepare residents for sleep for they are responsible for selecting clothes for the next day. Nursing must be intimately aware as to the resident's mood and emotions. This knowledge will direct the color of clothes the resident will wear and what music to play prior to sleep.

In fact, I would enforce the posting of music (and color) therapy in every room so all staff and families would be aware of what is needed for that day or night.

Music Heals Strokes?

Listening to music can help people who have suffered from a stroke recover faster, according to research at the Cognitive Brain Research Unit at the University of Helsinki, Finland. The results indicated that those listening to music showed a 60 percent improvement in their verbal memory, and a 17 percent improvement in being able to focus their attention (*Venture Inward*, July/August 2008, p. 12).

Families and staff will be taught music therapy with families being responsible for equipment needed. Families are to be reminded that all radios, earphones, and tape recorders must be engraved with the resident's name and items brought in are to be recorded on the inventory sheet.

Music Has Twin Soul . . . Color

Leonardo DaVinci said the power of meditation is increased tenfold if prayer and meditation is done under the rays of violet light falling through stained glass windows in a quiet place.

Every nursing-home needs a quiet place for both residents and staff. The quiet place should have colored stained glass windows. In all resident rooms, staff lounges, and offices, there needs to be colored crystal sun catchers in windows. When one looks at the color, we see the vibration of music, and when we hear music we hear the vibration of color. Music and color are twin souls.

According to Rosita Merrick, a teacher in the utilization of color, "color is one of the most beautiful gifts to us from the Universal Power."

Color is electromagnetic spectrums or rays of energy vibrations, just as the physical body is total energy, vibrating at different variables according to our moods.

The use of color is used as a mood setter and healer:

- *Red* is the color of courage, strength and determination, an action color . . . a physical color. Red is a good color for the introvert, the shy personality. Red is excellent for nursing-home residents who are in need of vitality, to improve one's health. One should not wear red when anger is evident.
- *Blue* is the opposite of red. Blue is a strong spiritual color. Blue is the color of harmony, patience, understanding, and tranquility. Blue is an excellent neutralizer of emotional outbursts. Residents who are on a diet and struggling in keeping to that diet, may consider wearing blue, having blue items in their room, taking meals on a blue tablecloth and dishes. Blue is not to be used if the resident is prone to isolation, inactivity, and loneliness. Blue is to be avoided when residents are feeling "blue."
- *Orange* is the color for optimism, health, and happiness. It is the color to use when a resident is feeling "down in the dumps." Orange encourages self-confidence, may overcome fears, shyness, and insecurity. Orange is a perfect color to assist in overcoming loneliness. Orange needs to be worn or used by nursing-home staff who are surrounded by residents who are depressed. The negative aspect of the orange hues is that too much orange can lead to egotism.
- *Yellow* is the color for mental activity as it brings forth wisdom and intelligence. Yellow is excellent for mental activities. Yellow is the "sunshine" color in the bringing of cheer to self and others. Dull yellows can precipitate the

161

emotions of "suspiciousness" or inadequacy . . . being yellow.

- *Yellow Gold* is the color of good communication and brings a feeling of comfort to the resident. Yellow-gold can be misused if used too much in the room. The resident can become selfish and hardened.
- *Purple* (violet) energizes mental powers, removes mental blocks from one's life, clams inner feelings of confusion. Purple is a highly powerful color and should be used with discretion.
- *Brown* is the color of work, reliability, and productivity. It denotes a sense of duty, responsibility, and solidarity; attracts rationality, patience, and sturdy character. It is the color of the soil which is always serving, producing, and working to serve mankind. The negative side of brown may bring the feeling of stagnation, heaviness and extremism.
- *Green* brings the feeling of abundance and prosperity, growth, and healing. All colors are healing colors at some level, but green is noticed in nature in an abundant amount. This makes green the physical healer. Green brings balance. Green is well adjusted, a solid citizen, and gives a youthful appearance. The negative side of green is envy. Residents who seem to be envious of others should not wear green. They should wear more pink.
- *Pink* is the color of love, beauty, and understanding. Pink represents the goodness of the emotions and promotes self-love, love for others, self-esteem, and with the combination of orange will improve self-confidence. Pink may elicit the feelings of harmony, femininity, goodness, togetherness, understanding, and adventurous spirit.
- *White* is the color of peace, truth, honesty, and all that is wholesome. The color white is connected with the power of God. If in doubt as to what a resident should wear, choose something white for peace of mind. This color is perfect to rid the person of nonacceptable habits such as smoking, nail-biting, hitting others, being critical. This color is used to dissolve emotions that are not acceptable

in the nursing-home such as anger, greed, and revenge. The color white is a "perfect" balancer.

- *Black* is the absence of light and the lack of all color. It is primarily a negative color. Black is only to be used in cases of extreme aggression. Black is a good color for concealing emotions or keeping the resident in solitude. Black protects the person and keeps them separate from worldly things. The negative aspect of the color black is that black repels people and makes the resident unapproachable or seen as overauthoritative. Residents in deep depression often appear with an "aura" of blackness about them.

Families need to be provided with both music therapy and color therapy information upon admission, as they will be responsible for the items and clothing needed.

Color therapy and music therapy charts should be placed in resident's room for family and staff to assist with the choice of music and color of clothing to choose.

Your Astral Colors

Your astral color is your special color. On your birthday, it is good to have your special candle color on your cake, the wearing of your special color, and these colors in your room to bring empowerment and encouragement throughout the year. Rosita Merrick has correlated colors with your birthday. They are as follows:

Zodiac Sign	Birthday	Your Special Color
Aries	March 21–April 19	Red and White
Taurus	April 20–May 20	Orange and Pink
Gemini	May 21–June 21	Red and Blue
Cancer	June 22–July 22	Green and Brown
Leo	July 23–August 23	Gold and Orange
Virgo	August 23–September 22	Blue and Brown
Libra	September 23–October 22	Blue and Pink
Scorpio	October 23–November 21	Red and Maroon
Sagittarius	November 22–December 21	Purple and Green

Zodiac Sign	Birthday	Your Special Color
Capricorn	December 22–January 19	Red and Brown
Aquarius	January 20–February 18	Blue and Green
Pisces	February 19–March 20	White and Green

Art Therapy

I cannot draw stick men to look like stick men, however, I was taught the value of art therapy at a soul level at the Oak House in Phoenix, Arizona, under the direction of Dr. William McGarey. I had success in offering art therapy in several nursing-homes with both staff and residents.

The Activity Director or Social Services need a box of colored chalk with no less than forty-eight pastel colors and large poster paper for each resident. Residents may sit or stand at a table or hold the poster paper in their lap or if the resident so chooses they may have the poster paper taped to a wall. Permit them a choice.

Art therapy requires no artistic ability. Art therapy intrinsically expresses inner feelings. Residents have a voice in art therapy without saying a word. They speak through the colors they choose and the lines and design they draw on paper.

Place all the colored chalk on a table. As the music plays, the residents should be able and encouraged to switch colors.

Music plays softly in the background with a variety of tempos such as soft and dreamy, the waltz, a military band, forties music, classical, Czech, Native American drums, religious, etc. The different tempos will produce different moods and will be reflected in the drawings. A satellite radio would be perfect to use.

Music will play for fifteen to twenty minutes. Ask the residents why they choose certain colors and what the drawing means to them or what the drawing reminded them of. The drawings are then displayed in the hallways or taken back to their rooms.

No more needs to be done. This is a therapy with which family or volunteers can assist. Art therapy should be held once a month for every resident.

There is a warning that I need to share. In one facility we

164

were told to stop and desist from saying, "art therapy" because none of us had a degree in art. This is where I say arrogance (and that degree) gets in the way of compassion.

Remotivation Therapy

Remotivation therapy is a lost art, and yet it proved its therapeutic value with hundreds of nursing-home residents. This gentle therapy can be held by families, social services, or activities or nursing. I hold a certificate in Remotivation Therapy, although you do not need to be certified to hold group remotivation. The therapy is very simple.

Needed are *large* pictures of any subject matter. For men I had *large* pictures of old farm tractors, farm equipment, horses, windmills, watermills, old cars, trucks, construction equipment or lumber mills. For ladies, I had a packet of *large* pictures of puppies, kittens, children, baby chicks, flowers. Usually the group is no larger than six and placed in a circle so all can see. In the group are usually one or two who are considered nonresponsive. One by one, the pictures are placed in front of the residents to reminisce or identify. The secret is patience and the ability to edge the nonverbal resident into remembering.

When the thirty-minute session is over, pictures enjoyed by residents are placed on their bulletin boards in their rooms for nursing and auxiliary staff to continue the conversation.

Remotivation is perfect for the family to utilize when they visit. When families bring in pictures of the old farm place, generations gone by, shucking corn, a threshing bee, old Dobbin the horse, or of the old family sheep dog, this is remotivation.

Aromatherapy

Aromatherapy means "treatment" using scents. Essential oils were mankind's first medicines. Aromas create environments that soothe, heal, relax, rejuvenate, and stimulate.

Aromas trigger impressions, memories, emotions, and healing responses.

Aromatherapy is a simple therapy designed for the family, a volunteer, social services, or nursing. Residents who have a difficult time relaxing or sleeping would have chamomile oil put in their aromatherapy diffuser. The cinnamon scent or lemon or eucalyptus would be used to keep residents more alert and has been used as an antidepressant. Lavender and sandalwood is used for calming. Those with claustrophobia and anxiety would do well with the aroma of vanilla.

After trying many different diffusers in residents rooms, I have found one by Aura Cacia that is very simple to operate. In my early days of experiments with aromatherapy, I used a smudge pot and set off the fire alarm. Then I tried the oil in a warming pot and, of course, would forget to turn it off when I went home. Diffusers are safe and easy to use.

I use lavender in my massage therapy room, which helps to relax the client. Above the head of the client is a full spectrum light and the best oil for massage is Almond Glow oil purchased at Home Health.

For every family to consider is my suggestion that before you move a loved one into a nursing-home room, you "cleanse" the room with a bit of sage. I was taught this by Native Americans, as sage removes any emotions left by the last occupant. The first night or two are usually difficult for the Elders, so I suggest the family use a lavender spray on the sheets and pillow case. To keep myself alert during the day, I use a rose body spray.

When I was on the Omaha reservation, medicine men would come to the facility and cleanse every room with sage. Sage and sweetgrass were used in outdoor ceremonies in which all residents took part, each having the wisps of smoke/aroma brushed over them with a feather held by the medicine men.

"Touch" Therapy

1. Nursing-home residents should sit on chairs in a circle. Choose partners. Take turns rubbing one another's feet using olive oil.
2. On a warm day, do these exercises outside, in a meadow of flowers.
3. Walk slowly through the trees, shrubs, and flowers. Touch each of them and thank them for their beauty.
4. Build a sand path. Walk barefoot every day.
5. Have a meditation garden. Touch the crystals, rocks, flowers.
6. Give one another a face massage.
7. Hold hands skyward and "touch" the clouds.
8. Play games like "pat a cake."
9. Beat a pillow. Release anger.
10. Rub hands together. Then move hands outward and feel the ball of energy.
11. Mirror therapy. Look into a full-length mirror and touch the different body parts.
12. Hold hands during the prayer before meals.
13. Designate one day to shake hands with one another.

We must all remember that ***Touch is manifesting God!!***

19

History of Homeopathy

I speak of homeopathy as being one part of the healing, compassionate care therapies for elders in nursing-homes. And it is with the use of homeopathy that the hope is to ease the work for nursing.

Homeopathy is a 200-year-old medical system for a wide spectrum of acute health problems. Homeopathics are made from plants, minerals, or the natural chemical kingdoms with no additives and no breakdown of targeted substances. Homeopathics gently stimulate the inner healing by the natural defense processes.

The best reason to use homeopathic medicines is that they work. When homeopathic medicines are prescribed correctly, they act rapidly, deeply, and curatively, *stimulating* the body's defenses, rather than simply suppressing symptoms. *There has never been a report of a side effect or a recall of a proven homeopathic remedy.* All homeopathic remedies are included in the U.S. Pharmacopeia.

Although rejected by the medical establishment of the nineteenth century, homeopathy spread rapidly throughout Europe and then to the United States. Few people, including the allopathic physician, are aware that the first national medical association in the United States was the American Institute of Homeopathy, founded in 1844. By the turn of the century fully 25 percent of all physicians in urban areas identified themselves as homeopaths. There were twenty-two homeopathic medical schools and over 100 homeopathic hospitals. William Cullen Bryant, noted journalist and poet, was the president of the Homeopathic Medical Society of New York City and County.

In the twentieth century, homeopathy declined because of

strong opposition by the AMA, which was controlled by the large and powerful pharmaceutical companies. A homeopathic remedy is inexpensive. There were very small profits in prescribing a homeopathic.

A sharp resurgence of homeopathic activity began in the early 1970s and homeopathy has continued to grow since that time. As of 1984, conservative estimates indicate there are over one thousand medical doctors and osteopaths actively involved in homeopathic practices in the United States. An equal number of other licensed health professionals—nurses, physician assistants, dentists, veterinarians, chiropractors, naturopaths, psychologists, massage therapists and an undetermined number of lay practitioners—suggest the use of homeopathics.

Homeopathy's current popularity is greatest in other countries especially in India, England, France, Russia, Mexico, Brazil, and Argentina. In India there are over 70,000 registered homeopathic practitioners, and it is widely practiced in Pakistan. Homeopathy is well-known throughout the United Kingdom and has been growing significantly in the last ten years. The royal family has been under homeopathic care since the 1930s. The queen is the patron of the Royal London Homoeopathic Hospital and the British Homoeopathic Association. In France 6,000 physicians actively practice homeopathy. Over 18,000 pharmacies sell homeopathic medicines and approximately 16 percent of the French population. In India there are 124 Homeopathic medical colleges and three homeopathic medical schools in Mexico.

There are over 300 homeopathic physicians in the USSR, with homeopathic medical institutions in many Soviet cities. The Central Homeopathic Polyclinic in Moscow has approximately sixty-eight full-time homeopathic physicians and many specialty departments.

In Brazil, the government requires schools of pharmacy to teach homeopathy, and at least four medical schools offer homeopathic classes as part of their regular curriculum. No homeopathics are used in nursing-homes in United States unless brought in and administered by family.

Is marijuana a homeopathic? One young man, paralyzed from the neck down, left the facility several times a week to meet with friends. Later, he came to me and told me his friends had obtained marijuana for him in order to decrease pain and provide a few hours of comfort. I looked at this young man, who, due to past life karma, would probably face an entire life in a nursing-home and said to him, "I did not hear what you said and would never repeat what you have just told me." If a bit of marijuana was of help to this human being languishing in a paralyzed state for the rest of his life, why is it not medicinally legal for him to use it in the nursing-home? This is a law that must be changed!

Marijuana is a tall, attractive plant often seen in ditches throughout rural states. It is picked in the bud state, crushed, and smoked in a pipe or in a rolled cigarette. We permit nursing-home residents to smoke tobacco, which is very addictive with its sugar, chemicals, and preservative coatings. We permit chemicalized white sugar to be in foodstuffs and aspartame (a chemical) in soft drinks, which has caused a myriad of illnesses and is also addictive. Should not tobacco, aspartame, all food products containing white sugar and soft drinks, be considered illegal, too?

Mary Furlong, a national expert in aging and technology, predicts the baby boomers will age differently from previous generations. Baby boomers have more time, more money, and more education than any previous generation. Boomers are interested in fitness, health, rejuvenation, and vitality. They prefer consumer-directed health care and will continue to strongly endorse alternative therapies, organic foods, vitamins, homeopathics (including marijuana) and exercise programs, such as yoga and tai chi.

Yes, allopathic physicians and nursing-homes will change, not by political choice, but by demands from the baby boomer generation.

20

Healing with Positive Thoughts

Intrinsically speaking, man knows, as an intelligent, spiritual being, that thoughts and words are a powerful builder.

Catherine Ponder states that man is 2 percent physical and 98 percent mental and spiritual, with the average person spending 98 percent of his/her time thinking about 2 percent of his/her physical nature. Nursing-home residents are constantly talking about all their ills and physical disabilities. Staff often support complaints with sympathy or a pill or what can I do, not realizing that what they say to a resident can enforce the illness or disability.

I use myself as a classic example. As an administrator in a small county-owned facility in which I inherited a serious financial deficit, I frequently said, "This is a pain in the neck." Within a month, I discovered a serious case of shingles . . . on the back of my neck. I vowed to never think or say that again.

Hindu scriptures say, "If a man speaks or acts with a negative or evil thought, pain follows him." One of the secret teachings of the ancient Egyptians was that a pained body is the result of pained thinking.

Psychologists find most diseases are self-inflicted. Criticism of others and self is said to be a major cause of ill health. Hermetic teachings state the primary cause of disease is excessive hate, resentment, condemnation of self, criticism of others, jealousy, and possessiveness.

Nursing-home residents in ill health must be taught to change their thinking, their words, thoughts, deeds, emotions, and utilize daily positive affirmations in their prayer life.

Plato pointed out to Greek physicians of his time, the word

"health" means a state of being WHOLE, in spirit, soul, words, thoughts, financial affairs, and relationships with others.

And then there are those residents who "enjoy" their ill health, daring anyone to try and heal them. Many health-care professionals are aware those who never respond to any treatment are really saying that they are attempting to escape life's responsibilities.

For those who wish to have "whole" health regardless of age and environment, there are a myriad of affirmations that must be said every day with posters placed in resident's room and hallways as daily reminders:

Lord, I am ready! I am ready to accept my complete healing in mind, body, affairs and relationships. Lord, I do accept my complete healing now.

I am the healthy child of God! I am! I am! I am!

There is nothing in all the world for me to fear, for greater is the miracle-working power of Jesus Christ here and now than any other appearance.

Praise the Lord anyway (regardless of the situation).

The above affirmations are found in the book *The Dynamic Laws of Healing*, by Catherine Ponder.

Healing Affirmations

- I am the radiant child of God. My mind, body, and affairs now manifest His radiant perfection.
- Every day in every way, I am getting better and better.
- I am blessed with divine desire and with divine fulfillment. I am satisfied with divine love, now!
- Health and harmony are now established in my mind, body, and affairs.
- Not my will but God's will is being done in, through, and around about me now.
- I willingly do the will of God, which is for my supreme good.
- There shall be no evil befall thee, neither shall any plague

come nigh my tent. For he will give his angels charge over thee, to keep thee in all thy ways. Psalms 91:10-11.
- There is nothing to fear. There is only good in this experience. Healing is now taking place in my world. I rest, relax, and let it.
- When a right-thinking person seems to lose something, it is because the inner self is clearing the way for better things.
- Any experience that causes me to grow, leads me to success and healing takes place.
- I give thanks for Divine fulfillment, which is now taking place.
- If I am having health problems, the someone that has to give . . . is me. Unless I give to others, I have no room to receive.

More About Affirmations

Affirmations work! The capable nursing-home residents may write out affirmations in the privacy of their rooms. Social workers may ask the questions and assist in the writing or place the affirmation on tape to be played on a daily basis. The resident must ask him/her self what his/her deepest desire is at this time. Don't be concerned with how "foolish" the desire is . . . just write it down. There can be more than one desire. There can be a dozen desires, if you wish.

I prefer to focus on one at a time. But affirmations come with a warning. You need to be careful what you write down, as you may pay the price of the asking and wonder afterward why this is happening to you!

The use of a pen or pencil is important, due to the fact all your energy and power is directed to the point of the instrument. The bedridden should be assisted to write their own affirmation. Write your affirmations ten to twenty times on a sheet of paper and be very specific. Several examples are:

"I need to lose fifty pounds in a safe and nutritional way."

"I am prepared to leave this earth plane quickly, pain free, and peacefully."

"I need my family to show their love to me on a frequent basis."

The purpose of affirmations is not only to give hope to the most hopeless of situations but to firmly plant in the minds of nursing-home residents that they have the power to change their life conditions. They are responsible for their health or their ill-health. Every nursing-home staff must be prepared to tell them in a gentle way to take control of their life! It belongs to them. They are the powerful co-creator of their being, their spirit, their soul! Hip! Hip! Hip! Hooray! And in Hebrew, we say again, again, again, shout ye!

God Is Not a God Of Disease!

God did not create disease so don't blame God if you are in ill health. Mankind creates its own ill health through its wrong thinking and actions. What is "wrong thinking" or "wrong spoken word?" Anger, jealousy, possessiveness, resentment, condemnation, hate, and negative thinking of any kind form disease germs.

And it is here, that I also add that ill health may be karmic from a past life, *however*, negative past karma can be alleviated by how one lives one's life in this lifetime. In fact, many of us have returned to earth to work through negative karma that we set up ourselves in past lives. Remember, *we have a God of many chances. And we must remember that there is moral anger*. When an elder is being abused in any way, one has the right and obligation to be angry, feel anger, and then do something about the situation.

Many return to assist others in their negative karma. An example is the teachers, prophets, and highly evolved spirits by the earth names of Jesus of Nazareth, Mohammed and Dalai Lama. Jesus came in the new age of Pisces (the symbol of the fish) to free mankind from his/her past bad karma by bringing forth the new law of "love one another" as the most powerful commandment. Jesus of Nazareth did not come to start a new religion nor to have mankind kill one another in wars nor to live a life in a diseased state. Jesus of Nazareth, Mohammed, and the Dalai Lama, were to be patterns for all mankind. Many spiritual teachers came before Jesus of Nazareth and Mohammed, and many teachers and prophets came after them in different names and titles.

21

Guardianships and Conservatorships

I am a Certified Guardian through the National Guardianship Foundation. I spent several months in study and then traveled to Minneapolis, Minnesota, to take a three-hour test. My reasoning was simple. I had been a court-appointed guardian and conservator for elderly persons and the indigent for years and did so by flying by the seat of my pants. There are rules and regulations to adhere to. With the study, I became more knowledgeable and competent.

In every nursing-home, there is a need for guardians and conservators. A regulation states that nursing-home staff cannot be guardians for nursing-home residents.

We usually find compassionate ministers and sometimes family members to take over as guardians; however, guardians and conservators are very difficult to find due to the responsibility, the time, and the money involved. State regulation says that Guardians for the indigent can not reimbursed.

Under *Guardianship Law, Article 81* by Rose Mary Bailly, guardianships are defined as:

Guardian: a person eighteen years of age or older, or a corporation or public agency appointed by the Court who is lawfully invested with the power and charged with the duty of taking care of the person and/or managing the property and affairs of another person who is determined by the court to be incapacitated.

Guardian ad litem: person appointed by the court in a proceeding that is in litigation (a temporary position as guardian.

Guardian of the person: appointed by the court given the authority to provide for personal needs of the person deemed incompetent.

Guardian of the property: appointed by the court with the authority to manage property and financial affairs.

Conservator: appointed by the court to manage the financial affairs of the person who needs financial management of property and finances.

In some states, if one is appointed guardian, it is assumed to be for both the guardian of the person and conservator of the property and finances. This is decided in the courts.

All interested parties are notified by the court of the guardianship proceedings. All attorney and court costs are paid by the Department of Health and Human Services if the guardianee is on Medicaid. A guardianee is one who has a court-appointed guardian.

Duties of the guardian and conservator begin by taking assessment of all personal property and finances to protect not only the guardian/conservator but to prevent any family issues that may arise. This inventory is presented to the court.

The guardian is to set up a special file for each guardianee. The guardian will be asked to present copies of court-appointed guardianship papers to the Social Security office, pension institutions, and to nursing-homes for their records, before any Social Security or pension checks are sent to the guardian in the guardianee's name.

- Have all of the guardianee's mail sent to you.
- Open a bank account with the guardianee's name and your name on the account. All funds must earn interest.
- Save all receipts and bank statements and file an income tax return each year.
- Don't commingle your funds with the guardianee's funds.
- Don't hand over any of your guardian responsibilities to others.

The guardian is responsible for payment of all bills; however, he/she is not responsible for any debts incurred prior to the guardianship if monies are not available and is not responsible for any debts incurred by an irresponsible guardianee (person of interest).

The guardian may assist in placement of a person in any living arrangement that is for the betterment and safety of the guardianee. Send a letter to the court of any change in living arrangement. Notify the court if the guardianee needs psychiatric institutional care.

The guardian will make health-care decisions. The guardian receives calls prior to any medical treatments, change of medications, visits to any health care professional, and injuries and altercations that have occurred.

The guardian may sell personal property to pay bills, if the guardianee is no longer in need of the personal property, i.e. admitted to a nursing-home.

Family is to be communicated with on an annual basis as to decisions made and a financial statement sent to them, if they are available and cognizant.

The court requires an annual report as to living arrangements, financial statement, physical or psychological changes, and the names of all health-care professionals. This report will cost the guardian $5.00 in court costs.

The guardian may elect to encourage the guardianee to fill out an Advance Directive, make decisions for or against a DNR (do not resuscitate) order, encourage funeral planning, or if the guardianee is not capable of making decisions, a family member or friends may know the wishes of the guardianee. Any medical decisions must be signed by the guardianee or the guardian and witnessed.

A guardian is to act as a surrogate for the guardianee. I always ask myself, how would the guardianee want this handled? It is important that the guardian become acquainted with family, friends, neighbors, and minister in order to make decisions in the best interest of the guardianee.

As a certified guardian, the Foundation requires $150 reregistration fee every two years plus eighteen hours of CEUs.

Most states do not offer guardianship workshops. As a volunteer guardian, to maintain registered and locate pertinent workshops is a hardship. For those who wish to be knowledgeable concerning guardianships, I offer an intensive three-hour workshop in my private home.

22

Passing through the Stargate

If you live well, you never have to worry about dying poorly. To live well means to love others, nature, and animals—all of God's creation.

Even if you, as the caretaker, hold the hand of an elder in the last moments of life on this Earth, you have served your purpose. You are assisting a spirit through a stargate in his/her last moments.

It is not enough to be a licensed social worker or physician or certified hospice worker, for knowledge alone is not going to help anyone in the dying stages. If you cannot use your head, your heart, and your soul, you are not going to help a single human being including yourself.

The dying person is there for your learning. Dying residents teach the caretaker about the stages of dying. They teach you how they go through the denial, the anger and the "why me?" stage, the rejection of God, the bargaining, and the depression. If they have a compassionate caretaker, the Elder may reach not only the stage of acceptance but of understanding "why."

Dying is an opportunity for the Elder and the caretaker to grow spiritually. An article by Shepherd Bliss entitled, "Walt Whitman Speaks to the Dying" addresses the art of lovingly telling someone he/she is to die. Walt Whitman, poet, has written:

To One Shortly to Die

From all the rest I single you out, having a message for you.
You are to die—let others tell you what they please, I cannot prevaricate.
I am exact and merciless, but I love you—there is no escape for you.

Softly I lay my right hand upon you, you just feel it. I do not argue, I bend my head close and half envelop it. I sit quietly by, I remain faithful. I am more than a nurse, more than parent or neighbor.

I absolve you from all except your spiritual body, that is eternal, you yourself will surely escape.
The corpse you will leave, it will be but excrementitious.
The sun bursts through in unlooked for directions. Strong thoughts fill you
with confidence. You smile. You forget you are sick, as I forget you are sick.

You do not see the medicines. You do not mind the weeping friends.
I am with you. I exclude others from you. There is nothing to be commiserated.
I do not commiserate. I congratulate you.

According to Shepherd Bliss' interpretation, the question was asked, "How does the poet approach the difficult assignment of lovingly telling someone he is to die?"

First, says Bliss, the poet does not hide behind the professionalism of doctors, (social workers and nurses), who neglect to tell the resident that he or she is to die soon. The poet recognizes that this information must be communicated clearly and yet compassionately and in the same sentence, the poet makes it clear in the plea that "I love you." The poet admits that he is exact and merciless in stating there is no escape for you (in the speaking of the truth that death is imminent).

Secondly, where doctors and social workers often withdraw from the dying resident, this poet actually moves closer, laying a hand on the patient, the head close by so the resident can hear and the resident knows the poet is always near. The dying need to have someone close just as they had their mother with them upon their birth.

Bliss continues, "The healing touch facilitates the person's leaving this world." How essential it is to touch the dying, the aging and others in pain. *Dying is not contagious*. Touch heals the soul, the spirit, the God within. What does the poet mean when he "absolves you"? Bliss explains that so many of the dying feel guilty for not having done something, or finished something, or said something. The poet is ready for this with the absolution from all.

"You surely will escape," says the poet. A spiritual belief in the nineteenth century, is the assurance that once a person has died, he or she will leave only their corpse.

According to Edgar Cayce readings, the spirit leaves the body and is immediately welcomed by family, friends, and co-workers who have passed on. Then the Book of Life (located in the heart center) is opened where the spirit-soul can see his/her life before her and judges her/him self. The many mansions are opened to the spirit-soul to receive its rewards and enter the many classrooms for learning and correction.

Calling the dying person's attention to the Sun fills the person with a higher level of spirituality, where the sickness, the medicines, and the weeping family and friends are there but no longer thought about. The Sun rises above all else. Life continues in death.

The poet remains faithful with the "I am with you," "I do not commiserate," and "I congratulate you." The poet feels the last moments before death is like a commencement . . . an ending which brings a beginning, not something to be dreaded, but something which is an integral part of life.

Shepherd Bliss, writer, ends by suggesting that, overall, the poet is saying, "If you would speak to the dying, be unafraid, touch them, draw close to them, tell them the truth, share your love with them, remind them of the Sun, let them know you are with them, be faithful."

Psychiatrist Elisabeth Kubler-Ross, MD, world-renowned authority on death and dying shares this story from near the end of her life on Earth:

My real job is to tell people that death does not exist. It is very important that mankind knows that, because we are at the beginning of a very difficult time. Not only for this country, but for the whole planet Earth. Because of our own destructiveness. Because of the nuclear weapons. Because of our greediness and materialism. Because we are piggish in terms of ecology. Because we have destroyed so many, many natural resources, and because we have lost all genuine spirituality. The only thing that will bring about the change into a new age is that the Earth is shaken, that we are shaken and we're going to be shaken. We have already seen the beginning of it.

You have to know not to be afraid of that. Only if you keep a very, very open channel, an open mind, and no fear, will great insight and revelations come to you. They can happen to all of you. You do not have to become a guru, you do not have to go to India, you don't even have to take a TM course. You don't have to do anything except learn to get in touch in silence within yourself, which doesn't cost one penny. Get in touch with your own inner self, and learn not to be afraid. And one way to not be afraid is to know that death does not exist, that everything in the life has a positive purpose. Get rid of all your negativity and begin to view life as a challenge, a testing ground of your own inner resources and strength.

There is no coincidence. God is not a punitive, nasty God. After you make the transition, then you come to what has been described as hell and heaven. That is not a right interpretation of the judgment, however.

What we hear from our friends, who passed over, from people who came back to share with us, is that every human being, after this transition, which is peace and equanimity and wholeness and a loving someone who helps you in the transition, each one of you is going to have to face something that looks very much like a television screen, where you are given an opportunity, not to be judged by a judgemental God, but to judge yourself, by having to review every single action, every word, and every thought of your life.

You make your own hell, or your own heaven, by the way you live.

Harold said that he "just wanted to go." I spent many hours by his bedside reading Bible passages or just being close to him. His pastor came to visit every day. In conversation with Pastor Bill, I was told to bend over close to his ear and whisper, "I give you permission to go." Pastor Bill believed that many elders just need to be given permission.

However, I knew this elder needed to forgive one very cantankerous resident who also resided in the nursing-home. I suggested to Harold to ask this resident to come to his room and ask his forgiveness. He did. Afterward, I whispered in his ear that he had my permission to pass over. Within twenty-four hours, Harold passed over.

Eddie was dying. He was a nonbeliever, so I was very careful not to pray with him, but, silently, to have his passing over be one of peace. The moment of death was with a very cold last breath and the feeling of a negative source in the room. I felt such sadness when I touched his hand and said good-bye.

A woman, I shall call Sara, was American Indian. She was dying of cancer and was unresponsive to my being in the room. However, her death song could be heard throughout the facility. She chanted through the night and was gone by morning. I still hear her mournful song in my soul.

Having the privilege to work in a Native American facility, I noted when an elder was dying, the entire tribe came to be with the elder and stayed until he/she passed over. Meals were prepared for any and all family and tribal members present. As a "white, capitalist woman" (as I was frequently called), I wanted the room to be cleaned, and all personal possessions taken home by the family so the room would be available for the next resident. With the gentleness of my Native American coworkers, I was informed that was not the Indian way. Following a death, the room was cleaned, personal possessions are placed on the bed, and a light was left on for three days and nights. Native Americans believe it takes three days for the spirit to leave the earth.

I am still embarrassed by this lack of knowledge concerning

Native American beliefs. It showed my ignorance and I ask for forgiveness by all who were aware of this mistake in thinking. I deserved the title of being a "capitalist," thinking only of income for the facility. I definitely had been with corporations too long.

I was privileged to help with arranging a Native American burial. The person lived several states away. He wanted to be buried with his own tribe. Several thousand dollars were sent to us for transporting the body, to hire drummers, to pay for the burial ground, and to celebrate his passing with a dinner for the entire tribe. What a send off he had!

The most wonderful, gentle elder was dying. Sara had no family. She was Catholic. Her room was so barren, so I asked her if she would like to have a cross or a picture of Jesus in her room, to which she agreed. I purchased both for her and then called for a priest to give her the last rites. The priest refused to come saying, "She has not been a member for many years." I was shocked and angry. I picked up the phone and called a pastor of a small Baptist church, told him what had happened. He was there within the hour. We both prayed with Sara. I thanked the pastor and later went to the little church and placed a check for $100 in the basket. I was so grateful for his compassion.

I returned to the facility to find Sara's evening meal at her bedside. When I checked to see what had been prepared, I saw a hot dog, chips, and a cup of coffee. I admit my hair almost stood up on end. I took the tray to the kitchen and chewed out the dietary manager and asked why she would not have sent a small bowl of chicken soup, a cracker, and tea to a dying person. The dietary manager was very apologetic, saying that she was never told. Another tray was prepared, which I took to Sara's side and assisted her with a spoonful of broth. As Sara seemed to sleep peacefully, I returned home thinking about all that had happened. Sara slipped into eternity during the night. I think of her often. I wonder if the Catholic priest thinks about her and what an opportunity he missed. And I did apologize to the Dietary Manager for my behavior.

Ted was comatose and in the last dying stage. He had no family. I took turns with the nursing staff being in the room in his last hour. Upon the moment of death, the room was so quiet, all I could hear was a fly buzzing around the room. Was that what this soul heard with his last breath. Then the nurse came in and immediately started packing up his meager possessions. I stopped her by saying that Ed was able to hear her actions. She looked at me like I had really lost it. I don't know. I said what my spirit told me to say.

As one elder lay dying, I asked God why, why did He not release this poor, fragile soul. Within my spirit, I was told, "He is here for you."

In several nursing-homes where I was administrator, residents would often choose to have the funeral service in the facility. Residents often say the nursing-home is where their family is, both residents and staff. It is a time when residents and all staff can say good-bye.

Another facility held bedside memorial services at the time of death for staff and residents, especially the roommate.

In direct opposition, one nursing-home owner would not permit a memorial notice or a rose to be put up upon the death of a resident. A once a month service was held for all those who had passed over during the previous month. My response is that those who reside in a nursing-home deserve (in the name of humanity) to know when a friend or tablemate passes away. All they hear is a scurry in and out of a room; then the rumble of the morticians gurney and out of the room comes a body covered in a black shroud. No one tells them anything and nothing posted?? Of course, there are whispers, but they are not sure. So you see residents stopping the staff to ask "Is it true that she/he passed away?"

In several facilities, a special table was placed in the foyer with a lace tablecloth, a few personal possessions of the one who just passed over, a small bouquet of fresh flowers and a picture of the elder. I noted that residents would also drop notes on the table or lay a small memorial in memory of their friend. Many asked to talk with family when family arrived at the facility. Elders need to say good-bye and shed a tear at the time of the passing, not a month later or as they read it in the paper. Administrators and Social Services need to take an active part in their residents' dying and death process.

One Social Services Director told me that she didn't get into things like sitting with the dying, or reading the Bible or just being in the room. I told her she needed to resign her job in Social Services and go work on an assembly line somewhere. Why do nursing-homes hire people with no compassion, no vision, no spiritual insight?

23

The Pros and Cons of Hospice

Florence Wald, a former Yale University Nursing School Dean, brought the hospice movement to the United States in 1971. Wald formed an interdisciplinary team of doctors, clergy, and nurses to study the needs of dying patients. The first hospice started in 1974 at the Connecticut Hospice in Branford. Today, about 3,200 hospice programs serve about 900,000 patients a year in the United States. The intent was meritorious.

Today, hospice is still alive and wealthy. At tremendous cost to the taxpayer, hospice talks with families creating an environment of guilt in order to place their loved one in a special hospice room usually designed in a hospital setting. Often with limited notification to the nursing-home, the dying resident is taken from the home she/he is familiar with and enters an often unknown and unfamiliar room with a myriad of staff such as a social worker (licensed), nurse, and minister who focus entirely on the dying elder. Sounds wonderful. With the exception that the elder is well aware that a hospice room means death, which can often create fear and despair for the resident.

If the resident receives hospice care in the nursing-home, all cares are taken out of the hands of the staff who have cared for the elder for many years and into the hands of strangers.

Is the purpose of Hospice compassion or profit? As I often come back into the facility in the evenings or late at night, I check on elders who are dying. I have found hospice workers asleep in the resident's room, or playing loud, irritating music, watching TV, or munching on snacks. I have rarely seen anyone pray, play soothing music, or touch the dying person. I have reported our unhappiness with the situation to both family and hospice.

In one case, Elsie was comatose, unable to respond to any cares or anyone in the room. I saw the social worker in the hallway (not with the resident) and asked how the resident was. The social worker said she spent a few minutes with her and then decided to leave. As the guardian, I received the Medicare billing and noted that hospice was reimbursed $250 for every "contact," even though the contact may have been for two minutes. I tried repeatedly to call Medicare to report fraud; however, I was unable to reach anyone. So much for reporting fraud.

The hospice regulation that states *only* a licensed social worker (not a counselor) can work with the dying and their family is absolutely disgraceful. One does not need a license, nor be degreed, nor ordained, nor have a degree in social work. One needs to be a highly evolved spiritual entity with deep compassion and knowledge of the pre-dying stage. Nursing-homes need to take a strong stand on the issue of the dying. If they have no one on staff who could be designated a "hospice" worker, better yet would be a retired elder who has the love, empathy, and time to spend with the dying person. The nondegreed hospice worker would also be the hostess for the family to make in-house arrangements for snacks, meals, sleeping areas, and just being there. The nondegreed hospice worker would be paid minimum wage.

From *Reclaiming the End of Life* fact sheet about dying:

- We are all going to die one day.
- We usually do not plan on dying.
- As a culture, we resist talking about it.
- 2.4 million people in the U.S.A. die each year; the majority are frail elders.
- Twenty-five percent to 35 percent die in nursing-homes.
- Only 20 percent die in their own homes, regardless of the fact this is where most elders choose to be when their time comes.
- By 2030, Americans sixty-five and older will more than double, going from 35 million in 2000 to 72 million. The number of elders eighty-five and older will double during that time from 4 million in 2000 to 9.6 million by 2030.

With 50 percent of our elders in the dying stage, the need for compassionate staff will be immense.

- In 1990, the average ratio of caregivers per elderly person was 11 to 1. With the current pattern, estimates will be 6 to 1 by 2030 and 4 to 1 by 2050.
- Nearly one-half of persons who live to age sixty-five will enter a nursing-home before they die.
- Again, more than 90 percent of nursing-homes have too few nurses to care for residents, which means little time to be with the dying resident.
- By 2010, nearly half of all nurses will be over age fifty; exacerbating what is already a national nursing crisis.

We need our community elders to assist nursing in the care of the dying. Families must stop and think about transferring their loved from the familiar nursing-home to the unfamiliar hospital hospice and what hospice is costing the taxpayer.

Hospitalization and Hospice, and the Dying Elder

A society that cannot face their own aging, the dying and death process endorses the dependent trend rather than the natural and spiritual way of aging, death, and dying.

Over the past ten years hospice has come to the forefront with tremendous cost to the taxpayer. The cost to care for a hospice resident has increased 1,200 percent faster than all other aspects of health care in the United States. Hospice promises pain control in the last days and hours (Illich, p. 101).

The conception of hospice began during the eighteenth century, when the elites refused religious assistance, rejected belief in an afterlife, had an intense fear of Hell, were horrified of being buried alive, and of utmost importance, had an intense fear of an unmedicated dying process. These fears and beliefs or lack of beliefs gave birth to a movement commandeered by the medical profession and hospitals, which, in turn, promoted the high cost of the dying chamber (Illich, p. 101).

Families of dying elders often demand hospitalization, be-

190

lieving that hospitalization will reduce pain or enhance longevity. Neither is true. Statistics show that 10 percent die on the day of admission to a hospital; 30 percent within the week; and 75 percent within the month (I. Illich, p. 104).

Hospitals require three times the equipment and five times the staff to care for an elder person during the dying stage. Public fascination with high technology utilized during the dying process is easily understood as a deep-seated need for man-made engineering of miracles (I. Illich, p. 106).

How much better are spiritual therapies for the resident long before the dying process is activated—when that precious time arrives, the resident remains in a comfortable, loving environment, passing over peacefully.

Yes, It Is Only a Body!

"Yes, it is only a body . . . but this body is precious to me." These were my words to one funeral director. His actions stirred my curiosity. Nursing informed me that this funeral director did not permit any staff to be in the room when he came for the body. So, I walked down the hallway, opened the door to see the funeral director had stripped all the clothes off the body and was literally throwing the naked body onto the gurney. Arms and legs were flopping all over. I was so shocked. I asked him if this was the way he honored the dead. He said, "It's only a body."

From that time on, a staff person was in the room when this funeral director came and our honored Elders' gowns were kept on. We picked up the gown at the funeral home following the services.

As I was helping a wonderful CNA by the name of Della, in preparing a body for family viewing before the family arrived at the nursing-home, we gently washed the face, the arms, legs, front and back, and the private areas. The entire body was lotioned, hair combed, teeth brushed (dental plates are taken out, cleaned, and placed in a clean glass for the undertaker to take with him.) A clean, fresh gown was placed on the body, all linens were changed and properly placed around the body with head uncovered. Gentle hands closed the eyes and a soft cloth was placed under the chin to keep the mouth from opening. All equipment was removed from the room and the room cleaned. Personal possessions remained until the family chose to take them home. What a privilege to care for the body!

Reading of the two Marys and Joseph of Arimathea, who so lovingly tended the body of Jesus of Nazareth with the washing of the body, the use of perfumes, and the laying of the cloth over His precious face, I ask, is not the tending to bodies of our elders just the same? Are we not all one in the Spirit? What a glorious moment!

A son came out of his dad's room. I looked into his eyes and in this moment the son said, "Dad's soul has already left." I nodded my head in agreement. The dad passed away during the night hours after the son had left his side. What did this son intuitively know?

Physicians have written that as a person dies, they have seen wisps curling into the air. What has left the body? Scientists in the medical profession report that a person who has just died weigh ounces less than when life was still with the body. What has left the body? I will have all these answers when I, too, pass over and celebrate my new birth. Until then, I will love, touch, and remain at their side during the dying process and speak the truth.

Those who Fear Death

It is the morbidness of the rituals, superstitions, and imaginary ideas associated with death that made this phenomenon seem terrifying to some. But to those who understand that it is a natural and rhythmic transformation of certain energies into other forms of power and that each individual is an inseparable part of an infinite universe and a part of eternity, death is an exodus and a freedom.

Such people know that there is no punishment after death and that the only hell is that created by man within himself when he deviates from universal law.

We begin to be part of that universal law when we listen to a beautiful symphony, enjoy a magnificent book, or contemplate a great piece of painting or sculpture. Our monotonous lives become stimulated by the beauties of nature and unite our consciousness with all that is beautiful, profound, and of true value.

If human kind continues on its own pathway of hate, violence, selfishness, quest for power over others, criticism, judgment of others, gossip, deceit, manipulation, wars, and destruction, man will remain in bondage to his lower self. And he will then always fear death because he has lived a life inharmonious with universal law.

It is not important to know what another believes following death. The following are several thoughts for the reader to think about.

The psychic Rudolph Steiner points out that after death the soul enters the space between earth and the moon. From this space, the soul is attracted to planets according to its need in development and improvement in preparation for reentry into the Earth plane as a born-again new life. William Henry, investigative mythologist, who has investigated many spiritual mysteries of the Universe, says that at the moment of death we pass through the Stargate into the stars and towards the planets. The Bible states there are many mansions awaiting us. Edgar Cayce states that these "rooms" or mansions are classrooms in which all of humankind becomes students. The purpose is to learn of our errors while we were on earth and make corrections before we reincarnate to make retribution for those errors. Our God is a God of many chances.

We live in the midst of death all the time. It is the most familiar thing to us. It is a phase of life. There could be no death if there were no life. Death is an event in life, in consciousness. When a man sleeps, he dies partially. This is one of the reasons why nursing-home residents have difficulty sleeping as they recognize they may never wake up . . . they fear death. Sleep is an imperfect death. Death is a perfect sleep. Death and sleep are brothers said the ancient Greeks . . . sleep and death are one. Every time we sleep, we rest and recuperate our minds and bodies. We die partially; that is why we rest. And when we dream, beau-

tiful or evil dreams, it is because our daily lives are lived beautifully or evilly. So it is with death.

Let us now leave written instructions in preparation for the
dying process and death on this Earth.

24

Leaving Written Instructions

It is imperative that all elders in a nursing-home leave written instructions concerning the dying process, death and burial wishes. This is a family issue that must be addressed and the nursing-home must have the basic information in the medical record.

Upon imminent death, who is to be notified?
Does the family wish to come to the nursing-home following the death?
Funeral home to be notified?
I have or have not a prepaid funeral plan?
I have or have not a prepaid burial plot? Where is the plot located?
Minister to be contacted?
I have chosen to be cremated? By what firm?
 Telephone #?
Embalming? By what firm?
Obituary in what papers? No obituary?
Location of funeral? Location of burial?
Eulogy by?
Music by? Special singer? Reader?
Burial clothes/jewelry?
Memorials to?
Lunch by?
Additional wishes:

Benefits of Preplanning a Funeral

1. Prearranging a funeral:
   - Involves your family in decision-making.

- Every detail can be arranged according to *your* wishes.
- Guarantees that personal records are organized.
- Saves family from the burden at an emotional time.
2. Prefunding a funeral:
   - Spares your loved ones from financial worry.
   - Fits your budget with various payment plans.
   - Funeral expenses can be taken care of today.

Key Reasons Why More People are Choosing Cremation:

1. Migration to retirement areas leaving no one to tend to the grave site.
2. Cremation is more acceptable now.
3. Environmental concerns.
4. Level of education has led to understanding cremation.
5. Costs, which are usually lower.
6. Origin of immigrants are changing with acceptance of cremation.
7. Wishes of those who don't like the thought of being underground.
8. Wishes of survivors especially when there are no burial arrangements.

One may wish to donate his/her body to science. If this action is taken, family must be informed as the body is usually taken immediately to the School of Anatomical Science at a medical center. Within one year, the body is cremated with the ashes buried on site or given to the family for burial. There is no cost to the family.

With permission from the National Hospice and Palliative Care Organization and a special thank you to the State of South Dakota, the following information is provided for the reader's convenience. *Each person should check the law / regulations in his or her own state.*

SOUTH DAKOTA
Advance Directive
Planning for Important Healthcare Decisions

Caring Connections
1700 Diagonal Road, Suite 625, Alexandria, VA 22314
www.caringinfo.org
800/658-8898

Caring Connections, a program of the National Hospice and Palliative Care Organization (NHPCO), is a national consumer engagement initiative to improve care at the end of life, supported by a grant from The Robert Wood Johnson Foundation.

Caring Connections tracks and monitors all state and federal legislation and significant court cases related to end-of-life care to ensure that our advance directives are up to date.

It's About How You LIVE

It's About How You LIVE is a national community engagement campaign encouraging individuals to make informed decisions about end-of-life care and services. The campaign encourages people to:
    Learn about options for end-of-life services and care
    Implement plans to ensure wishes are honored
    Voice decisions to family, friends and healthcare providers
    Engage in personal or community efforts to improve end-of-life care

Please call the HelpLine at 800/658-8898 to learn more about the LIVE campaign, obtain free resources, or join the effort to improve community, state and national end-of-life care.

If you would like to make a contribution to help support our work, please visit www.nationalhospicefoundation.org/donate. Contributions to national hospice programs can also be made through the Combined Health Charities or the Combined Federal Campaign by choosing #11241.

**Support for this program is provided by a grant from
The Robert Wood Johnson Foundation, Princeton,
New Jersey.**

Your Advance Care Planning Packet

Using these materials

BEFORE YOU BEGIN
1. Check to be sure that you have the materials for each state in which you may receive healthcare.

2. These materials include:
   - Instructions for preparing your advance directive.
   - Your state-specific advance directive forms, which are the pages with the gray instruction bar on the left side.

PREPARING TO COMPLETE YOUR ADVANCE DIRECTIVE
3. Read the HIPAA Privacy Rule Summary on page 4.

4. Read all the instructions, on pages 7 through 9, as they will give you specific information about the requirements in your state.

5. Refer to the Glossary located in Appendix A if any of the terms are unclear.

ACTION STEPS
6. You may want to photocopy these forms before you start so you will have a clean copy if you need to start over.

7. When you begin to fill out the forms, refer to the gray instruction bars - they will guide you through the process.

8. Talk with your family, friends, and physicians about your advance directive. Be sure the person you appoint to make decisions on your behalf understands your wishes.

9. Once the form is completed and signed, photocopy the form and give it to the person you have appointed to make decisions on your behalf, your family, friends, healthcare providers and/or faith leaders so that the form is available in the event of an emergency.

If you have questions or need guidance in preparing your advance directive or about what you should do with it after you have completed it, please refer to the state-specific contacts for Legal & End-of-Life Care Resources Pertaining to Healthcare Advance Directives, located in Appendix B.

Summary of the HIPAA Privacy Rule

HIPAA is a federal law that gives you rights over your health information and sets rules and limits on who can look at and receive your health information.

Your Rights

You have the right to:
- Ask to see and get a copy of your health records.
- Have corrections added to your health information.
- Receive a notice that tells you how your health information may be used and shared.
- Decide if you want to give your permission before your health information can be used or shared for certain purposes, such as marketing.
- Get a report on when and why your health information was shared for certain purposes.
- If you believe your rights are being denied or your health information isn't being protected, you can:
  - File a complaint with your provider or health insurer, or
  - File a complaint with the U.S. Government.

You also have the right to ask your provider or health insurer questions about your rights. You also can learn more about your rights, including how to file a complaint from the Web site at www.hhs.gov/ocr/hipaa/ or by calling 1-866-627-7748.

Who Must Follow this Law?

- Doctors, nurses, pharmacies, hospitals, clinics, nursing homes, and many other healthcare providers.
- Health insurance companies, HMOs, most employer group health plans.
- Certain government programs that pay for healthcare, such as Medicare and Medicaid.

What Information is Protected?

- Information your doctors, nurses, and other healthcare providers put in your medical record.
- Conversations your doctor has had about your care or treatment with nurses and other healthcare professionals.
- Information about you in your health insurer's computer system.
- Billing information about you from your clinic/healthcare provider.
- Most other health information about you, held by those who must follow this law.

Summary of the HIPAA Privacy Rule (continued)

Providers and health insurers who are required to follow this law must keep your information private by:

- Teaching the people who work for them how your information may and may not be used and shared,
- Taking appropriate and reasonable steps to keep your health information secure.

To make sure that your information is protected in a way that does not interfere with your healthcare, your information can be used and shared:

- For your treatment and care coordination,
- To pay doctors and hospitals for your healthcare,
- With your family, relatives, friends or others you identify who are involved with your healthcare or your healthcare bills, unless you object,
- To protect the public's health, such as reporting when the flu is in your area, or
- To make required reports to the police, such as reporting gunshot wounds.

Your health information cannot be used or shared without your written permission unless this law allows it. For example, without your authorization, your provider generally cannot:

- Give your information to your employer.
- Use or share your information for marketing or advertising purposes, or
- Share private notes about your mental health counseling sessions.

INTRODUCTION TO YOUR SOUTH DAKOTA ADVANCE DIRECTIVE

This packet contains two legal documents that protect your right to refuse medical treatment you do not want, or to request treatment you do want, in the event you lose the ability to make decisions yourself:

1. The **South Dakota Durable Power of Attorney for Health Care** lets you name someone to make decisions about your medical care – including decisions about life support – if you can no longer speak for yourself. The Durable Power of Attorney for Health Care is especially useful because it appoints someone to speak for you any time you are unable to make your own medical decisions, not only at the end of life.

2. The **South Dakota Living Will Declaration** lets you state your wishes about medical care in the event that you can no longer make your own medical decisions and are diagnosed to be in a terminal condition. Your Living Will goes into effect if it is determined by your attending physician that you are in a terminal condition , death is imminent and you are no longer able to communicate decisions about your medical care.

Note: These documents will be legally binding only if the person completing them is a competent adult.

COMPLETING YOUR SOUTH DAKOTA DURABLE POWER OF ATTORNEY FOR HEALTH CARE

Whom should I appoint as my attorney-in-fact?

"Attorney-in-fact" does not refer to a lawyer. Your attorney-in-fact is the person you appoint to make decisions about your medical care if you become unable to make those decisions yourself. Your attorney-in-fact can be a family member or a close friend whom you trust to make serious decisions. The person you name as your attorney-in-fact must be an adult who clearly understands your wishes and is willing to accept the responsibility of making medical decisions for you. (An attorney-in-fact may also be called an "agent" or "proxy.")

You can appoint a second person as your successor or alternate attorney-in-fact. The alternate will step in if the first person you name as attorney-in-fact is unable, unwilling or unavailable to act for you.

How do I make my South Dakota Durable Power of Attorney for Health Care legal?

The law requires that you have your Durable Power of Attorney for Health Care witnessed. You can do this in either of two ways:

1. Have your signature witnessed by a notary public,

   Or

2. sign your document, or direct another to sign it, in the presence of two adult witnesses, who must also sign the document to affirm that they know you, that you signed or acknowledged the document in their presence, and that you appear to be of sound mind and under no duress, fraud, or undue influence.

Should I add personal instructions to my South Dakota Durable Power of Attorney for Health Care?

One of the strongest reasons for naming an attorney-in-fact is to have someone who can respond flexibly as your medical situation changes and deal with situations that you did not foresee. If you add instructions to this document, you might unintentionally restrict your attorney-in-fact's power to act in your best interest.

Talk with your attorney-in-fact about your future medical care and describe what you consider to be an acceptable "quality of life." If you want to record your wishes about specific treatments or conditions, you should use your South Dakota Living Will Declaration.

COMPLETING YOUR SOUTH DAKOTA DURABLE POWER OF ATTORNEY FOR HEALTH CARE (CONTINUED)

What if I change my mind?

You can revoke your South Dakota Durable Power of Attorney for Health Care at any time. You may revoke your document orally, in writing, or by destroying the document. You must then notify your attorney-in-fact or doctor of your intent to revoke your document.

What other important facts should I know?

- Your state law restricts your attorney-in-fact's power to make decisions to withhold or withdraw comfort care. In addition, your state law generally restricts your attorney-in-fact's power to withhold or withdraw artificial nutrition and hydration unless you express in your Durable Power of Attorney for Health Care that artificial nutrition or hydration is to be withheld, or expressly authorize your attorney-in-fact to direct the withholding of artificial nutrition or hydration.

- Due to further restrictions in the state law, your attorney-in-fact cannot authorize the withholding or withdrawal of life-sustaining treatment and artificial nutrition and hydration if you are pregnant, unless your doctor and one other doctor certify that such treatment will not permit the development and live birth of the unborn child, or will be physically harmful to you or prolong severe pain which cannot be alleviated by medication.

COMPLETING YOUR SOUTH DAKOTA LIVING WILL DECLARATION

How do I make my South Dakota Living Will legal?

The law requires that you sign your document, or direct another to sign it, in the presence of two adult witnesses.

Can I add personal instructions to my Living Will?

Yes. You can add personal instructions in the part of the document called "Other directions."

If you have appointed an attorney-in-fact, it is a good idea to add the following statement to your Living Will Declaration: "Any questions about how to interpret or when to apply my Declaration are to be decided by my attorney-in-fact."

What if I change my mind?

You may revoke your Living Will Declaration at any time and in any manner, regardless of your mental or physical condition. Your revocation goes into effect once you notify your doctor or other healthcare provider, who must then make the revocation part of your medical record.

What other important facts should I know?

- Due to restrictions in the state law, life-sustaining treatment and artificial nutrition and hydration must be provided to you if you are pregnant, unless your doctor and one other physician certify in writing that the continued application of life-sustaining treatment will not allow for the live birth of the unborn child, or will be physically harmful to you or cause you to suffer prolonged severe pain which cannot be alleviated by medicine.
- If an individual has executed both a declaration and a durable power of attorney, the later executed document will control to the extent that there are conflicting provisions.

INSTRUCTIONS

PRINT YOUR NAME
AND ADDRESS

PRINT THE NAME,
ADDRESS AND
TELEPHONE
NUMBER OF YOUR
AGENT

PRINT THE NAME,
ADDRESS AND
TELEPHONE
NUMBER OF
YOUR ALTERNATE
AGENT

© 2005 National
Hospice and
Palliative Care
Organization
2008 Revised.

I, _____, of
(name of principal)

_____
(address)

hereby appoint _____ , of
(name of attorney-in-fact)

_____

_____
(address and telephone number of attorney-in-fact)

As my attorney-in-fact to consent to, to reject, or to withdraw consent for medical procedures, treatment or intervention.

2) In the event the person I appoint above is unable, unwilling or unavailable to act as my health care agent, I hereby appoint:

_____ , of
(name of successor attorney-in-fact)

_____

_____ .
(address and telephone number of successor attorney-in-fact)

3) I have discussed my wishes with my attorney-in-fact and my successor attorney-in-fact, and authorize him/her to make all and any health care decisions for me, including decisions to withhold or withdraw any form of life support. I expressly authorize my agent (and successor agent) to make decisions for me regarding the withholding or withdrawal of artificial nutrition and hydration in all medical circumstances.

4) This power of attorney becomes effective when I can no longer make my own medical decisions, and is not affected by physical disability or mental incompetence. The determination of whether I can make my own medical decisions is to be made by my attorney-in-fact, or if he or she is unable, unwilling or unavailable to act, by my successor attorney-in-fact, unless the attending physician determines that I have decisional capacity.

206

PRINT YOUR NAME AND THE DATE

I, _____, of

the principal, sign my name to this instrument this _____ day of
                                                                    (date)
_____, 20_____, and being first duly sworn, do
(month)   (year)
hereby declare to the undersigned authority that I sign it willingly (or
willingly direct another to sign for me), that I execute it as my free and
voluntary act for the purposes therein expressed, and that I am eighteen
years of age or older, of sound mind, and under no constraint or undue
influence.

SIGN THE DOCUMENT

_____
                                    (signature of principal)

WITNESSING PROCEDURE

A NOTARY PUBLIC MUST COMPLETE THIS SECTION

NOTARY

The State of South Dakota
The County of _____

Subscribed, sworn to, and acknowledged before me by _____

OR

_____, the principal, this _____ day of

_____, 20 _____.

TWO WITNESSES MUST SIGN YOUR DOCUMENT ON THE NEXT PAGE

(Seal)

_____
                                    (notary public)

207

OR

WITNESS STATEMENT

I declare that the person who signed or acknowledged this Durable Power of Attorney for Health care is personally known to me, that he/she signed or acknowledged this durable power of attorney in my presence, and that he/she appears to be of sound mind and under no duress, fraud, or undue influence.

Witness #1:

Witness #1:

Signature: _____ Date: _____

Print Name: _____ Telephone Number: _____

Residence Address:_____

_ _

Witness #2:

Witness #2:

Signature: _____ Date: _____

Print Name: _____ Telephone Number: _____

Residence Address:_____

_ _

Courtesy of Caring Connections
1731 King St., Suite 100, Alexandria, VA 22314
www.caringinfo.org, 800/658-8898

208

INSTRUCTIONS

This is an important legal document. A living will directs the medical treatment you are to receive in the event you are in a terminal condition and are unable to participate in your own medical decisions. This living will may state what kind of treatment you want or do not want to receive.

Prepare this document carefully. If you use this form, read it completely. You may want to seek professional help to make sure the form does what you intend and is completed without mistakes.

This document will remain valid and in effect until and unless you revoke it. Review this document periodically to make sure it continues to reflect your wishes. You may amend or revoke this document at any time by notifying your physician and other health care providers. You should give copies of this document to your family, your physician and your health care facility. This form is entirely optional. If you choose to use this form, please note that the form provides signature lines for you, the two witnesses whom you have selected and a notary public.

TO MY FAMILY, HEALTH CARE PROVIDER, AND ALL THOSE CONCERNED WITH MY CARE:

PRINT YOUR NAME

I, _____,
direct that you follow my wishes for care if I am in a terminal condition, my death is imminent, and I am unable to communicate my decisions about my medical care.

With respect to any life-sustaining treatment, I direct the following:

INITIAL THE STATEMENT THAT REFLECTS YOUR WISHES ABOUT LIFE-SUSTAINING TREATMENT

(Initial only one of the following optional options. If you do not agree with either of the following options, space is provided below for you to write your own instructions).

_____ If my death is imminent, I choose not to prolong my life. If life sustaining treatment has been started, stop it, but keep me comfortable and control my pain.

_____ Even if my death is imminent, I choose to prolong my life.

ADD PERSONAL
INSTRUCTIONS
(IF ANY)

_____ I choose neither of the above options, and here are my instructions should I become terminally ill and my death is imminent:

_____

_____

_____

(Artificial nutrition and hydration: food and water provided by means of a tube inserted into the stomach or intestine or needle into a vein.)

With respect to artificial nutrition and hydration, I direct the following

INITIAL THE
STATEMENT THAT
REFLECTS YOUR
WISHES ABOUT
ARTIFICIAL
NUTRITION AND
HYDRATION

(initial only one):

_____ If my death is imminent, I do not want artificial nutrition land hydration. If it has been started, stop it.

_____ Even if my death is imminent, I want artificial nutrition and hydration.

ORGAN DONATION
(OPTIONAL)

ORGAN DONATION (OPTIONAL)

Under South Dakota law, any individual 18 or older or an emancipated minor, by signing a written document, may donate all or any part of his body, the gift to take effect upon death.

The donor may amend or revoke a gift by: (1) A writing signed by the donor; or (2) Any other writing used to identify the individual as refusing to make an anatomical gift. During a terminal illness or injury, the refusal may be an oral statement or other form of communication if the statement is addressed to at least two adults, one of whom is disinterested.

Initial the line next to the statement below that best reflects your wishes. If you do not complete this section, your agent will have the authority to make a gift of a part of your body pursuant to law unless you give them notice that you do not want a gift made. The donation elections you make below survive your death.

_____ In the hope that I may help others, I hereby make this organ and tissue gift, if medically acceptable, to take effect upon my death. The words and marks (or notations) below indicate my desires. **Default** choice is (a).

I give:
(a) _____ any needed organ or tissue
(b) _____ only the following organs or tissues:

My donated organs and tissues may be used for:
_____ any legal purpose;
_____ transplantation or therapy,
_____ medical research;
_____ education

(c) _____ my body for anatomical study if needed.

_____ I do not want to make an organ or tissue donation and I do not want my agent or family to do so.

_____ I have already signed a written agreement or donor card regarding organ and tissue donation with the following individual or institution:

Name of individual/organization:_____

_____   _____
(your signature)   (date)

- -
(your address)

- -

- -
(type or print your signature)

INTIAL THE STATEMENT THAT REFLECTS YOUR WISHES

NAME OF INDIVIDUAL/ ORGANIZATION

SIGN AND DATE THE DOCUMENT THEN PRINT YOUR ADDRESS AND NAME

WITNESSING PROCEDURE

The declarant voluntarily signed this document in my presence.

Witness: _____

WITNESSES MUST SIGN AND PRINT THEIR ADDRESSES

Address: _____

_____

Witness: _____

Address: _____

_____

NOTARY (OPTIONAL)

THIS SECTION IS TO BE COMPLETED BY A NOTARY PUBLIC

On this the _____ day of _____, _____, the declarant,

_____, and

witnesses_____ and _____,

personally appeared before the undersigned officer and signed the foregoing instrument in my presence.

Dated this _____ day of _____, _____.

_____
Notary Public

My Commission expires: _____

© 2005 National Hospice and Palliative Care Organization 2008 Revised.

Courtesy of Caring Connections
1731 King St., Suite 100, Alexandria, VA 22314
www.caringinfo.org, 800/658-8898

You Have Filled Out Your Advance Directive, Now What?

1. Your South Dakota Durable Power of Attorney for Healthcare and South Dakota Living Will Declaration are important legal documents. Keep the original signed documents in a secure but accessible place. Do not put the original documents in a safe deposit box or any other security box that would keep others from having access to them.

2. Give photocopies of the signed originals to your attorney-in-fact and alternate attorney-in-fact, doctor(s), family, close friends, clergy and anyone else who might become involved in your healthcare. If you enter a nursing home or hospital, have photocopies of your documents placed in your medical records.

3. Be sure to talk to your attorney-in-fact and alternate, doctor(s), clergy, and family and friends about your wishes concerning medical treatment. Discuss your wishes with them often, particularly if your medical condition changes.

4. If you want to make changes to your documents after they have been signed and witnessed, you must complete new documents.

5. Remember, you can always revoke one or both of your South Dakota documents.

6. Be aware that your South Dakota documents will not be effective in the event of a medical emergency. Ambulance personnel are required to provide cardiopulmonary resuscitation (CPR) unless they are given a separate order that states otherwise. These orders, commonly called "non-hospital do-not-resuscitate orders," are designed for people whose poor health gives them little chance of benefiting from CPR. These orders must be signed by your physician and instruct ambulance personnel not to attempt CPR if your heart or breathing should stop.

   Currently not all states have laws authorizing non-hospital do-not-resuscitate orders. We suggest you speak to your physician for more information. **Caring Connections does not distribute these forms.**

Appendix A

Glossary

Advance directive - A general term that describes two kinds of legal documents, living wills and medical powers of attorney. These documents allow a person to give instructions about future medical care should he or she be unable to participate in medical decisions due to serious illness or incapacity. Each state regulates the use of advance directives differently.

Artificial nutrition and hydration – Artificial nutrition and hydration supplements or replaces ordinary eating and drinking by giving a chemically balanced mix of nutrients and fluids through a tube placed directly into the stomach, the upper intestine or a vein.

Brain death – The irreversible loss of all brain function. Most states legally define death to include brain death.

Capacity - In relation to end-of-life decision-making, a patient has medical decision making capacity if he or she has the ability to understand the medical problem and the risks and benefits of the available treatment options. The patient's ability to understand other unrelated concepts is not relevant. The term is frequently used interchangeably with competency but is not the same. Competency is a legal status imposed by the court.

Cardiopulmonary resuscitation - Cardiopulmonary resuscitation (CPR) is a group of treatments used when someone's heart and/or breathing stops. CPR is used in an attempt to restart the heart and breathing. It may consist only of mouth-to-mouth breathing or it can include pressing on the chest to mimic the heart's function and cause blood to circulate. Electric shock and drugs also are used frequently to stimulate the heart.

Do-Not-Resuscitate (DNR) order - A DNR order is a physician's written order instructing healthcare providers not to attempt cardiopulmonary resuscitation (CPR) in case of cardiac or respiratory arrest. A person with a valid DNR order will not be given CPR under these circumstances. Although the DNR order is written at the request of a person or his or her family, it must be signed by a physician to be valid. A non-hospital DNR order is written for individuals who are at home and do not want to receive CPR.

Emergency Medical Services (EMS): A group of governmental and private agencies that provide emergency care, usually to persons outside of healthcare facilities; EMS personnel generally include paramedics, first responders and other ambulance crew.

Healthcare agent: The person named in an advance directive or as permitted under state law to make healthcare decisions on behalf of a person who is no longer able to make medical decisions.

Hospice - Considered to be the model for quality, compassionate care for people facing a life-limiting illness or injury, hospice and palliative care involve a team-oriented approach to expert medical care, pain management, and emotional and spiritual support expressly tailored to the person's needs and wishes. Support is provided to the persons loved ones as well.

Intubation- Refers to "endotracheal intubation" the insertion of a tube through the mouth or nose into the trachea (windpipe) to create and maintain an open airway to assist breathing.

Life-sustaining treatment - Treatments (medical procedures) that replace or support an essential bodily function (may also be called life support treatments). Life-sustaining treatments include cardiopulmonary resuscitation, mechanical ventilation, artificial nutrition and hydration, dialysis, and other treatments.

Living will - A type of advance directive in which an individual documents his or her wishes about medical treatment should he or she be at the end of life and unable to communicate. It may also be called a "directive to physicians", "healthcare declaration," or "medical directive."

Mechanical ventilation - Mechanical ventilation is used to support or replace the function of the lungs. A machine called a ventilator (or respirator) forces air into the lungs. The ventilator is attached to a tube inserted in the nose or mouth and down into the windpipe (or trachea).

Medical power of attorney - A document that allows an individual to appoint someone else to make decisions about his or her medical care if he or she is unable to communicate. This type of advance directive may also be called a healthcare proxy, durable power of attorney for healthcare or appointment of a healthcare agent. The person appointed may be called a healthcare agent, surrogate, attorney-in-fact or proxy.

Palliative care - A comprehensive approach to treating serious illness that focuses on the physical, psychological, spiritual, and existential needs of the patient. Its goal is to achieve the best quality of life available to the patient by relieving suffering, and controlling pain and symptoms.

Power of attorney – A legal document allowing one person to act in a legal matter on another's behalf regarding financial or real estate transactions.

Respiratory arrest: The cessation of breathing - an event in which an individual stops breathing. If breathing is not restored, an individual's heart eventually will stop beating, resulting in cardiac arrest.

Surrogate decision-making - Surrogate decision-making laws allow an individual or group of individuals (usually family members) to make decisions about medical treatments for a patient who has lost decision-making capacity and did not prepare an advance directive. A majority of states have passed statutes that permit surrogate decision making for patients without advance directives.

Ventilator – A ventilator, also known as a respirator, is a machine that pushes air into the lungs through a tube placed in the trachea (breathing tube). Ventilators are used when a person cannot breathe on his or her own or cannot breathe effectively enough to provide adequate oxygen to the cells of the body or rid the body of carbon dioxide.

Withholding or withdrawing treatment - Forgoing life-sustaining measures or discontinuing them after they have been used for a certain period of time.

Appendix B

Legal & End-of-Life Care Resources Pertaining to Healthcare Advance Directives

LEGAL SERVICES

The South Dakota Adult Services and Aging (SDASA) website provides a list of resources and referral of legal information and advice. The services are for individuals 60 and older with low to moderate incomes.

The website can assist older individuals to get legal information and advice on most issues, including:
- Advance Directives and Healthcare Planning
- Living Wills and Trusts
- Power of Attorney
- Civil issues and more

- Must be 60 and older
- Free for individuals with low to moderate incomes

Visit their website at: http://www.state.sd.us/social/asa/Services/legal.htm

OR

Call toll free: 1-866-854-5465 or 605-773-3656

END-OF-LIFE SERVICES

The South Dakota Adult Services and Aging (SDASA) provide a variety of services and programs for disabled adults and older individuals with low to moderate incomes. In-home services are available to those who need assistance.

SDASA resources and services include, but are not limited to:
- Adult Day Care
- Respite
- Home maker services
- Food program
- Information and referrals and more

- Must be 60 and older
- Free for individuals with low to moderate incomes

Visit their website for more information about the services:
http://www.state.sd.us/social/asa/Services/index.htm

OR

Call toll free: 1-866-854-5465 or 605-773-3656

217

The Empty Chair

A man's daughter had asked the local minister to come and pray with her father. When the minister arrived, he found the man lying in bed with his head propped up on two pillows.

An empty chair sat beside his bed. The minister assumed that the old fellow had been informed of his visit. "I guess you were expecting me," he said. "No, who are you?" said the father. The minister told him his name and then remarked, "I see the empty chair and figured you knew I was going to show up."

"Oh, yeah, the chair," said the bedridden father. "Would you mind closing the door?" Puzzled, the minister shut the door. "I have never told anyone this, not even my daughter," said the man. "But all of my life I have never known how to pray. At church I used to hear the pastor talk about prayer, but it went right over my head. I abandoned any attempt at prayer," the old man continued, "until one day about four years ago my best friend said to me, 'Johnny, prayer is just a simple matter of having a conversation with Jesus. Here is what I suggest. Sit down in a chair, place an empty chair in front of you and in faith, see Jesus on the chair. It's not spooky because he promised, "I'll be with you always." Then just speak to him in the same way you are doing with me right now.'

"So, I tried it and I've liked it so much that I do it a couple of hours every day. I'm careful though. If my daughter saw me talking to an empty chair, she'd either have a nervous breakdown or send me off to the funny farm."

The minister was deeply moved by the story and encouraged the old man to continue on the journey. Then he prayed with him. Anointed him with oil, and returned to the church.

Two nights later, the daughter called to tell the minister that her daddy had died that afternoon. "Did he die in peace?" he asked. "Yes, and when I left the room about two o'clock, he called me over to his bedside and told me he loved me and kissed me on the cheek. When I returned an hour later, I was informed he had died. But there was something strange about his death. Apparently, just before Daddy died, he leaned over and rested his head on the chair beside his bed. What do you make of that?"

The minister wiped a tear from his eye and said, "I wish we could all go like that."

Thanks to friend Ken Wagner, who sent this to me via email. The source is http:/www.moytura.com/reflections/the-empty-chair.htm.

25

Sex, Companionship, and Marriages in Nursing-Homes

Can we agree that, as human beings, sexual feelings, thoughts, and actions are a human normal behavior? Then would you agree that there can be these same sexual behaviors, feelings, and thoughts in a nursing-home? The answer is, yes, of course. The only persons horrified at two consenting adults having sex in the nursing-home is the staff and the families.

One married woman, whose roommate was her husband, came by the nurse's station with such a sad face. The Charge Nurse, Rena, asked her what the problem was. The Elder said nothing, but simply bent her finger in a limp manner as if to say, "No sex." The charge nurse and I (as the social worker) chuckled and then concocted a little scheme. I went out and bought a sheer sexy nightgown for her. The "gift" was placed on her bed. Next day, we asked if "things" were a bit better. The answer was a broad smile.

I say men never lose the desire for sex, even at the age of 105. Nurses often report men reaching for their breast, pinching bottoms, or having an erection during personal care, and I was the chosen one to have a little chit-chat with them.

However, one woman left her bed every night and paid a visit to several men in the facility. The men, interestingly, were irate, and, again, I had the privilege to talk with the lady about her "nightly visits."

There are couples in most nursing-homes who just wish to sit and hold hands. One couple decided to marry. The lady had money. Her family vehemently objected. The gentleman had no money. His family thought it was a great idea. He bought her a ring; however, the marriage never took place. They just enjoyed one another's companionship.

Companionship is one thing, but "fondling" while in sitting areas is a situation that needs a bit of counseling. It must be determined if both parties are consenting adults and then the touching must be in the privacy of their rooms.

When two love bugs are identified by staff, usually the staff is very careful about entering their room without the traditional knock on the door and asking for permission to enter.

An elderly male volunteer came to the facility almost every day and was loved by every lady. He would often be seen walking down the hallways with his arm around a female resident. One LPN thought this was inappropriate. With the need to be needed, loved, and touched, I felt the LPN was out of touch herself, not understanding the real needs of our elders. And I said so.

As a social worker and administrator who walks the floor five or six times a day to talk with residents, staff, families, and any volunteers, I am very aware of any improprieties that may occur. Holding hands, walking arm in arm, a hug, or a kiss are just not one of my concerns.

One day I was walking down a hallway toward the dining room when a tall, attractive male resident came up to me and said, "sure would like to wear one of those earrings you got on."

Since I wear clip-ons I quickly slipped one gold ear ring off and placed it on his ear lobe. We continued to walk down the hallway, arm in arm, giggling and laughing. Then I heard him say softly, "I guess we're engaged now . . . but I don't know what we are engaged in."

And then there was a wedding in one facility that brought the news media. Two lovebirds decided to be married in the facility chapel. Families were invited, a resident played the organ, a staff member sang, all residents were invited. The service was videotaped. A wonderful reception was hosted by the bride and groom and the couple took off for parts unknown. But of course they came back in a few days looking the part of a happy couple.

Several months later this couple decided to transfer to another facility to be closer to family. The last I heard was that they divorced. Perhaps, they, like so many other elder couples, would have been better off just being boyfriend and girlfriend.

26

Smoking Habits in Nursing-Homes

Smoking in nursing-homes has always been and still is controversial for both residents and staff. I do not smoke. However, I have always been very sensitive toward smokers, realizing the addictive properties of tobacco. One facility would not admit any elders if they smoked. Most facilities provide outdoor smoking rooms, which I have found to be very uncomfortable and often cold and drafty in the colder climates.

In nursing-homes of today, with no spiritual therapies, residents have very little to look forward to except TV, sugary snacks, beer, bingo and smoking. Tobacco must be addressed as an addiction that needs special therapy. For untrained staff to work with an addict is to increase the level of agitation for the resident. Encouraging residents to quit is nonproductive.

The benefits of tobacco can be a type of self-medication, reducing anxiety and helping to relax. Unless the facility or the family has a therapist who works with addicts, the smoker should be left alone except when endangering others.

What most smokers do not know is that they are not addicted to tobacco, but the chemicals and sugar that coats the tobacco. One brand that is nonaddictive and chemical free is the Natural American Spirit.

In a large Midwestern veterans campus, smoking and drinking were part of the day's activities. A problem arose when one veteran, who was on continuous oxygen, refused to stop smoking in his room. The nurses told him he would not only blow himself up but all his buddies, too. I was called to intervene. I told him that if we found him smoking in his room and endangering others, he could be evicted. Several hours later, I received a call from the nurses' station to go to the window and look towards the building next to me. Would you believe, this veteran had taken the screen off his window, was leaning out the window, smoking. When I went back to his room his response was, "Well, you said I could not smoke IN my room and I'm not!" I laughed and he laughed. I was outsmarted by one of the best. When the little power pull was over, the veteran went to the smoking room, which was supervised.

Another resident smoked in his room, which was filled with old newspapers and magazines. I threatened him several times to just clean out his room. Finally the showdown came when I called the Fire Marshal, who had conveniently neglected to write up this fire hazard for years. The room was cleaned out, and Mr. Smoker smoked his last cigarette in his room. He went outside with everyone else.

William Campbell Douglass II, MD wrote the following story about a friend's grandmother:

> Granny was one hundred years old and in perfect health. Her children thought she needed a check up, which would be her first. The only advice her doctor could provide her was to give up smoking, which she had been rolling her own for over fifty years.
>
> To keep the peace, she agreed to cut back on the number of cigars she smoked daily. True to her word, she, indeed, cut back on the number smoked. What she didn't tell her children was that each of her new stogies was now ten inches long and as fat as a Polish sausage. She lived to the ripe old age of 106.

27

Railing Against Bed Rails and Restraints

Restraints are a raging debate in nursing-homes concerning the use of soft restraints for residents in wheelchairs and the use of bed rails during sleeping hours.

Many families have insisted restraints be used to prevent falls. Their requests and occasionally a threat of a lawsuit falls on deaf ears of regulators. The nursing-home industry has valiantly tried many alternative options, such as alarms placed on the residents clothes so when they try to get up, the alarm goes off. Half bed rails are used only for residents to assist themselves up while in bed. The geri-chair, which provides more movement, is still considered a restraint. Staff takes off any soft restraint during activities and while eating, which provides more movement, and then we have the Broda chair, which tips back so the resident cannot fall out and comfortable easy chairs in rooms and lounges. Lower beds have been initiated. The placement of mats next to the lowered bed are another alternative. I have personally assisted residents up from the "mat" position and will say, like most nursing staff, it is very difficult, especially with an obese resident. The mats are also difficult to keep clean, and it is very difficult to do personal cares with the mat in the bathroom or against a window. A recent Danish study tested external hip protective pads in a nursing-home where hip fractures had been extremely common. The risk reduction was 60 percent.

In *Annals of Internal Medicine*, it has been reported there are about 1,800 fatal falls each year in nursing-homes. Nursing-home residents also have a disproportionately high incidence of hip fractures than those elders residing in the community. Hip fractures usually lead to further functional decline, depression, feelings of helplessness, social isolation, use of physical or chemical restraints by physicians' orders, which they believe will prevent elders from falling again.

Frail, high-risk persons living in nursing-homes tend to have a higher incidence of falls caused by gait disorders, weakness, and confusion, with weakness and confusion accounting for 25 percent of reported cases. Gait disorders affect 20 percent to 50 percent of elderly persons, with nearly three quarters of nursing-home residents requiring assistance with ambulation. Even among the healthier Elders, their score on strength tests are 20 percent to 40 percent lower in comparison to young adults.

Much of the weakness seen in nursing-home residents stems from prolonged bed rest, limited physical activity or chronic debilitating medical conditions, decreased visual acuity, and drug side effects. Drugs frequently have side effects that result in impaired thinking and gait instability, especially drugs such as sedatives, antidepressants, antihypertensives, diuretics, vasodilators, and B-blockers.

Accidents or falls stemming from environmental hazards account for 16 percent of reported injuries attributed to decreased lower extremity strength or poor posture control while reaching or bending. Most falls occurred during transferring from a bed, chair, or wheelchair. Falls have also been reported to increase when nurse staffing is low, such as during breaks and at shift changes.

To address the fifteen-minute breaks is to acknowledge a little known fact that these breaks are not a regulation but a privilege of the facility. If resident's call lights are on and resident's needs have not been met, the charge nurse is not to permit CNAs and CMAs to take the fifteen-minute break. The sole purpose of working in a nursing-home is to care for the residents, not demanding fifteen-minute breaks. Smokers usually take longer than the fifteen minutes, which can be interpreted as elder abuse, neglect, or abandonment. The thirty-minute lunch break is a regulation but can be shortened in case of an emergency. Staff will then be paid for the entire thirty minutes.

To alleviate the lack of staff supervision during shift changes the following policy can be enforced by the DON and Administrator:

- Implement twelve-hour shifts from 6 am to 6 pm. (only two shift changes).
- Eight-hour shifts should begin at 5:55, 1:55, and 9:55 to permit the oncoming shift to walk into every resident room with those going off shift to discuss any issues, thus creating an environment of safety and knowledge of the resident's condition during shift changes.

In several facilities the DON and I would warn and warn that only one CNA could take a break at a time; however, warnings and writeups were often ignored. It takes constant vigilance to keep everyone on task. The DON, charge nurses, and administrator do not have time for unending paperwork. Their "soul" purpose must be in the care of the residents.

In one large veterans facility, mattresses were so short and ill fitting, blankets were folded at the ends and sides to keep the resident safe. And this facility received a "deficiency-free" survey. As I knew of dozens of deficiencies, I asked the surveyors how they could say this facility was deficiency free. The answer was, "If we cite deficiencies, then this state-owned facility would have to correct the deficiencies and that would cost taxpayer money." So much for state favored facilities and discrimination against the private and corporately owned facilities.

With all the alternatives used, nurses can still be seen running at the speed of lightning to prevent a resident from falling. And falls are still happening.

Today, with 2.5 million hospital and nursing-home beds in use in the United States, there have been 691 incidents of patients and residents caught, trapped, entangled, or strangled in beds with rails. The Food and Drug Administration reported the statistics over a period of twenty years. Of these reports, 413 people died, 120 had a nonfatal injury, and 158 were not injured because staff intervened. Most patients (residents) were frail, elderly, or confused. That is thirty-five incidents per year in both hospitals and nursing-homes. Although these incidents are horrifying, regulators created the "no restraints" requirements without providing alternatives. Bean bags were one alternative.

However, surveyors decreed them to be undignified. In several facilities, the "fall prevention" units were implemented, where additional CNAs worked and were specifically trained to use creative methods of preventing falls.

Residents get up and out of their chairs in a split second. Even with a chair or bed alarm and fully staffed, falls are going to occur. Again, the most promising alternative is to strengthen the body through natural therapies.

I contend that daily passive and/or active exercises would strengthen the bones and muscles of residents. For passive exercises is the Chi machine, physical therapy, an exercise chair, or gentle massage on the hips and legs to stimulate circulation. Imperative is fresh air, sunshine, full spectrum lights in every room, and nutritious food and vitamins targeted to build bones and muscles. The Rife machine also is useful in targeting weakened areas of the body. None of the above therapies need a licensed, certified staff member. Family members could easily assist with these nonharmful, noninvasive therapies. What would the benefit be for elders not to have a fear of falling or in the degree of pain or hospitalization following a fall and at what cost savings to the taxpayer? If 50 percent of falls could be alleviated through the strengthening of leg and back muscles, how many nurse hours could be saved?

28

The Hard Subject of Constipation

Constipation is a serious and degrading malady for residents in nursing-homes. I have witnessed pain, the degradation of a resident digging one self out, and the horror of having a nursing staff dig hardened feces out.

The ideal is that every nursing-home resident empty his/her bowels two to three times a day, usually following a meal.

I heard nursing staff say that it is normal to have bowels move every two to three days! Think of the putrefied food mass impacted in the bowels, leaking into the entire system to poison and destroy! Is it a wonder that the elderly suffer from bowel cancers! And have you ever wondered why there is such an odor in nursing-homes? And why so many nursing-home residents have bad breath? The answer is usually from the rotting of food in the bowels when the bowels do not empty every day.

Nursing-staff time, resident pain, and degradation can be averted through diet, massage, castor oil packs, and resident attitude. In order to have normal bowel function properly, the daily diet must contain a majority of whole grain foods, vegetables as well as fresh fruits, oils (not fats), such as olive and flax oils, at least four glasses of water per day, and exercises, and any movement that allows the pelvis to move and the spine to be flexed.

To assist with daily bowel movements, incapacitated residents must have weekly spinal massages with monthly osteopathic or chiropractic treatments.

When daily bowel movements do not occur, another gentle method to utilize is the castor oil pack. The warmed castor oil, placed over the bowel area for one hour, is picked up by the lymphatics of the skin, carried to the deeper lymphatics, which in turn assists the peristaltic movements within the bowel itself.

A castor oil pack is made by soaking a flannel cloth with castor oil, placing the pack directly on the skin over the bowel area. A heating pad, wrapped in Saran Wrap to prevent the soaking of the pad with castor oil, is placed over the flannel cloth. The heating pad is turned on low. The pad stays in place for one hour. As the pad is removed, the skin is washed with a mild warm baking soda-water solution in order to stop the action of the castor oil. The castor oil cloth may then be wrapped in the Saran Wrap or plastic bag and used again as needed. The castor oil treatment may be repeated once a day for three days.

I endorse the use of Dr. Miller's Holy Tea herbs and herbs such as senna as gentle methods of keeping nursing-home residents free of constipation.

According to Edgar Cayce readings, to avoid constipation, one must not hold on to anger, resentment, fear, or any negative emotion such as grudges, animosities, or hatred, which causes the body to tighten up and not eliminate properly. Here, positive affirmations, thoughts, attitudes, serving others, loving self, understanding life's purpose, prayer, and meditations are essential for nursing-home residents' proper elimination.

The key players in keeping nursing-home residents free from constipation are dietary, the massage therapist, social services, and, lastly, if all else fails, nursing staff.

Colon Therapy

Natural health professionals are well aware that the bowel itself is the most abused organ in the human body due to the fact that hardened fecal matter remaining in the colon creates toxins that are thrown throughout the entire body. The fecal matter consists of not only new wastes but wastes that are decaying.

Over seven million Americans, many in nursing-homes, suffer from bowel abnormalities due to the eating of soft, overprocessed foods.

Hardened fecal matter makes it difficult for the body to adsorb mineral and nutrients through the intestinal wall, thus causing a nutritional deficiency no matter how good the eating habits or how many supplements are taken.

Colonics are part of preventive care. It is imperative that nursing-home residents receive a colonic upon admission and again each month for two months and yearly thereafter.

Colonics are not painful, nonharmful and are often called a high enema. The procedure takes about forty minutes.

Colonic equipment could be an investment for the nursing-home. At this time, colonists receive training but are not licensed. Nursing staff or massage therapists could administer colon therapies. The use of alternative methods to alleviate constipation is not only one of gentleness for the resident, but would be a time saver for nursing.

29

Vaccines and the Immune System

I have often been asked about flu shots. I have never advised an elder not to take the shots nor have I condoned them. The following is a synopsis of an article by Dr. Joseph Mercola:

> Vaccines, all vaccines, are immune suppressing; that is, they depress the immune functions. The chemicals in the vaccines depress the immune system; viruses present depress immune function and foreign DNA/RNA from animal tissues depress immunity. You are trading a total immune system depression, which is your only defense against all known disease, for a temporary immunity against the one disease you believe you are being protected from. The trade off is the risk of getting many more diseases. The best method to protect yourself from diseases is to strengthen the immune system by eating properly and getting all the essential vitamins and minerals that the body needs.

I personally take one small homeopathic pellet before any flu breakout at a cost of $2.00 per pellet. The decision to receive a flu shot must be carefully researched by residents and their families, not through scare tactics by the pharmaceutical industry.

30

Vitamins and Minerals

My experiences with nursing-home residents wanting to take vitamins is one of the greatest shams in the care of the elderly. First, one must have a physician's order for a "multiple" vitamin, and then there must be a physician's order if the resident wishes to take his/her own brand and the resident must be able to take the vitamins him/herself. Medicare and Medicaid do not pay for most vitamins.

Vitamins were developed when it was discovered that certain foods could cure specific diseases, such as the use of lemons and limes (the C vitamin) in the prevention of scurvy; vitamin D to prevent rickets; iodine to prevent goiter; and iron to prevent anemia.

Vitamins are concentrated, isolated compounds directed towards the prevention of a specific disease or to boost the immune system to fight off ill health.

The vitamin industry is a billion-dollar-a-year business. And not all vitamins are "pure" and useful to the body. It is my personal opinion that the majority of vitamins are useless.

Nursing-home residents should never take vitamins unless the resident has been tested for what their body needs. This can be done through hair analysis or through muscle testing provided by a natural health care professional. Muscle testing or with the use of a pendulum can be given by any staff person or family member.

There is no need for the state department to control the use of vitamin intake by demanding an allopathic physician's order, for the majority of allopathics have had no training in the testing for vitamin needs. Statistics prove there has never been an overdose of vitamins taken by a nursing-home resident that resulted in death or a negative reaction. Nor are hospital beds full of patients who have had an adverse reaction to vitamins.

Elderly nursing-home residents need vitamins and minerals on a daily basis, primarily because the food in nursing-homes is overly processed, boiled, canned, refined, chemicalized, formaldahydized, colorized, nonflavorized, imitationalized, additivized, and homogenized. With all the "izeds," nutritional deficiencies in the elderly are not only possible but probable which results in multiple diseases, heavier care and additional cost to the taxpayer. Ask yourself, who is benefiting from nursing-home resident's ill health?

Of utmost importance is vitamin D (sunshine, which is free), chondriton/glucosome for the building of bones, calcios (calcium spread on crackers) which is easily assimilated and is taken in place of milk products and vitamins and minerals for mental alertness.

Let's check out inexpensive vitamins, such as sunlight.

The Healing Power of the Sun

An Activity Director again and again defied my request to take residents outside in the sun following breakfast. This facility was very fortunate to have lovely French doors off the dining room leading to a beautiful garden with walking paths, flowers, trees, bird houses, a bridge over a stream, and a pagoda, where residents could sit and enjoy the fresh air. I send my forgiveness and peace to her wherever she is as she just did not realize the importance of the natural healing of the sun. It is of utmost importance that all staff be knowledgeable in the many aspects of alternative therapies. For this activity director, she just did not realize the importance.

In almost every nursing-home, elders rarely feel the healing power of the sun. Most are never taken outside.

The human race evolved under the sun and for thousands of years benefited from its heat and light. A little more than fifty years ago, doctors in Europe and North America used sunlight treatments for a number of diseases. In fact, sunlight not only increases one's energy and general well being, sunlight also

- Disinfects the skin and triggers the manufacture of Vitamin D, which is essential for healthy bones and the immune system.
- Lowers your cholesterol.
- Treats multiple sclerosis and osteoporosis.
- Is a preventative for cancer.
- Lowers blood pressure.
- Increases the value of exercise.
- Improves the body's ability to detoxify.
- A light tan on exposed skin is a preventive against melanoma.

Nursing-home residents should be outside for no less than thirty minutes daily without eyeglasses and without any sunguard, preferably while doing exercises in the early morning or evening sunshine.

Facilities in northern states are encouraged to purchase a suntan board from Mercola.com. Suntan board treatments for every resident would be one time a day. A suntan board consists of eight full spectrum lights, six feet tall and three feet wide. The resident stands or sits in front of the lights, with protective eye coverings, for about fifteen minutes. A perfect place would be in the shower room for total body sunlight.

In northern states during winter seasons, it is imperative for all nursing-home residents to have in their room full spectrum lamps that are positioned over their bed or used as a reading lamp. Daily sun and full spectrum lighting is often used to treat depression.

In one facility I purchased full spectrum lights for my office, the business office, and the nurse's station. Corporate officers denied payment, so I paid for the lights out of my own pocket because I knew those of us working all day in poorly lit offices can easily become depressed and lethargic. I encouraged families to purchase full spectrum lamps for their elder.

Family, friends, and volunteers should be encouraged to

take a resident or two for daily walks in the sun and fresh air, selecting those who have no family and never get outside. Sit with them in the sun, just hold their hand. You need say nothing. Their spirit knows you are there.

Then who may tell the rose where and when to bloom? For it takes from whatever may be its surroundings, and when encompassed even by man it does the best possible to be the beauty, to be the joy, and to give out that which is pleasing in the service to God. Thy whole lesson is in that.

—Edgar Cayce reading 2778-2

31

The Psychological / Spiritual Reason for Alzheimer's

Research and statements by professionals has revealed many and varied reasons for the development of Alzheimer's. It is said that aluminum is found in the brain of those with Alzheimers, and it has been suggested that one is to avoid all aluminum products such as food in aluminum cans, cookware, and products such as fluoridated toothpaste and mouthwash. Others say that there has been brain damage from falls or an accident. The medical profession has targeted strokes, illegal drugs, lack of oxygen for those who are obese and do not exercise. Natural health professionals target prescription drugs, an acidic diet with too much sugar, white refined flour products, dairy products, vaccinations, and silver and mercury fillings in the teeth as likely causes of Alzheimer's. Then there is the theory that the brain has atrophied from lack of water.

There are approximately 4.5 million victims of Alzheimer's in United States. Many nursing-homes have designated one wing for those diagnosed with Alzheimers due to their degree of confusion and often violent behaviors. Nurses who work in Alzheimer's units are specially trained to be calm, patient, and accepting of the multitude of behaviors.

These units are usually kept quiet. Meals are served on individual tables, and snacks are available at any time. One unit was situated so residents could walk around and around and never have to be stopped by a locked door. This seemed to quiet the mind. One facility had a door that opened into a garden area, where residents could pass the time of day. A clothes line was put up so dish towels could be hung out to dry by the residents who were doing their own dishes. At times, nurses reported that if they tried to take some residents outdoors, their confusion worsened.

An LPN played old-time rag tunes on the piano and always drew residents around the piano. I never saw aromatherapy, massage, or homeopathy used in an Alzheimers unit.

During a stay at the Oak House in Phoenix, I asked the question, "What is the psychological or spiritual reason for Alzheimers?" Dr. McCarey, Medical Director for the Oak House, answered that he felt the person was, in his/her life time or in a past life time, the head of the family, or a controller, or was in a seat of authority. As the person aged, he/she saw this authority fading away. Thus the person shut down the brain so as not to see or feel what was happening.

If this is true, the treatments provided must be of total love, compassion, soft music, and alternative therapies such as reflexology, touch, recordings of the Lord's Prayer, prayers, meditations, affirmations, sun therapy, and walks outdoors as tolerated.

I have witnessed the use of prescription drugs and seen Alzheimers residents behaviors go from quiet to the point we had to call for police back-up. It is only my opinion, but the less prescription drugs the better, for if the reason is psychological, then Alzheimer's residents should be treated as such. Let's take a look at this next true story:

> Once upon a time there was a retired businesswoman who had moved to Virginia Beach, Virginia. In searching for volunteer work, she was asked to come to the house of a very wealthy gentleman to look after his needs for a few hours every day.
>
> She was horrified to see the man in a cage, completely nude, with food strewn over the cage floor. He was evidently deranged (an Alzheimer's victim?). Each day she sat patiently near his cage, praying for him. Many months passed. The caregivers began to notice a change in his behavior. Soon the man began to dress himself. Then he ate his food using utensils. There came a moment when he began to talk to the volunteer. The day came when he no longer needed the caged environment.

The volunteer was so curious as to her experience that she requested a reading from the medical intuitive Edgar Cayce. She was shocked to hear the man was her husband in a former life. He was a wealthy man in a prior life; however, he had physically and mentally abused his wife, keeping her in a caged, controlled environment. He was now reaping what he had sown. The retired volunteer, his past-life wife, had entered his life again with prayers and patience to release him from his karmic cage. Think on these things. How many elders enter life in a nursing-home for one purpose, and that is to release *us or them* from a karmic debt?

32

Nursing-Home Departments

Are Housekeepers Social Workers In Disguise?

Housekeepers not only spend seven-and-a-half hours a day pushing a mop, changing buckets of dirty water every third resident room, cleaning windows, swabbing out toilets, disinfecting rooms and hall railings, picking up trash, moving furniture, taking down curtains to be washed, sweeping down cobwebs, keeping their carts clean, waxing and buffing floors, vacuuming and cleaning spots on carpets, putting away supplies, creating work schedules, and sometimes painting. The housekeeping department head does inventory, ordering, hiring and firing, attends requested meetings, and all housekeepers attend required in-services. In one state, housekeepers, with state mandated training, transport residents to and from meals and assist with feeding residents.

Their hands are often rough from the water and chemicals they use, and they occasionally will suffer a back injury from trying to lift furniture that is far too heavy for them.

Housekeepers are a quiet bunch. They go about their duties, rarely complaining. They are happy over a new cart! However, I discovered their secret. Housekeepers are really social workers in disguise. They are loved by the residents. Elders will talk with housekeepers with ease, sometimes telling them how they really feel, their desires, about family and friends long gone. Housekeepers often come into my office and whisper what a resident has just told them, as they feel I needed to know or sometimes remind me of someone's birthday (resident or staff) or if something needs to be done, such as a sign put up. And, of course, there was the day I misspelled a word in a sign and who could hardly wait to tell me? Of course, a housekeeper!

I rarely directed housekeepers, as the department heads were very good managers. However, housekeepers have legitimate complaints.

This all too true email was found on the Internet from a housekeeper:

> I work at a local nursing-home as a housekeeper. Our Administrative staff is so rude, along with the rest of the staff. They expect us to do work that is not in our job description . . . for example, picking up trash that they throw down on purpose, leaving BM diapers on the floor or thrown in the wastebasket and saying things like, "Oh that's okay, the housekeeper will get it." We already do part of the CNAs job, also resident escort, and make sure they are turned every few hours, reporting abuse and neglect, falls, and then are expected to clean up spills that the CNAs do or it will be there all day. We get treated like we are no one, but can you imagine what the place would look like if not for us? Our job is as important as theirs so why do they look down on us?

And then there was one set of housekeepers who decided to have fun (while on duty) by calling on-duty staff via phone. When the staff answered, the housekeepers hung up. One staff had a very sick husband and received one of these anonymous calls. She nearly fainted because she thought her husband was in trouble and was trying to call her. When I found out, I placed both housekeepers on probation. Did that stop them? No. Several more incidents, and both were fired. However, over thirty years, most housekeepers are like angels, just doing their work and are rarely recognized for what they do.

The email found on the Internet is not an exaggeration. I have heard and been shown nurses throwing disposables and needles in wastebaskets, spilling medications on the floor and never wiping up, and not flushing the BM down in the hopper room, not getting a mop out for a urine spill, just letting it dry for the housekeepers when they come in the next day.

This is why I not only acknowledge housekeepers with a hug and a smile every day and continually say thank you, but also I have so much respect for the work they do. Yes, they should have paid workshops to attend and must be acknowledged with tiny gifts, cards, and gift certificates for a massage one time a year. I acknowledge the fact that there should be a nursing-home Housekeepers Day when they are honored guests. The administrators can do the housekeeping for the day. I will guarantee you the residents would get great joy out of seeing the administrator scrubbing the floors!

Chemicals Used in Nursing-Homes

It's time we talked about (of all things) the chemical called chlorine. As consumers, we are most familiar with chlorine's role as a bleaching agent for paper and as an ingredient in household cleaners.

In October 1993, the American Public Health Association unanimously passed a resolution urging American industry to stop using chlorine. Dioxins, a byproduct of the paper industry's using chlorine to whiten paper products, are believed to be the most carcinogenic chemicals known to science, finding dioxins to be 300,000 times more potent as a carcinogen than DDT, which was banned in the United States in 1972.

Recent research has conclusively linked dioxins to cancer and immune system breakdowns. Dioxins are not only in our food chain but in nursing-homes as chlorines used in dishwashers, housekeeping supplies, in laundry, toilet paper and tissues, napkins, disposable diapers, decorations used by Activity Directors, and in paper used in business offices.

Firms that offer non chlorine bleaches are Bi-O-Kleen, Country Save, Ecover, Seventh Generation, and Earth Friendly. Unbleached paper products are offered by Earth Friendly, Frontier Herbs, Green Forest, If You Care, Natural Brew, and Seventh Generation. Nursing-home residents and staff deserve a healthy environment.

Let us take a moment and examine antibacterial soaps. Researchers have proven that antibacterial soaps are no more effective against germs than common soap. Frequent handwashing is the answer. The massive use of antibacterial soap is leading to stronger drug-resistant germs and mutated bacterial strains. Myron Genel, a chairman of the AMA's Counsel on Scientific Affairs: "There's no evidence that they do any good, and there's reason to suspect that they could be contributing to problems. Antibacterial soap kills beneficial bacteria on the skin, and it has the potential to also get into the body and cause harm. Not all bacteria is bad!" Big pharma is, again, cashing in on antibacterial products at great expense to the nursing-home industry and to the detriment of nursing-home residents (Crusador, March/April 2008, 41, p. 18).

All staff and families must be willing to assist in housekeeping chores. If a spill occurs, wipe it up. If a wastepaper basket needs to be emptied, take it to the dumpster. Families must keep the residents' closet cleaned out as I have found it near-impossible to clean when closets are stuffed full of unused items and ill-fitting clothes, and a year's supply of holiday decorations.

The best gift for housekeepers is hand lotion with olive oil in it or a massage. Housekeepers usually make minimum wage.

Laundering Money

An elderly gentleman was brought to the facility in the early evening by the local police. Neighbors had called because they had not seen any movement in the house for several days. The police found the man on the floor. When brought in, his clothes were ragged and dirty. The nurses undressed him in preparation for a bath. I took his clothes to the small washer in the laundry room and started up the machine. The man was furious telling us he had money sown into his clothes. I panicked. What I found in the washer was several hundred dollars in small denominations. Fishing the money out of the water, I took the money to the man and told him to count it and then I would dry it in my office and put it in the safe for the night. His son was called and informed of the incident.

I never thought I would be involved in laundering money . . . but I must confess, I am guilty.

It takes a strong stomach to spend even a little time in a soil room of a laundry that handles medical waste. Laundry workers must pick up, sort, wash, dry, fold, and deliver hundreds of garments every day. Linens are often soiled with blood and fecal matter, and at times linens contain needles, syringes, and residents' personal items such as rings, watches, money, and dentures.

Personal clothes are often unmarked. Because of unmarked clothing, laundry personnel are accused of losing clothes. Then families purchase clothes and bed throws that are to be dry cleaned, and, of course, when picked up by laundry personnel, there is a good chance the clothes will be shrunk and the facility pays for replacements.

Laundry employees work hard, and it's not only dirty work but also hot and heavy pulling wet clothes from washers. At times, when I would go into the laundry, I could not find the laundry gal because she was hidden with ten feet of clothes and linens. My favorite hiding place was in the laundry room helping to fold linens. But I only saw the end product.

While the risk of disease predominantly affects those working in laundry rooms, there is always the risk of ergonomic problems and heat hazards from the huge dryers.

Department heads have their own little idiosyncrasies. For example, Leona would not hire anyone unless she checked out the laundry hanging on the applicant's clothesline.

One department head started to mark the large container of laundry powder, as she felt it was disappearing. Several weeks of investigation brought forth that a night nurse was bringing her family clothes to the facility to wash and dry.

In a facility that had a serious financial problem, the laundry department head was bringing her knitting with her to work. I, again, investigated and found the system was a time waster, so hours were changed and hours cut much to consternation of the community.

In one facility, a husband of a dietary cook was coming in at 5 p.m. to work until 8 p.m. in laundry. Both the husband and the wife got off duty at 8 p.m. but not before they were spotted taking boxes of food with them. I let the husband go without any accusation—just simply that I was changing the system. As an administrator, did I just solve the immediate symptom but not the moral problem? What would you have done?

In another facility the administrator came out every evening one block from the facility, with a pair of binoculars. Linens were not only disappearing, but staff had reported they had seen linens marked with the facility name being sold at a garage sale. The administrator caught not only the laundry worker but the maintenance man handing linens out a back window of the facility. They were both fired; however, no charges were filed.

A newly hired laundry worker lasted three days. When I inquired as to what had happened, the department head said that a resident had left $20 in a jacket pocket. The jacket was washed by the new hire. The money was never found. The facility reimbursed the resident.

Family and volunteers can help in the laundry area by checking clothes that are unmarked, keeping a maximum of five sets of clothes in the closet, packing away or donating excess clothing, or throwing away clothes that no longer fit or stained and ragged. Families need to take their loved one's clothes home to be laundered. Before any clothes are taken out of the facility, the family or volunteer must document and sign the intake inventory sheet, which is located in the back of the resident's medical chart. Ask the Social Services Director for assistance or leave a note posted on the residents' bulletin board. Laundry staff usually make minimum wage.

Business Managers

Heads down, always writing, typing, computing, figuring, answering the phone, faxing, copying and answering questions. Today, the business manager is often involved in payroll, Medicaid, Medicare, and insurances. Business managers are, for the most part, competent, friendly, intelligent, well organized persons. However, not all have a halo on their heads.

I took one business manager out of a closet room, gave her a well-deserved office, and an increase in wage because I saw her degree of dedication to her job. For my reward, she became angry and resentful because she felt she needed to be paid the same as an administrator. She manipulated the monthly budget so that if I did not carefully check it, it would get me in trouble with the nursing-home board. Eventually, being a home town gal, she assisted the board in getting me fired.

Another secretary spent her time with a board member every morning over coffee, telling him everything that was going on in the nursing-home. The board member never came to the administrator. When surveyors checked the Resident Trust Fund and found questionable activity, the secretary broke into wails and cries, so the surveyors did not continue auditing the books. However, when she left her position, with my encouragement, we found the Resident Trust Fund short by several thousand dollars, and our postage expenses went down 100 percent. The board member (with whom she sat visiting every day) simply told me to take the money out of the general fund, replace the monies, and write to the families that "we" had made an error. Who lost in this one?

Another business manager was taking classes to become the nursing-home administrator. I was kept in the dark when first hired. I resigned when I discovered the plot. Several years later she was fired. Karma?

All the attributes of a good business manager were exhibited in "Pat." Always on time, organized, keeping the administrator on course, very knowledgeable, and, most of all, with a smile and acceptance of others.

Business managers need a large office with ample space for files and a table to work on special projects. The office needs a window, full spectrum lights, and live plants. The office must be clean and well organized for often this is the first office family approaches. I do not believe business managers should do initial resident admissions except for the signing of financial papers.

In the practice of feng shui, the back of the business manager (and the administrator, Director of Nursing, and Social Services) must be to the wall. Chimes must be placed in these offices, as their gentle movements increase energy. No office or resident room should be in total mauve or pink colors, as research has proven these colors produce anxiety. Wall pictures should be of streams and running water that depict movement. Business managers make an average of $15 per hour.

If families wish to be of assistance in this department, they can sign over the resident's Social Security check to the facility to prevent repetitive billings to the family. If the resident has nursing-home insurance, they should pay the facility and then bill the insurance company. The saddest situations that I was involved in were families keeping and spending residents' Social Security monies, leaving the nursing-home without proper payment.

Many families do not understand the method of payment when an elder is on Medicaid. The nursing-home is paid first with the resident's Social Security check minus $50 taken out for personal needs. Then Medicaid makes up the balance.

If the family chooses to be the payee for the Resident Trust Fund monies (the $50 per month), make sure the resident's needs are met, i.e., clothes, hair care, TV, satellite radio, comfortable reclining chair, well-fitted wheelchair, cosmetics, bird feeders, large clocks and calendars, bed throws, a bottle of wine for special occasions, and a few dollars for the purse or billfold.

Medicare is grossly misunderstood by most families. Medicare does not pay for nursing-home care except following a hospitalization and a physician's order for physical therapy, which may last for one day or a week or two. When physical therapy is no longer needed, Medicare no longer pays.

How Nursing-Homes Are Reimbursed

In the beginning a check was issued from the village, the county, or the state on a monthly basis to the caretakers of private homes, county farms, or at a later date to owners of nursing-homes. It was a simple system.

In 1998, a new computer system came into being called the MDS (minimum data set), which collected all data on a nursing-home resident and was transmitted electronically to the state and federal government for payment. However, this method brought information to both state and federal surveyors, HIPPA, the Census Bureau, and OBRA, creating a trillion-dollar business with the software mandated, updated computers, accounting and billing firms, and thousands of government personnel to analyze all the data.

MDS Coordinators

Training workshops to become an MDS coordinator are held throughout the nation which created another nationwide business. MDS coordinators who enter all the necessary data are considered of significant value due to the fact reimbursement is dependent on the data entered. All data entered is based on the medical model, i.e. pain management, behaviors, prescribed medications, falls, accidents, restraints, therapies offered, care plans, visual, dietary, weight, and dental. Tracking what the allopathic physician prescribes is known by hundreds of thousands of state and federal employees and surveyors, and the pharmaceutical companies. Nothing is private once in a nursing-home.

Coding errors on the MDS affect a skilled nursing facility's reimbursement in several ways. One is downcoding (not crediting for services rendered), which is a loss to the facility. Coding errors cost the facility extended hours of correction and loss of reimbursements in a timely manner.

Upcoding (fraudulent billings) brings in the federal auditors in an unannounced visit. The number one fraud is the allopathic physician or other providers who visit a nursing-home, walking through the facility and then billing for a number of nursing-home visits without rendering any specific service to each resident. (Judy Griffin workshop lecture). This occurred in one facility where I was administrator. The physician came in on Christmas Eve to wish all his patients a "Merry Christmas" and then charged for the calls. In one facility, an Activity Director was documenting on the MDS form activities that were not being carried out. I charged her with upcoding. She was released from her position because her actions were not only fraudulent but the residents were not receiving activities as scheduled.

248

There is no regulation, at this time, that an MDS coordinator must be a nurse; however, in my personal opinion, the nurse is the person of choice and must work the floor at least one shift, one time a week in order to be familiar with all facets of the residents needs.

A medication aide is an excellent choice for the MDS coordinator position and is paid an average of $15 per hour. An RN MDS coordinator can make an average of $60,000 per year. The MDS coordinator, a 40-hour-a-week position, is again, another position in a nursing-home that has little impact on the personal and intimate care of the residents. Training courses for MDS certification costs approximately $2,000.

The Jack and Jills of All Trades

I could not write this book without talking about maintenance men and women. Especially one who insisted on calling me "grandma," much to the consternation of the staff. I loved it!

The "to do" list is always long and sometimes repeated again and again to change light bulbs, fix a toilet, repair the furnace, the water heaters, the facility is too hot or too cold, paint this and that, fix the van, repair a piece of resident furniture, mow the yard, plant flowers, put up holiday lights, pull weeds, water the yard, put up bulletin boards, fill the bird feeders and waterers, check the fire extinquishers, hold monthly fire alarm drills, check air conditioners, moving furniture, and on and on. The work is never done.

One maintenance man took the cake or should I say took a walk. I was serving as an interim administrator and noted that the physical plant was in bad shape—the patios needed cleaning and garbage needed to be taken out every day. I walked the facility with my little pen and paper in hand and handed a list of what needed to be done to the maintenance man. The next day, a staff person came to me and repeated what the maintenance man was saying, "If she thinks I come to work to work, she has another think a-comin.'" A little chit-chat was held, at which time I released him permanently. No ifs, ands, and buts.

Certificates are of no value without common sense. One gentleman held a certificate in heating and mechanical work. He came to my office and wanted permission to wear earphones to listen to music while on duty. Guess what my answer was?

Then came the day when he jumped into the laundry chute, not only scaring the laundry gals when they opened the door, but the thought of this 180-pound person breaking down the chute was more than a bit disturbing. So a write-up was in order. This was followed by his weekend on call. He turned his cell phone off, and the nursing-home had an emergency. Eventually, he was released. I was accused by his father of discrimination. I took out his son's file and showed him multiple write-ups and asked the father if this was his employee what would he do? The father left the office and never came back.

And the shameful episode when maintenance and the housekeeping department head were arguing as to who should be watering two fern plants I purchased for the foyer.

Maintenance persons are not highly paid, and most are not only valuable but respected, especially those who have a good relationship with staff and residents.

How can families and the community assist in the maintenance area? I have been blessed with community service clubs planting flowers, pulling weeds, painting, and wallpapering resident rooms. The Aid to Lutherans organization built and placed flower boxes by every resident's windows. Ladies and school children have come in to decorate the doors and hallways for special holidays, and a large mall contributed decorations that, to them, were outdated but we loved them. Flowers were donated by a large greenhouse, and one business donated seasonal table decorations. With every little donation is a lifting up of the soul by the giver and a delight to the elders. Families must take care of bird feeders and waterers, their loved one's reclining chair, especially the lift chair, a wheelchair, and any other equipment the elder uses. It is phenomenal how much time is spent on repairing personal belongings. Wage? $15 to $20 per hour.

Now we go on to those who support elders in a nursing-home setting, the volunteers, the therapists, nursing-home boards, and last but not least are the surveyors.

33

Nursing-Home Therapists

Physical Therapy

Physical therapies and Restorative Aides are reimbursed by Medicare when an elder returns from the hospital in need of physical therapy. PT is completed on a daily basis. When PT is no longer necessary, Medicare payments stop. The resident must then pay privately, return home, or go back on nursing-home Medicaid. Restorative Aides may continue limited therapies, which becomes a nursing-home reimbursable cost under nursing.

Physical therapists provide services that restore function, improve mobility, relieve pain, and prevent or limit permanent physical disabilities. Treatment often includes exercises, especially for Elders who have been immobilized or who lack flexibility, strength, or endurance. Physical therapists may use electrical stimulation, hot packs or cold compresses, and ultrasound to relieve pain and reduce swelling. Therapists also teach elders to use assistive and adaptive devices such as crutches, walkers, and wheelchairs. They measure devices to fit the size and height of the elder.

According to the American Physical Therapy Association there were 209 accredited physical therapy education programs in 2007. Only two-year master's degree and three-year doctoral degree programs are accredited. All states require physical therapists to pass national and state licensure exams before they can practice.

About six out of ten physical therapists work in hospitals or in private offices. Other areas are in nursing-homes and home health centers.

Employment of physical therapists is expected to grow 27 percent from 2006 to 2016, much faster than the average for all other occupations. The increasing elderly population will drive this growth in the demand for physical therapy services. I have found it very difficult to find a physical therapist, especially in rural areas. When a bordering state offered classes for physical therapy certification, there were over 200 applicants, but only a few were accepted. It is my opinion that the reason for denial into the physical therapy program is one of control by the Physical Therapy Association to limit the number of physical therapists in order to always assure a deficit of physical therapists, which in turn guarantees higher wages. Median annual earnings for physical therapists is $66,000. I have never met a physical therapist or restorative aide that I did not like. They are very special people.

Occupational Therapy

The occupational therapist teaches the residents how to re-adapt to a degree of independence with the use of specially designed equipment such as the cup, drinking glasses and utensils, self-help buttoning devices, special clothing for the handicapped, canes designed to pick up articles from the floor, and visual assistance.

The occupational therapist holds a master's degree, is licensed, and is under contract with most nursing-homes for consulting when a resident is admitted and as needed.

Employment for occupational therapists is expected to increase by 23 percent between the years 2006 and 2016, much faster than the other occupations due to the influx of the baby boomers and the growth in the seventy-five-plus years of the older generation.

Average annual earning for the occupational therapist is $60,000.

Most nursing-homes have ample equipment to assist an elder in need of adaptive devises. A perceptive director of nursing, administrator, or social services director could replace the services of the occupational therapist and often does.

Speech Therapist

The speech therapist has a very difficult position in assessing problems involving difficulty chewing or swallowing food or with a speech impediment of the resident. The speech therapist is under contract with the nursing-home to do an initial admission assessment with an order from the resident's allopathic physician.

The speech therapist works with stroke victims who are aphasic or have swallowing dysfunctions. Speech therapists are skilled in the use of communication devices to use and are well versed on the types of food to give the resident when recovering from a swallowing problem.

The speech therapist holds a master's degree and is licensed. The speech therapist works on a one on one basis with residents, however, orders for the nursing staff to follow through in her/his absence are rarely followed. As a social worker, I made rounds with the speech therapist and carried out her directions because the nursing staff did not have the time to do so. I became very adept in the therapies used and was fascinated with the results. Speech therapy with whomever carries out the program, needs patience and time.

Speech therapy is expected to grow 11 percent between the years 2006 and 2016. Average annual earnings is $58,000.

In one small nursing-home, a dedicated nurse aide volunteered her time to work with a friend who was aphasic due to a stroke. The nurse aide volunteer came every day and spent thirty minutes in retraining. After months, we saw little improvement, but what did develop was a deep bond between the resident and the volunteer-friend-nurse aide. Family must take responsibility in assisting a speech therapist.

Podiatrist (DPM)

The podiatrist is a college graduate who has four years of additional training at a recognized school of podiatry and is licensed. The podiatrist can medicate, perform treatments, or perform surgery on the foot.

The podiatrist has taken over a nursing responsibility regarding the care of the feet of the elderly. With poor circulation elderly people can suffer severe problems with toes, feet, and heavy calcium deposits developing under toenails.

Nursing-homes contract services with a podiatrist, who usually make rounds at least once a month. A podiatrist does not delegate his/her services to anyone else. She/he works on an individual basis. The podiatrist is an essential part of the health-care team in the care of the elderly, although the care of the feet was a nurse responsibility in the past.

The question should be asked, "Could not nursing take back this duty if they had less paperwork?"

Podiatrists held 12,000 jobs in 2006 with an anticipated increase of 9 percent in employment needs between the years 2006 and 2016. Average annual earning is $114,000.

The podiatrist is reimbursed through Medicaid, Medicare, and usually by private insurances.

Families can, with approval of the podiatrist, gently massage the elder's feet, which stimulates the blood flow. Massage therapists call this reflexology, and it can be easily learned by family members. A highly moisturized oil should be used, not lotions, as the feet are usually very dry. Hain's peanut oil or olive oil and Home Health castor oils are best. Then cotton stockings put over the feet for the night in order to enhance the skin.

34

The Wave of the Future ... Getting Rid of Licensing?
(Synopsis taken from Healthy Competition and Crisis of Abundance by Michael F. Cannon, Michael D. Tanner, and Arnold Kling. Cato Institute 2006/2007)

Regulation can be used as a tool for crippling one's competitors. Regulations bar individuals from entering a profession or providing certain services. States have enacted numerous laws that restrict who may provide health care services. Such laws restrict not only the freedom of individuals to choose their profession but restrict the consumer's choice.

Evidence suggests such barriers increase health-care costs and have a negative effect on health care quality.

Various state licensing boards have taken steps to restrict "allied health professionals" and telemedicine. Allied health professionals include nonphysician medical workers such as dental hygienists, diagnostic medical sonographers, dietitians, medical technicians, nurse midwives, nurse anesthetists, nurse practitioners, occupational therapists, physical therapists, physician assistants, psychologists, radiographers, respiratory therapists, and speech language pathologists.

In the restriction of so-called allied health professionals, it is understandable that licensing boards would also not approve of any natural health care professionals having direct access to residents in a nursing-home (author's observation).

A number of studies demonstrate that licensing laws reduce the availability of medical care and increase costs. William Allan

Pusey, former Medical Association President states, "As you increase the cost of the license to practice medicine, you increase the price at which medical service must be sold and you correspondingly decrease the number of people who can afford to buy this medical service."

Christopher Conover, in *Health Care Regulation*, estimates that licensing of medical professionals costs Americans $6.5 billion per year, $4.7 billion of which is channeled to licensed professionals in the form of higher (personal) incomes. *That is largely the purpose of such laws.* Economist Chris W. Paul also found that licensing was created to limit applicants into the medical profession, thus increasing the cost of medical care.

A 2002 survey found that nearly six million Americans turned to alternative medicine (i.e. herbal remedies) to treat illnesses like chronic pain or depression because traditional medical care was too expensive.

In 1962, Milton Friedman wrote, "I am persuaded that licensure has reduced the opportunities available to people who would like to be physicians . . . that it has forced the public to pay more for less satisfactory medical service. I conclude that licensure should be eliminated as a requirement for the practice of medicine."

The first move from licensure will be certification as to competency. The second move is to be registered in your profession without having to meet any government standards. Thus any health-care professional would focus on high-quality service and ratings from consumer groups. Attorneys would continue to protect patients from willful or negligent harms. Harmed elders would be compensated by the courts.

Licensure boards were created to control their peers, limit the number of applicants into their profession, and increase their professional incomes . . . not necessarily to be of service to the public.

Interestingly, the word "licensure" is a derivative from "licentious," meaning pursuing desires aggressively and selfishly, unchecked by morality.

Licensure boards are not always friendly to their members, especially, if a member goes over their line of control. How many allopathic physicians have lost their licenses because they prescribed alternative medicines or therapies? How many pharmacists have been threatened if they suggest a vitamin or a homeopathic to a customer? And we are well aware that licensed nutritionists dare not get out of line.

I have held a Nebraska nursing-home license since 1977. In 2006, I completed eighteen courses toward a Ph.D. in philosophy with the majority of the courses directly towards the care of the elderly in nursing-homes. Each course took approximately forty hours of study and testing. When I called the licensure board for CEUs, I was told that maybe they would grant me three CEUs for 720 hours of study. For the reader who needs to understand CEUs, one CEU = one hour of workshop attendance. My dissertation, entitled *Introducing Natural Health Care in Nursing-Homes* took another four months of research. So, according to the board they will grant me three hours toward my license renewal.

What this board is saying is that they have no intention of encouraging nursing-home administrators (or anyone) to advance in their knowledge to create a more compassionate and healthy environment for elders in a nursing-home setting.

35

Surveyors

The public is told that nursing-homes are surveyed at least annually and the facilities know when they are to arrive. That is a
gross error in thinking. Following the annual survey, surveyors
make a revisit (unannounced) to see that all deficiencies have
been corrected. Even though all the first deficiencies have been
corrected, during this revisit if they see another deficiency, this
invites them back for another revisit, and if during the third revisit, all prior deficiencies are cleared, but they see another deficiency, this will bring them back again for a revisit. Then if
someone calls in a complaint (and the complaint can be from a recently fired employee), the surveyors are again in the facility
checking the complaint. The complaint may be found to be not
true, but on this revisit they see another deficiency, they will
again cite the facility and be back for another revisit.

I was an interim administrator in a Kansas facility that was
run very well, but we could not shake the surveyors. We just expected them to appear on our doorstep every month or so. To say
surveyors are in facilities one time a year is the grandest mis-
statement of the year.

Most surveyors are very nice and respectful. They expect the
facility to make corrections as soon as possible. I never had a
problem with correcting deficiencies; however, I challenged the
deficiencies such as three out of fifty-two beds had paint off the
undersides, and it was winter in the North Country. The surveyor gave us thirty days to correct. We were at 100 percent occupancy, with no extra beds, so it was a hardship to find extra beds
in order to take the three out of the facility to have them re-
painted. Why did the surveyors not give us six months to permit

us to bring in three older beds when the weather was warmer and to have a warm place to touch up the undersides of the beds?

Dietary received a deficiency when they used a wooden cutting table. We were told to varnish the table. We did. The next set of surveyors gave us a deficiency because dietary was using a wooden table that was varnished. We took the varnish off. The next year surveyors gave us a deficiency for using the wooden cutting table, so we purchased a stainless steel table.

Dietary received a deficiency for one dish that had been put away and had drops of water on it. Maintenance received a deficiency because there was floor tile that did not match and one tile was broken out. One facility received a deficiency because they saw a note I had written to the nurses to be sure and dress residents with sweaters because the temperature was dropping to below zero outside. The surveyors thought there was something wrong with the furnaces, which there was not; however, we were cited, and I learned not to put notes up on the nurses' bulletin boards.

One classic example is when surveyors wrote up a facility for using red plastic bottles filled with applesauce used on the med cart. The bottles had caps to prevent any contaminations and were washed each day in the Hobart dishwasher. The bottles were immediately taken off the medication carts and replaced by the more expensive single portion applesauce cups. Although the deficiency was immediately corrected, it still appeared on public records.

Nursing received deficiencies usually due to lack of documentation or improper documentation (paper compliance). Activities have received deficiencies for having a storage closet in disarray or not having evening activities.

Deficiencies are given for improper documentation on the MDS sheets, which if falsified in any way can result in a fine for the facility. Resident care plans must be followed and many are not. All are paper compliance issues.

No doctors orders for bed rails or restraints brings a deficiency. Proper staffing must be documented, although in one facility I found the Director of Nursing falsifying the number of staff on duty to satisfy surveyors.

Resident Trust Funds are examined thoroughly. A comptroller and I examined not only the Resident Trust Funds but the entire payment system in one facility to find criminal intent to defraud. The bookkeeper spent five years in prison. This facility had been surveyed many times, however, they did not find this tampering with resident funds.

Do nursing-homes "fix" the paperwork for surveyors? The answer is yes. Especially corporate facilities and facilities who have management firms. Many consultants earn an excellent income "fixing" paperwork to please surveyors.

We certainly can not be so naïve as to think that surveyors who want to keep their jobs don't capitulate to pressure from their bosses, who are in bed with management firms and corporate officers sitting on licensure boards. And how many surveyors have been hired, not because of their knowledge and experiences in nursing-homes, but because of who they knew in a state office. After many years as a nursing-home social worker and administrator, I applied for a surveyor position and was told I did not possess the proper credentials.

I have noted that facilities that have management firms have a tendency to be "deficiency free." In actuality, management firms have consultants setting up paperwork to appear as if the facility has no deficiencies. Rarely are these "deficiency free" facilities providing any better care than the neighboring facility down the road. Politics and consultants pay dividends in the nursing-home industry.

Surveyors are doing their job to the best of their abilities. Surveyors make mistakes and are sometimes pressured to "pick" on certain facilities. Nursing-homes are also doing their jobs to the best of their abilities. Nursing-homes make mistakes and sometimes "pick" on unreasonable surveyors. Overall, surveyors need to check on the physical, psychological, and spiritual care of the residents and not be nitpicking at what I consider irrelevant issues.

Surveyors have often been heard to say, "We must find something or else we will be suspect of not doing our job." These are the saddest fifteen words in the field of surveys.

36

Volunteers

Volunteers are an integral part of a resident's daily life. Elders recognize volunteers as the giving of their time and creative abilities especially for them.

And who are the volunteers in a time when most are struggling to hold one or two jobs just to pay the bills? According to Hunter and Linn, 20 percent of elders over the age of sixty-five are doing volunteer work . . . somewhere. The research states that elder volunteers are significantly more satisfied with life, have a stronger will to live, and report fewer somatic or depressive symptoms than those elders who do not volunteer their time to any cause.

This research refutes the earlier data from Carp (1968), who concluded that elder persons have increased happiness, self-esteem, and richness of social life when they are engaged in paid rather than volunteer activities.

Paid or volunteer, it is human nature to be compensated in some small way. Nursing-homes need to consider supplementary ways to say "thank you."

In one community church, ladies baked homemade pies and brought them to the nursing-home. They requested a staff person to help unload the pies and then the ladies left. They said they abhorred the thought of coming in to visit with all those old people. However, we were thankful for the delicious pies.

Many elders did not have the opportunity to obtain a high school diploma. I talked with seven residents and they were delighted to know they still could "study" for that diploma. A GED instructor volunteered her time. Months later, we had a graduation party when Certificates of Completion were handed out to all seven.

A very compassionate radio station owner and announcer came frequently to the nursing-home to broadcast an activity. In another and larger city, I approached the owner of a radio station to broadcast some of our special activities. He looked at me as if I had lost my mind. His answer said a lot about him, "Certainly not! Listeners are not interested in that type of coverage!"

Churches are usually supportive of nursing-homes, bringing in the word of God and some mighty good singing. Prior to the Christmas season, I approached the ministerial council to do a skit around Christmastime. Wonderful, wonderful ministers dressed as the three wise men came bearing gifts of great tidings, gifts of love, and hugs for the residents.

Then there was the day when we took a busload of very handicapped residents to the local circus. Waiting for us was all the circus crew to help unload the residents and push/carry them to the front row, bought them spun candy cones, and assisted several residents up on the back of camels. I often wonder if they knew the happiness they brought to all those "old people."

Only nursing-homes in northern states would understand the devastation of the mighty winter blizzards. Snowmobile buffs are out in numbers to provide emergency service to nursing-homes. All they ever received (in this world) is a thank-you. But I know, secretly, they receive the greatest payment of all . . . a little notation in that big Book of Life.

Ladies have donated hundreds of hand-sewn napkins, bed throws, blankets, and aprons. And those blessed with song and music have brought their talents to nursing-homes. One vocalist said that singing was like talking to God . . . twice.

School children and babies are more precious than gold. Elders love them. It is a habit for elders to touch small children and babies on top of the head. Unknowingly, most do not realize the soft spot on the top of the head is where the child's silver cord was attached to the Universe. This soft spot emits spiritual energy. Elders touch this spot to give them energy. As the child grows and becomes more attached to material earth, the soft spot closes.

Staff brought in their babies for a "swim meet." The facility purchased a shallow plastic pool, filling it with warm water in which the babies played much to the delight of the elders.

I was thankful for a young man bringing his new motorcycle into the foyer so all the men could come and see how motorcycles have changed and near fainted when told the cost . . . more than their first John Deere "B" tractor.

In one facility we had over one hundred volunteers, and in another facility we were fortunate to have one volunteer who came and helped with bingo.

Once a year is volunteer day, in which volunteers are asked to come to the facility and be honored with a luncheon and gifts. Again, I believe volunteers are rewarded with far greater gifts when they pass over and the Book of Life is opened. Recently, I read that the Book of Life is really our hearts that will be opened as all that we do and say is written on our heart. Possible volunteer benefits for volunteering eight hours every month:

1. Free lectures (in-services) monthly.
2. One free six-hour workshop every year of the volunteer's choice.
3. One free meal every week.
4. Free Nurse Aide training.
5. Free CPR training.
6. One Sunday meal every month with a guest.
7. Pay for out-of-pocket expenses (mileage, etc.).

According to the IRS, volunteers are valued at $12.45 per hour. This is calculated with training time plus benefits plus time donated.

The most profound statement by a resident to be remembered: "I love when volunteers come because I know they are not being paid to be here."

263

Beauty and Barber Services

Beauticians and barbers are usually not volunteers, however, some are. There are times when family, friends, and staff volunteer their time to fix, cut hair, and trim a beard or two.

Hair care professionals usually have a contract with the facility and pay a small amount to use the beauty/barber shop.

A social services director was a former beautician. Our ladies looked absolutely gorgeous. Since the SSD was on facility payroll, she was fixing hair for no fee to the residents. Then came the day we were threatened with a letter from the beautician state board that the SSD could not fix hair without a license. Who would even think of turning us in when the ladies looked so grand and at no cost? The SSD was forced to stop, much to the consternation of the female residents and families. Would you say a beautician somewhere in the neighborhood needed the business?

Families are always welcome to use the beauty/barber shop if they bring their own supplies and clean up afterward.

37

Nursing-Home Boards, Regional Managers, and Owners

City and county nursing-home board members are appointed by the mayor or county commissioners. Appointments tend to fall into five personality types: the politically motivated, the financial reward, the need for power and importance, the inept, or the compassionate person who has an altruistic interest in the care of the elderly.

Examples are: One board member was a building contractor who benefited from any remodeling or building projects. Another board member, owner of a local food market, provided all milk and food products for the facility. A board member came to the facility and complained that I was purchasing paint from a competitor. I told him the paint he carried was not washable. I promised to purchase all wallpaper from his store, which I did.

A woman board member owned stock in a car dealership where the facility purchased their van. Were their prices fair and competitive? Was it a good deal for the facility? In one facility, the nursing-home paid for a board member's health insurance.

In my observation, insecure people need to have power over others. They are often the most critical of the administration. Although most appointed board members have never worked in a nursing-home, they believe that only they understand how the policies and procedures should be written, how to communicate with the staff, and how the nursing-home should be operating.

One male board member refused to listen to nursing-home staff when they told him of sexual harassment by a male administrator towards staff. The reason was obvious. The male board member and the male administrator sat in the bar nightly and went fishing together on weekends.

I was privileged to work for a board that never came into my office and shared with me any complaints or compliments. One board member encouraged the staff to come to him with their complaints. Another board member listened to staff complaints and then discussed them with her bridge partners, but never with the administrator. One four-year board member had never walked through the nursing-home prior to my hire. I took him on "tour" to meet the staff and view the facility.

To city, county, state, corporate, or privately owned facilities, I make one strong statement, and that is that no nursing-home board member or owner or corporate officer should permit a staff person to come to their house or call them with a complaint. There is a chain of command to follow and if followed, the complaint will be heard and cleared up 100 percent of the time.

It is my personal opinion that any staff that goes over the head of the administrator is not only constitutionally weak, but is a troublemaker and should never be permitted to work in a nursing-home. Our soul's purpose is to care for the elders, not be complaining to others outside of the facility.

I ask board members to gently tell the staff person to go back to the administrator and their department head to discuss the problem.

If this is not done, the administrator and department heads lose their authority. Board members who listen and make judgments without knowing all the facts are deliberately undermining the administrator and department heads. Only board members who have a need to feel important will listen to an errant employee.

The Director of Nursing, Assistant Director of Nursing, and I examined the files of three nurse aides who repeatedly missed work or were hours late for their shift, causing distress among their peers. We fired all three. The next day, they were back on duty. They went to a board member. He hired them all back. I never fired another employee in that facility. It was a waste of time and who, overall, suffered? And what did this do to the morale for the rest of the nursing staff?

A board member who possesses traits of compassion for the elderly residing in the nursing-home and has altruistic motives is usually one who is of service to others and the community. The most competent board members are those who are active and interested who:

1. Visit the nursing-home frequently.
2. When they visit, they are friendly to all staff, speaking to and with them about any concerns. These concerns are brought to the attention of the administrator.
3. Visits with the residents.
4. The physical plant is surveyed inside and out on a monthly basis.
5. With no advance notice, board members ask to see the financial sheets/donation ledger and especially the Resident Trust Account.
6. The board member takes meals occasionally at the facility and eats with the residents.
7. Occasionally volunteers to make beds, helps serve meals, scrubs a floor, transports residents to activities.
8. Gets a bird's eye view of how daily routines are accomplished.
9. Attends most special events.
10. Compliments staff and administration when truly deserved.
11. Makes small donations to the home to show his/her support.
12. A compassionate board supports the administration upon the firing and chastisement of staff when the facts are made clear on both sides.
13. Board members support the staff, and administration when in conversation with anyone from the community.
14. Board members do not listen to staff complaints against administration unless the staff is willing to talk with the administrator first. Then documentation must be

made available to the board as to the results of the conference.

15. Boards turn over all signed and unsigned letters of complaints against administration to the administrator, discuss the letters, and then call for a meeting between the staff person, the family member or a member of the community, and administration.

Requirements for City and County Board members should be:

1. One six-hour workshop annually developed by state health-care associations or colleges.
2. City and county board members must be reimbursed no less than $100 per month, with the stipulation that they have visited the facility during the month and have committed no indiscretions against the operation of the facility.
3. No less than three out of the five board members will be former nursing-home staff.
4. Board members will not have a vested interest in the facility.
5. Attend one facility in-service annually.
6. Review Employee Handbook annually.

38

Exciting In-Service Training at the Healing Place

Staff in-services in the new, innovative "Healing Place" will be exciting and intense as well as useful for staff, residents, volunteers, board members, and family. The state mandates twelve in-services per year. In-services are paid time for staff. Subjects will be:

a. Music therapy. What music is best for residents.
b. Color therapy. How to use color for healing.
c. Light therapy.
d. How to make massage, reflexology, and touch therapy the most effective.
e. Understanding the spiritual self and others.
f. Understanding the soul's purpose on this Earth.
g. How to respond to the dying resident. Understanding hospice.
h. Understanding proper nutrition.
i. Alternative therapies.
j. Advance directives, wills, powers of attorney, guardianships.
k. State mandated: fire and storm safety/infection control/ resident rights.

The Ten Beatitudes to Work in a Nursing-Home

1. You feel joy in coming to work and during work hours.
2. You do your job well.

3. You feel the presence of a higher power in what you are doing.
4. You recognize that what you do is benefiting others.
5. You feel you are in the right place at the right time at this time in your life.
6. When needed, you have energy that comes from beyond yourself.
7. You are in a constant sense of wonder about life itself, seeing the beauty around you.
8. Innovative ideas come to you easily.
9. You carry your enjoyment in your work outside of the facility.
10. You have a willingness to serve others, with humility.

If you are a staff person presently working in a nursing-home, and feel, very strongly, that you do not fit in the above pattern, *and want to change and know that you can change,* you must admit to yourself that you have behaviors not conducive to caring for elderly persons and/or you are not able to get along with your peers, you gossip, and continually complain, you must say daily:

1. I forgive myself for what I have done in the past.
2. I forgive those who have hurt me.
3. I will begin each day with a prayer of thanksgiving.
4. I will end each day with five minutes of meditation.
5. I will listen to my inner guidance as to how to respond to every given situation that develops during working hours.
6. I will begin to remember my dreams and use them for guidance.
7. I will work on an ideal as to how I will guide every day of my life.
8. I will use daily affirmations in correcting my behavior.
9. I will stop judging and criticizing others, *today*, in my thoughts and verbally.

39

What Is It Like in a Day in the "Healing Place?"

The day would be filled with natural therapies such as dream therapy, with groups scheduled on a daily basis—sharing dreams that may reveal feelings, emotions, and solutions to any existing concerns. Dreams reflect meaning in lives, the residents' destiny and purpose for life and their own potential during their time in a nursing-home setting (W. Tanner, p. 1).

Healing with Mind Power therapy is held on an individual basis for residents in order to promote spiritual, mental and/or physical healing (R. Shames and C. Sterin, p. 19).

Aromatherapy, financially underwritten by family members in the purchase of aromatherapy kits, would be placed in the resident's room to stimulate or calm the senses (J. Rose, p. 295).

Color therapy is for individuals in surrounding themselves with the psychologically correct colors in dress and in their room. A nervous person or one suffering from insomnia must have the room in soft green tones. A lonely, solitary person will benefit by their clothing and surroundings in shades of pink. North rooms would be painted in shades of yellow. Residents who tend to be cold would have rooms painted in warm coral colors (C. Heline, pp. 59-61).

Palma Christi therapy is the use of castor oil for a multiple of ailments. Castor oil is not only inexpensive, but is said, when absorbed by the skin into the tissues that it carries some remarkable therapeutic property to the afflicted areas, thereby expediting the natural healing process (McGarey, p. 144).

Therapeutic Touch is the use of energy in the hands from the person playing the role of healer to the elder resident. The process is derived from the Christian "laying on of hands." Therapeutic Touch is used in hospitals and by massage therapists. Workshops are held throughout the nation and the process could be taught to all nursing home staff (D. Krieger, p. 23).

Laying-on-of-hands therapy is held for large or small groups and at any time of the day or night. The staff person asks the resident to write down any special request or concern. Hands are placed on the head or shoulder with prayers offered. Touch is an essential therapeutic activity. In our predominantly no-touch society, touch can serve to soothe, reenergize, or encourage residents (Harpur, p. 139).

"A Death as a Beginning" gathering would be held one time a month, open to residents, family, and the public. Regardless of religious beliefs or lack of them, death and the dying process frightens most elderly. Those attending discuss feelings concerning the dying process, death, and life-after-death experiences (Anderson, p. 5).

The ion effect is a therapy for residents suffering from breathing problems that advocates that electrically-charged particles in the air may control moods and overall health. During this therapy residents are encouraged to wear only natural clothing, such as cotton or wool (Anderson, pp. 5 and 117).

Volunteers, family, church members, or staff provide pet therapy on a weekly basis. Residents are also encouraged to have their own birds, fish, a puppy dog, or kitty to care for. Pets speak a special language to the deaf, the blind, the confused, or the physically impaired (Fox, p. 31).

Animals Speak is a daily therapy with walks through the gardens that activate all bodily senses and enable communing with the souls of plants, flowers, trees, grass, rocks, birds, and animals. It is a time to permit Nature to speak to residents, bringing a gentle peace and contentment (Andrews, pp. 60–61).

Music therapy is a mood setter. Music brings back memories and orients those who tend to be disoriented to their surroundings. It is indicated in many of Edgar Cayce's readings that the way to mental, physical, and spiritual harmony is found in the vibrations of music (S. Winston, p. 1). Rock music would be verboten. Hard rock music is meaningless noise that wears resident and staff nerves to a frazzle and was devised to prevent a relaxed atmosphere, disrupting the mind during meditative and prayer time. Dr. Joyce Brothers also pointed out that psychotic symptoms follow hard rock music (D. Noebel, p. 5).

Reflexology is the massaging of the feet. There are ten zones of the limbs and all parts of the body, with all zones ending in the feet. Gentle pressure placed on one or all zones will stimulate that part. Reflexology is offered one time a week for a period of ten minutes and can be initiated by any staff with limited training by a massage therapist (E. Ingham, p. 7).

Vision therapy is the process of learning how to change inappropriate visual habits to habits more compatible with living appropriately with self and others. Vision therapy would be provided by a Behavioral Optometrist (Kavner and Dusky, p. 32).

Light therapy is the placing of a full spectrum light lamp beside the bed or chair of every resident so they receive full color spectrum of natural daylight. Each resident would receive a fifteen-minute, twice a week, sun therapy with a suntan bed (Dr. Mercola). Kavner and Dusky have stated most fluorescent lighting is unhealthy, using up large quantities of Vitamin A (p. 139). The majority of nursing-homes have only florescent lighting.

Massage therapy is the gentle manipulation of the soft tissue of the body. It provides effective and often quick relief through the art of strokes, friction, and tapping. Most important is the compassionate touch and healing prayers by the therapist during the massage (Triance, pp. 9, 11, 16, 17).

Feng Shui (the energy of wind and water) is practiced in every resident's room involving the color and décor. Feng Shui therapy is the art of designing a resident's room to promote the highest level of health and happiness. To consult with a Feng Shui professional would be the responsibility of the family (Brown, p. 5).

Homeopathic Therapies are natural herbal substances suggested by a health-care professional trained in the art of homeopathies. Homeopathies act rapidly, deeply and curatively stimulating the body's defenses rather than suppressing symptoms (S. Cummings and D. Ullman, p. 1).

Rife therapy is the use of a Rife machine, fully computerized, to experiment with energy balancing and regulating energy pathways. The Rife machine is operated by trained personnel. The electrical currents are noninvasive (Rife Instructional Booklet).

Never again will residents be bored, depressed, or angry. Their days will be filled with useful activities and therapies. And in the evening they will kick off their shoes, relax in a comfortable chair, have a glass of wine, and know who they are and what their purpose is as a family member in this Healing Place.

Natural health therapists are usually accepting of all religious beliefs as therapies are both spiritual and practical. The spiritual side is in the promotion of the brotherhood of man and explores the hidden powers latent in man (L. Thomas, p.89). Residents elect to believe what they like.

Elders in a nursing-home can be Buddhists or Baptists. There is a difference in doctrine and that is healthy. A common denominator is the belief in karma. Karma is "the good law," whereby every action in this world has its inevitable consequence, or reaction. Christians call this "you reap what you sow." In other words, in this life or in succeeding lives, each shall reap as he has sown. The idea is that all souls were created in the beginning and through consecutive lives are given the opportunity to experience, understand, and correct those situations and inner mistakes that must be faced again and again and again for correction (S. Winston, p. 19). Gradually, through the experience of countless births, the soul learns the lessons of karma and attains to the kingly wisdom of why he/she is in a nursing-home. Without understanding Karma, elders seemingly become bitter about their "lot" in life. The teachings of karma would be part of spiritual conversations.

These and many more natural and inexpensive therapies have been negated by allopathic geriatric physicians in the care of nursing-home residents illustrated by these examples:

Case History #1

In February 1990, Dr. Rasmussen, nutrition consultant in the American International Hospital, Zion, Illinois, endorsed the use of magnets to treat bed sores, which are rampant in nursing-homes. Of minimal cost and less healing time, other physicians began to order magnet therapy. Then came visits by the FDA with threats to all physicians ordering magnet therapy to stop promoting magnetic usage (J. Carter, p. 13).

At the same time, unethical medical research was uncovered in New York City. Cancer cells were being inoculated into nursing-home patients to determine what would happen to them, unbeknownst to the patients or their relatives (J. Carter, p. 156).

Case History #2

In the spring of 2006, Dr. Oliveto, Omaha, Nebraska, MD, Ph.D, in psychiatry, was notified by his insurance company they would no longer provide liability insurance for his chelation therapy clinic. Dr. Oliveto was treating coronary patients in a series of chelation for $3,000. Cost of a coronary by-pass is well over $50,000 plus the pain of recovery (S. Kraemer, chelation client). Organized medicine refuses to acknowledge chelation's thirty-plus-year track record in the prevention and healing of heart disease, stroke, senility, diabetic gangrene, and many other vascular related conditions (J. Carter, p. 1).

40
The Allopathic Physician. Iatrogenics. Polypharmacy

Permit me to say Natural Health Care Professionals, like me, have the deepest respect for reputable allopathic physicians. *We work with them, not in opposition to them.* Alternative health-care practitioners do not diagnose or prescribe any medications. We search for the cause of disease and suggest corrections by a change of life style, thoughts, the implementation of organic food in the daily diet, meditation, prayer, a myriad of natural therapies, and, most importantly, the understanding that the human body is total vibration, known as the Vital Force. Where there is a vibration blockage in the body, there is disease. The Vital Force cannot be cured with prescribed medication. The Vital Force must be rebalanced. And yet, every time an elder takes a prescribed pill, the Vital Force is weakened. On the average, the American people take 25 million pills *every hour*. (Hardy and Nonman, p. 247).

According to the American Iatrogenic Association, iatrogenic means diseases caused by physicians (N. Martin Mar. 2001 article). However, induced iatrogenic illnesses are often caused by synthetic drugs, which means the drug is not natural to the body due to the fact every drug inevitably affects a natural enzyme system within the body (R. Strand, p. 9). So, should iatrogenic really mean diseases caused by both research pharmacists and physicians who create, endorse, and prescribe pharmaceutical drugs?

The major problem with the synthetic drug is that it can create adversity for all other enzyme systems. Pharmaceutical researchers have discovered portions, and use only that portion of herbs or natural substances that may assist the body with pain; however, they cannot or choose not to duplicate how the portion will react to the entire body without knowledge of how the rest of the natural herb or substance reacts to protect the entire body system (J. Carter, p. 240). According to the *Journal of American Medical Association* (Lazarou, J. *JAMA*, April 15, 1998; 279; 1200-1205) an estimated 106,000 Americans die from adverse drug reactions every year. These deaths are the direct result of FDA-approved drugs. ADRs are the fourth leading cause of death in this country after heart disease, cancer, and strokes (JAMA). Some 1.7 million people in this country received improper administered pharmacy prescriptions.

There are an estimated 1,500,000 nursing-home-induced (iatrogenic) illnesses reported annually (N. Gingrich, p. 41).

Polypharmacy is an accepted practice in nursing-homes. A year 2000 study of nursing facilities revealed that individual nursing-home residents receive an average of 6.7 routine prescription drugs per day plus 2.7 additional medications on an "as needed" basis. According to the National Health Policy Forum, there are 261 different drugs in development to treat diseases of aging, as well as 122 medications for heart diseases and 402 medications for cancer (D. Mendelson, National Health Forum, Policy 2002).

I was one of a research team in a large midwestern veteran nursing-home facility to find out why the veterans were taking a multiple of prescribed medications. The results revealed triple the number of medications taken versus the national average. During interviews with the veterans, it was found:

- The veterans were bored and lonely.
- The veterans felt the VA "owed" them the medication they demanded.
- The majority of veterans were without family support.
- Newly admitted veterans were told by other veterans they needed to fabricate illnesses in order to receive medical attention, which resulted in additional prescribed medications.

- No spiritual counseling and natural health therapies were available.

The Food and Drug Administration (FDA) was once considered the consumer's greatest protector. Today, the FDA has formed a deadly partnership with the pharmaceutical industry. It is here that manufacturers produce synthetic drugs in a lab, which knowingly or unknowingly, researchers produce medications that tend to block the natural enzymatic reaction in the body (R. Strand, p. 30).

Due to the number of induced iatrogenic illnesses and the practice of polypharmacy, the cost of litigation insurance in Long Term Care facilities is the leading cause of facilities closing their doors or selling to large and often dispassionate corporations.

In Florida, Long-Term Care facilities are paying as much as $12,000 per bed per year in litigation insurance. That is $1,000 per month, per resident, that could go toward better care (N. Gingrich, p. 128) and more than underwrite the cost of natural health therapies. With the assistance of families, religious organizations, and society lawsuits could decrease or be totally alleviated.

When will the people wake up to polypharmacy and big pharmacy putting out unsafe prescribed drugs with the approval of the FDA?

As fascist dictator Adolph Hitler once said, "How fortunate for the governments which administer to them . . . that those people don't think for themselves."

41

OBRA

Omnibus Budget Reconciliation Act of 1987. Only a governmental agency could have thought that one up. OBRA brought to the forefront that the resident was to be at the center of all cares and decisions. Wall posters went up with Resident Rights, care plans were initiated with residents in attendance, Resident and Family Councils were formed. Restraints and psychotropic drugs were decreased. Water was pushed to prevent dehydration.

OBRA is twenty years old. Overall, OBRA has failed in the majority of facilities. Care plans are rarely adhered to, resident rights are ignored, there continues to be serious dehydration plus a lack of nourishing food. Restraints have all but disappeared; however, falls continue at an alarming rate and psychotropic drugging continues.

OBRA failed due to the fact that in twenty years nursing-home residents are older and sicker, nursing-homes are not reimbursed for wellness nor alternative therapies, the loss of professional nursing staff due to retirements, inadequate training of nurse aides, low wages for nurse aides and auxiliary staffing, the continued practice of polypharmacy by allopathic physicians, and the lack of responsibility by families, religious organizations, and society in providing additional compassionate care. Competition is factored in due to swing beds in hospitals, and the rise of the assisted-living complexes, home health agencies and hospital-based hospices. Again, the nursing-home industry was a follower, not a leader in the care of the elderly.

HIPAA

Health Insurance and Portability Accountability Act. Another governmental fiasco. It simply implies that no nursing-home employee may discuss any health condition of a resident or of a coworker outside of the facility to any unknown or known entity. When a charge nurse calls a hospital to find out the condition of one of our own residents, the hospital is not permitted to reveal the prognosis. Only family members/guardians may be told diagnosis and prognosis.

I served as a HIPAA officer in two facilities. My name was posted for any complaints. I spend approximately forty hours in developing policies and procedures and placing forms in my side desk. I doubt to this day that those forms, policies, and procedures have ever been used. According to one HHS report, HIPAA implementation and follow-up for all medical facilities has cost the taxpayer three billion dollars. And I ask . . . has HIPAA improved the care of nursing-home residents?

OSHA

OSHA is another government agency inspecting nursing-homes. OSHA is the acronym for Occupational Safety and Health Administration. I have had one inspection that was so similar to the facility's workers compensation insurance inspection, that in my opinion, OSHA needs to be phased out to save billions of taxpayer dollars and lessen the paperwork in nursing-homes.

42

The Cabbala Says

Rabbi Herbert Weiner, an authority on the Kabbala, tells a beautiful traditional story about the beginning of life . . .

It is said that before a person is born, he carries a light on his head which enables him to see from one end of creation to the other, perhaps that means he is given a full picture, a preview of all the things that are going to happen to him in life ahead. All the good and the bad, all the difficulties and the accomplishments, the joys and the sorrows, the highs and the lows, those individuals whom he will spend time with . . . the whole story.

Then he is told that he must choose, for choice is always one of man's sacred gifts from the Creator and the final choice is his. If, then, the answer is "yes," the angel of forgetfulness touches him on the center of the upper lip, he forgets everything he saw . . . and he is born.

The Cabbalist, in Jewish lore, teaches that every human is born with the potential for greatness.

Know that each sojourn or indwelling may be compared to that as ye have in your mental experience as a lesson, as a schooling for the purpose for which each soul . . . entity enters an Earth experience; and why an entity under such environments come into that experience.
Reading No: 1158–5 Edgar Cayce.

And the Gods Listen

Once upon a time far beyond the stars, each individual spirit sat within the essence of the Energy Source, the Word, the All in One, the Creators, to design its life destiny upon a planet called Earth. What would assist their spiritual growth the most in preparation toward their next level of enlightenment?

Some chose to lose a loved one in infancy or to lose a teenager or to be in a tragic accident and become handicapped. There are those who chose to come into the world physically and mentally handicapped. And those who chose to come to Earth as caregivers, to become elders in a nursing-home. There are those who hated those of another race, then choosing to enter Earth as that very race because they needed the experience to feel the hardship of discrimination.

Dispassionate male spirits selected to become female with the difficulty of childbirth and struggles of motherhood. Others chose to remain single to best serve others in need. Then there are those who chose to live a long life, eventually residing in a nursing-home, where they could feel the pain of loneliness and fear of not being cared for, and loved by family and staff. When each soul has felt these experiences and added compassion, love, and experiences to their energy, then and only then will the soul choose to leave the body and begin another life experience in another realm.

A beautiful analogy is that we all wear a cloak of invisible threads. With each positive experience we weave more threads into the cloak. With each negative experience, we unravel threads.

Without these experiences, many souls would not develop and grow spiritually, thus not having the opportunity to return over time to a heavenly mother-father God in the Milky Way of stars.

Understanding the Spiritual Purpose of Nursing-Homes

Nursing-homes were intended to allow mankind to give expression for service toward those who were elder and infirm.

Overall, the nursing-home industry has failed its soul's pur-

282

pose. Many of those involved have lost their opportunity to serve with compassion and altruistic love. The industry that might have gained in soul experience and opportunity have lost through unethically profiting and their craving for power.

Governmental entities have failed to protect elders from abusive pharmaceutical industries, the medical profession, the chemical companies, and the food industries that have found themselves in a world of hurting and destruction.

Nursing-homes are our classroom for staff, residents, family, and society. Each day we enter the door, we are tested . . . spiritually tested.

43

Changes to Come . . .

First and foremost, is family support of the elder residing in a nursing-home. Although there is no legal obligation on the part of families to assist financially, physically, or emotionally, there is a moral obligation for family to assist in personal cares as well as financially for natural healing therapies.

Secondly religious organizations must heavily support elders in assisting with activities, social services, and positive teachings, plus financial support for those who are without family and resources to pay for natural health therapies.

With the influx of the baby boomers, who may need some assistance in a nursing-home, there already has been a resurgence in spirituality. Baby boomers will not only bring spirituality forward but will demand natural therapies.

Third, the Minimum Data Set forms will include time spent by families and natural health therapies. Facilities will be reimbursed for family and spiritual cares.

Fourth, there will be no reimbursements for consultants and seminars.

Fifth, the nursing-home industry will demand regulation changes that will decrease paperwork, demand no licenses for social services and hospice care workers, and result in a complete change in meeting the nutritional needs for elders.

Sixth, nurse aides will no longer take tests, but be trained in house by a nurse trainer who should be another nurse aide who has proved her/his ability to more than adequately care for the physical and spiritual needs of the elders.

Seventh, the nursing-home industry will demand that each state mandate a two-year specialized college course designed only for nursing-home administrators. There will be no mandate for a four-year college graduate.

Eighth, any deficiencies cited by state surveyors will be those where the elders are in jeopardy. Deficiencies can be deleted if the facility corrects while the surveyors are in house. Surveyors can not cite another completely different deficiency when doing a revisit unless a resident is in jeopardy. Surveyors will write "suggestions," which are not a deficiency. If suggestions would be made, it would not be for public view. Suggestions will be followed up in the next annual survey.

Ninth, nursing-home board members and owners will attend no less than one workshop annually targeted towards morals and ethics, how to communicate with nursing-home staff, their duties as a board member, and understanding nursing-home policies and procedures.

Tenth, the implementation of strong exercise and alternative therapy programs for staff to alleviate the cost of injuries and missed days of work and decrease workers compensation costs and more importantly, to build their self-esteem and self-worth, which will decrease staff turnover.

Eleventh and, most importantly, is the prayer power and citizen knowledge to restrict the control of the medical profession by the pharmaceutical industry. Today, the pharmaceutical industry hires 625 lobbyists (more than one for each member of the House and Senate) spending $177 million on lobbying efforts and another $20 million in campaign contributions and $65 million for ads aired by Citizens for Better Medicare, plus billions for medical research that often sidesteps clinical results. The pharmaceutical industry also funds more than three-fifths of doctors continuing education, with pharmaceutical instructors pushing their drugs. In 2003, the drug companies were spending more than $1,500 per year on education workshops for every doctor in the United States (excerpts taken from *Overdosed America* by John Abramson, MD).

The manipulating of doctors by the pharmaceutical industry started slowly and insidiously, like an addiction, and has ended up influencing the very nature of medical decision-making by the allopathic physician.

Pharmacist Christopher Terf is one of many titled "natural pharmacists" practicing a team approach called integrative medicine in the use of both conventional and alternative methods. Terf says that the users of integrative medicine know that treating certain conditions requires the strength of both conventional and alternative therapies.

This is the ultimate (spiritual) test! Will the pharmaceutical industry, the medical profession, and the nursing-home industry join integrative medicine to provide a more compassionate level of care for elders in a nursing-home setting, which in turn would decrease the cost of care for the taxpayer?

44

The Last of the Chapters

In review of all that has been written, in understanding the concept of natural or alternative health therapies and the implementation of these therapies in nursing-homes, it is first and foremost imperative that residents have a deep desire to take personal responsibility for their own health and wellness.

Resident decisions must be supported by staff, family, religious organizations, and communities. Natural health is all inclusive of spiritual, mental, and physical therapies that promote the highest level of quality care and dignity in the lives of nursing-home residents. It is with the understanding that the soul's desire is to search for its full potential, regardless of age or place of residence. In that search, it is essential that society is knowledgeable as to the growth of the nursing-home industry, how and why the family relinquished responsibility for their elders, and the infringement of the pharmaceutical and medical profession in the decision-making for elders in a nursing-home setting.

Natural health therapies in nursing-homes are the wave of the future for a nation that no longer is able to underwrite the tremendous cost of eldercare. Without natural therapies and without any outside assistance, society continues to complain bitterly concerning the care of their elders.

Today's generation-tomorrow's elders will demand natural/alternative/drugless therapies in a compassionate, spiritual environment.

The new age of Aquarius brings the promise to expose those who are in untruthful, manipulative, or deceitful situations. Those who are now in high positions and have played a part in abusing nursing-home elders will be brought down.

Those who have served well, will be brought to the forefront, not only in recognition, but in promulgating the uplifting of their own spirituality. The positions we are holding today, in a "Healing Place" nursing-home, are so important and powerful, spiritually, that we will bring in the New Consciousness of change. Nursing-home staff can be the forerunners of peace as peace is the unity between heaven and earth.

In the past forty years in the nursing-home industry, souls have gained and souls have lost. All of us have had the same opportunity to gain or lose.

The hope is now, today, as the New Age brings in a heightened enlightenment and spirituality to all humans on this Earth, with change, elders in nursing-homes will never again lack compassionate and spiritually enlightened staffing.

Who Are We?

We are a Tribe of Soul Beings with no separation of religions and races.

Today, we are enlightened by those who have been visiting us, by whom we have often called "aliens," although I prefer to call them Star Beings. Humans who are in contact with Star Beings have asked them to comment on the concept of "God." Star Visitors say that God is a transcendent matrix of consciousness that underlies everything transcending all manmade religions.

Dr. Carl Sagan was reported to have said in a private remark, "The Star Visitors are here as missionaries. They are very concerned for the Earth, its ecosystem, and for human kind. The Star Visitors have scolded many humans, including government leaders, for bad choices, which have harmed the environment or caused great human distresses.

The Star Visitors have commented on life spans. All (those on Earth) have had previous lifetimes, and after death from this current life, go on to successive lifetimes. Subsequent lifetimes are not necessarily on the same planet. There is no support in Star Visitor theology for the doctrine of only a single lifetime, after which the soul is judged and assigned a permanent fate.

The Conclusion

Most nursing-homes today are secular, even though research has proven over and over that compassion, nurturing, touch, and daily spiritual activities can produce peace of mind, soul, and body. Personal spirituality makes good *health* sense! In test after test, scientists have found that spiritually active people are generally healthier and heal faster than those who have no spiritual dynamic in their lives. (*Personal Spirituality Newsletter*, September 30, 2002).

Even though there are millions of hard-working, compassionate nursing-home staff throughout the nation, their training is of the medical modality. The nursing-home industry *must* move to a higher level of collective consciousness. Again and again and again I say that all of us created the crisis that now besieges the nursing-home industry because we were followers. I have often told families that we only take orders! We make no decisions. We are, at the present, totally controlled by the medical profession, the pharmaceutical industry, and policy makers who are unenlightened beings. However, it is time to WAKE UP! We are the essence of God and gods in training!

We are in the Age of Aquarius . . . the age of information when those who have abused our elders and disabled persons will be put down and those who have remained faithful to themselves and those in their care will rise.

The new generation of elders will not demand a beautiful foyer with a water font, hallway carpet, and expensive wall and holiday decorations. However, they will demand what they instinctively know to be in their best interest . . . natural health therapies with compassion and spiritual ideals.

Changes will not be forthcoming from the medical and pharmaceutical industry, nor the government that is in bed with the pharmaceutical industry. The nursing-home industry is reimbursed on the MDS (minimum data set) system—being reimbursed for the number of cares provided for the resident and the number of medications given. Therefore, the sicker the resident and the more medication taken, the higher the reimbursement. Today, the average nursing home is operated on the concept of high profitability, and would not be willing to be a leader in advocating for natural health therapies.

However, the wind is changing. Elders and the family will be change agents. Nursing-homes will no longer be feared but embraced as the new Healing Place, where holistic healing is embraced.

Let us applaud those who have implemented the new and innovative Green Houses throughout the nation; however, the cost of residing at a Green House is more than at a traditional nursing-home, therefore, for private pay only? Or will Medicaid increase its reimbursement for those who choose to reside in Green House complexes?

"Healthy people are those who live in healthy homes, on a healthy diet, in an environment equally fit for birth, growth, work, healings, and dying; they are sustained by a culture that enhances the conscious acceptance of limits to population, of aging, of incomplete recovery, and ever imminent death. Healthy people need minimal bureaucratic interference to mate, give birth, share the human condition, and die." (I. Illich, pp. 274–275).

The Taxi Driver

When I arrived at 2:30 a.m., the building was dark except for a single light in a ground floor window. Under these circumstances, many taxi drivers would just honk twice, wait a minute, and then drive away.

But I had seen too many impoverished people who depended on taxis as their only means of transportation. Unless a situation smelled of danger, I always went to the door as some passengers might need my assistance.

I walked to the door and knocked. "Just a minute," answered a frail, elderly voice. I could hear something being dragged across the floor. After a long pause, the door opened. A small woman in her nineties stood before me. She was wearing a print dress and a pillbox hat with a veil pinned on it, like somebody out of a 1940s movie.

By her side was a small nylon suitcase. The apartment looked as if no one had lived in it for years. All the furniture was covered with sheets. There were no clocks on the walls, no knickknacks or utensils on the counters. In the corner was a cardboard box filled with photos and glassware.

"Would you carry my bag out to the car?" she said. I took the suitcase to the cab, then returned to assist the woman. She took my arm and we walked slowly toward the curb. She kept thanking me for my kindness. "It's nothing," I told her. "I just try to treat my passengers the way I would want my mother treated." "Oh, you're such a good boy," she said.

When we got in the cab, she gave me an address and then asked, "Could you drive through downtown?" "It's not the shortest way," I answered quickly. "Oh, I don't mind," she said. "I'm in a no hurry. I'm on my way to a hospice." I looked in the rear-view mirror. Her eyes were glistening. "I don't have any family left," she continued. "The doctor says I don't have very long."

I quietly reached over and shut off the meter.

For the next two hours, we drove through the city. She showed me the building where she had once worked as an elevator operator. We drove through the neighborhood where she and her husband had lived when they were newlyweds. She had me pull up in front of a furniture warehouse that had once been a ballroom where she had gone dancing as a girl. Sometimes she'd ask me to slow in front of a particular building or corner and would sit staring into the darkness, saying nothing.

As the first hint of sun was creasing the horizon, she suddenly said, "I'm tired. Let's go now."

We drove in silence to the address she had given me. It was a low building, like a small convalescent home, with a driveway that passed under a portico. Two orderlies came out to the cab. They were solicitous and intent, watching her every move. They must have been expecting her.

I opened the trunk and took the small suitcase to the door. The woman was already seated in a wheelchair.

"How much do I owe you?" she asked, reaching into her purse.

"Nothing," I said.

"You have to make a living," she answered.

"There are other passengers," I responded.

Almost without thinking, I bent and gave her a hug. She held onto me tightly.

"You gave an old woman a little moment of joy," she said. "Thank you."

I squeezed her hand, and then walked into the dim morning light. Behind me, a door shut. It was the sound of the closing of a life.

I didn't pick up any more passengers that shift. I drove aimlessly, lost in thought. For the rest of the day, I could hardly talk. What if that woman had gotten an angry driver or one who was impatient to end his shift? What if I had refused to take the run, or had honked once, then driven away?

I don't think I have done anything more important in my life. We're conditioned to think that our lives revolve around great moments. But great moments often catch us unaware—beautifully wrapped in what others may consider a small one.

PEOPLE MAY NOT REMEMBER EXACTLY WHAT YOU DID, OR WHAT YOU SAID—BUT—THEY WILL ALWAYS REMEMBER HOW YOU MADE THEM FEEL.

The taxi cab driver remains unknown. Wherever he is, without a doubt, he has reaped many rewards for his compassion towards this elderly woman. Thanks to my forever friend Mary Newman for sending me this story.

A grand opening celebration for a new beginning.

Resource Material

AARP Magazine—Jan/Feb 2007.

Abramson, John. *Overdosed America. The Broken Promise of American Medicine*. Harper and Collins, 2004.

Alcena, Valiere. *The African-American Health Book*. Birch Lane Press.

Baker, Beth. *Old Age in a New Age*. Vanderbilt University Press, 2007.

Bassano, Mary. *In the Flow*. Mary Bassano, 1983.

Birren, Faber. *Color In Your World*. Collier MacMillian, 1962.

Brantl, Virginia M., and Brown, Sister Marie. *Readings in Gerontology*. C.V. Mosby Co., 1973.

Braun, Leo M. *Apocalypse*. Vantage Press, 1993.

CATO INSTITUTE, *Crisis of Abundance*, by Arnold Kling. *Healthy Competitor*, by Cannon and Tanner.

Cayce, Edgar. Readings at the Association of Research and Enlightenment. Virginia Beach, VA.

Cayce, Hugh Lynn. *God's Other Door*. ARE Press, 1958.

David, William. *The Harmonics of Sound, Color and Vibration*. DeVorss and Co., 1980.

Don, Frank. *Color Magic*. Destiny Books, 1977.

Forrest, Mary Brumby and Forrest, Christopher B., *Nursing-Homes, The Complete Guide*. Facts on File, 1990.

Fulder, Stephen. "Remedies For Life Extension." In *Pharmocology and Gerontology*. Destiny Books, 1983.

Gale Research, Inc. *Statistical Forecasts of the U.S.* Washington, D.C.

Gerber, Richard. *Vibrational Medicine*.Bear and Company, 1988.

Griffin, Judy. *Medicare Part A & B. Reimbursement for SNFs and Sub-acute*. Cross Country Education, 2008.

Hardy, Mary and Nonman, Dotty. *The Alchemist's Handbook to Homeopathy*. Delta K. Trust, 1994.

Henry, William. DVDs. *Potential to Follow the Path to Become Beings of Light*. 2007.

Hrachover, Josef P. *Keeping Young and Living Longer. How to Stay Alive and Healthy Past 100*. Sherbourne Press, 1972.

Kra, Siegfried, MD. *Aging Myths: Reversible Causes of Mind and Memory Loss*. McGraw Hill, 1986.

Lingerman, Hal A. *The Healing Energies of Music*. Quest, The Theosophical Publishing House, 1983.

Maddox, George L. and Busse, E.W. *Aging: The Universal Human Experience*. Springer Publishing, 1987.

McGarey, Gladys T. *Born to Live*. Gabriel Press, 1980.

McIntire, Virginia Allen. *Color Energy*. Virginia Allen McIntire, 1986.

Nelson, Portia. *There's A Hole In My Sidewalk*. Beyond Words Publishing, 1994.

Newsweek Magazine 6/27/1994. "This Is My World."

Peterson, Richard. *Miles to Go. The Spiritual Quest of Aging*. Harper and Row, 1989.

Pieper, Hanns G. *The Nursing-Home Primer*. Betterway Publications, 1989.

Purucker, G. De. *Studies in Occult Philosophy*. Theosophical University Press, 1945.

Rivlin, Alice M. and Wiener, Joshua M. *Caring for the Disabled Elderly*. The Brookings Institution. 1988.

Robbins, John. *Diet For A New America*. Stillpoint Publishing, 1987.

Soyka, Fred and Edmonds, Alan. *The Ion Effect*. Bantam Books, 1991.

Springer Publishing Co. *The Encyclopedia of Aging*.

Szekely, Edmond Bordeaux. *The Essene Book of Creation*. First Christians (Essene) Church, 1968.

Works Cited

Anderson, George. *We Don't Die*. New York: Berkley Publishing Group, 1988.

Andrews, Ted. *Animal Speak*. St. Paul: Llewellyn Publications, 1993.

Bealle, Morris A. *Medical Mussolini*. Washington D.C.: Columbia Publishing Co., 1939.

Brown, Simon. *Feng Shui*. London, England: Carrol and Brown Limited, 1997.

Carter, James P. *Racketeering in Medicine. The Suppression of Alternatives*. Charlottesville: Hampton Roads Publishing Co., 1992.

Cummings, Stephen and Ullman, Dana. *Everybody's Guide to Homeopathic Medicines*. Los Angeles: Jeremy P. Tarcher, Inc., 1984.

Fox, Nancy. *How to Put Joy into Geriatric Care:* Ashland: Geriatric Press, 1979.

Garavaglia, Brian. "Avoiding Drug-Induced Depression in Nursing-Home Residents." *Find Articles*. Oct. 2004. Epidemiologic Catchment Area Survey. Mar. 2002. http://www.findarticles.com/p/asticles/mi_m3830/is_10_53/ai_n6359044.

Gingrich, Newt. *Saving Lives and Saving Money*. Washington D.C.: Hampton Roads Publishing Company, 2003.

Harpur, Tom. *The Uncommon Touch*. Toronto, Canada: McClelland and Stewart, 1994.

Harvard Public Health Review. "*Returning Medicine to Its Roots*." Harvard School of Public Health. 23 Feb 2007.http://?/?www.hsph.harvard.edu/?review/?_2000/?almkorn.htlm.

Haumann, Barbara. "Organics R Us," *Readers Digest*, March 2001, 228.

Heline, Corinne. *Color and Music in the New Age*. Marina Del Rey: Devorss and Company, 1964.

Hendricks Gay, and Hendricks, Kathlyn. *At the Speed of Life. A New Approach to Personal Change Through Body-Centered Therapy*. New York: Bantam Books, 1993.

Humphry, Derek. *Lawful Exit. The Limits of Freedom for Help in Dying*. Junction City: Norris Lane Press, 1993.

Illich, Ivan. *Medical Nemesis*. New York: Pantheon Books, 1976.

Ingham, Eunice. *Stories the Feet Can Tell Through Reflexology*. Saint Petersburg: Ingham Publishing, 1984.

Kavner, Richard S. and Dusky, Lorraine. *Total Vision*. New York: A. and W. Publishers, 1978.

Kraemer, Shirley A. "Elder Abuse/Social Services Workshops." Delivering workshops and thirty years experience in nursing-homes throughout the Midwest. Yankton, SD. Health Services/Nebraska Health Care Association. Throughout the States of South Dakota/Nebraska/Iowa/Kansas, Various Cities and States.

Krieger, Dolores. *The Therapeutic Touch*. New York: Simon and Schuster, 1979.

Lapane, Kate L. and Resnik, Linda. "Obesity in Nursing-Homes; An Escalating Problem." *Journal of the American Geriatrics Society*. Aug. 2005. Department of Community Health. Brown Medical School. Providence, RI. Feb. 2007.

Lidell, Lucinda. *The Book of Massage*. New York: Simon and Schuster, 1984.

Martin, Nicolas S. "What Does the Word 'Iatrogenic' Mean?" *American Iatrogenic Association*. 2002. American Iatrogenic Association. 01 Mar. 2001 http://www.iatrogenic.org/define.html.

McGarey, William A. MD. *Healing Miracles. Using Your Body Energies*. San Francisco: Harper and Row, 1988.

Melendy, Mary Ries. *Medical Manuals Nineteenth Century, Perfect Health and Beauty for Parents and Children*. Chicago, 1906.

Mendelson, Dan. "Prescription Drugs in Nursing-Homes: Managing Drugs and Quality in a Complex Environment." *National Health Policy Forum*. NHPF Issue Brief No. 784/November 12, 2002. The George Washington University. 01 Mar. 2007 <http://www.aval erehealth.net/research/docs/iB784_RxDrugsNurs Homes_11-12-021.pdf—Cached>.

Myers, Michael. *Elder Law*. School of Law. University of South Dakota, Vermillion. Feb. 2002.

Noebel, David A. *The Marxist Minstrels*. Tulsa: American Christian College Press, 1974.

Nutritional Health Profiler. *Healthy, Older and Wise—Just Say No To Drug Combos*. 15, 9. 2004. WDDTY Archives (1991-2006). 26 Feb. 2007. <http://www.healthy.net/scr/Article.aspId=4501&xcntr=2>.

Oslie, Pamala. *Life Colors. The Colors of Your Aura*. San Rafael: New World Library, 1991.

Reilly, Harold J. and Brod, Ruth Hagy. *The Edgar Cayce Handbook for Health Through Drugless Therapy*. New York: Macmillan, 1975.

Rife, Royal R. "Sweep Function Generator." *Operating Manual*. Ed. Royal R. Rife. Vol. 1. AAA Production, 2002.

Ritberger, Carol. *Your Personality, Your Health*. Carlsbad: Hay House, 1998.

Rose, Jeanne. *The Aromatherapy Book*. Berkley: North Atlantic Books, 1992.

Shames, Richard and Sterin, Chuck. Healing with Mind Power. Emmaus: Rodale Press, 1978.

Simons, Raphael T. *Feng Shui Step by Step*. New York: Crown Trade Paperbacks, 1996.

Stevens, Judith. *Venture Inward*. "Nature As Healer." (volume 23) p.22. March/April 2007.

Strand, Ray D. *Death by Prescription*. Nashville: Thomas Nelson Publishers, 2003.

Tanner, Wilda B. *The Mystical, Magical, Marvelous World of Dreams*. Tahlequah: Sparrow Hawk Press, 1988.

Thomas, Lowell. *India, Land of the Black Pagoda. Garden City: Garden City Publishing Company, 1930*.

Triance, E.R. *Massage At Your Fingertips*. New York: Thorsons Publishers, 1984.

Wayne, Anthony and Newell, Lawrence. "Radiation Ovens. The Proven Dangers of Microwaves." *Lawgiver.org*. 2000. *Christian Law Institute and Fellowship Assembly*. Feb. 2007. <http://www.herbalhealer.com/microwave.html>.

Winston, Shirley Rabb. *Music As the Bridge*. Virginia Beach: Association for Research and Enlightenment, 1972.

Wood, George P. and Ruddock, E.H. Medical Manual Used in the 19th C. *Encyclopedia of Health and Home*. Chicago: Donohue and Henneberry Printers, 1887.

Yost, Nellie Snyder. *Evil Obsession; The Annie Cook Story*. Midgard Press, 1991.

About the Author

As a school dropout and after raising seven children, Shirley Ann Kraemer entered college at the age of thirty-seven completing her GED and a college degree (magna cum laude) and obtained a license as a nursing-home administrator—all in a three-year period. A spiritual calling led to five years working with the elderly as a nursing-home consultant social worker. After completing a master's degree in educational counseling, Kraemer, known for her compassion for the elderly and the need for change, worked for twenty-five years as a nursing-home administrator, became a licensed massage therapist, obtained a bachelor's degree in Divinity-ordained, is a Registered Guardian for the elderly, completed one semester of Elder Law, was a Nebraska Senate candidate, was awarded a Ph.D. in philosophy, and is a member of the Nemenhah Band as a Medicine Woman. Dr. Kraemer travels throughout the Midwest as an interim nursing-home administrator and is the CEO of the Academy of Natural Healing Arts, offering a suite of natural health services. Kraemer resides on five acres, where she has gardens, orchards, and walking paths for spiritual growth. Her website: proelder.net. Email: sakraemer@conpoint.com.